Team up a British Pekingese and an American Shihtzu with an international journalist, and you get two canine reporters with an attitude!

The little dogs have packed more into their years than most people will into a lifetime. From Operation Desert Storm to Willie Nelson, from Aids Wards to Texas Death Row, Tiny and Mike have been there, done that and reported on it. They are cute as can be, but tough as nails beneath their sweet exteriors; a team of furry jetsetters who charm people and animals wherever they go.

Mike dated Willie Nelson's drummer's dog. As is fitting for "stars", they are groomed courtesy of an international newsmagazine. They are intimately acquainted with diverse groups of people, from Robert Kennedy Jr to the inmates of America's toughest prison. True to their motto "Life is short, live it while you can", they travel around the world. Mike had his picture painted by a death row inmate, days before he went to his execution. In their spare time, the little dogs cheered up Mexican slum children in the barrios of Texas. But this was before they became involved in Operation Desert Storm and the TWA 800 crash.

The canine reporters stay in luxury hotels where they charm staff and guests alike. As American Airshow VIPs, they flew high with the world's most daring pilots. Everywhere, they reached out with a nose-lick of comfort to those who needed it. For their charity work, Tiny and Mike travel with a cat and a horse.

This unique book allows the reader to share Tiny and Mike's amazing escapades as they witness the joys and miseries of human existence. They have collaborated with their Human in this deeply moving narrative, softening the world of international journalism through their unique canine eyes. Their memories are funny, sad, or intriguing, but always charming. Each of their encounters unfolds into a unique story as the tail-wagging adventurers meet the Famous, the Infamous, the Poor, the Rich, the Sad, or the Triumphant. They meet people who live in different parts of the world. Who belong to different classes of society. Who may not even want to know each other. And yet, whether it is a POW from the gulf war, a death row inmate or a celebrated rock star, they all have something in common; they own a photo of Tiny and Mike.

Tiny is a British Pekingese, who first started in journalism in 1987.

Mike was born in Houston, Texas and began his journalism career in 1990.

About the Authors:

Tiny, Mike and Tess Crebbin are a team of former international journalists. Tiny is a British Pekingese, who first started in journalism in 1987. He loves Vanilla ice cream, and enjoys participating in pet therapy, beaches, horse-riding, editing manuscripts, listening to Mozart and going for walks with Mike. He hates cigarettes, pop music and most vets. Tiny is multi-lingual and has an enormously long tongue that can to the bottom of most jars and glasses. Mike was born in Houston, Texas and began his journalism career in 1990. He likes beaches, swiping cats aside, dancing, eating anything, checking into motels, hanging his head out of a driving car, and running in circles. He hates horses and cows. Tiny and Mike both are fond of airplanes. They have extensively travelled in three continents, and have lived in England, the United States, Canada, Germany and France. Tess Crebbin studied journalism and biology. She has worked all over the world, in many different fields of journalism, and for the most part of her career has been accompanied by Tiny and Mike. She has most recently acted as US correspondent for an International Wildlife Magazine. Tess Crebbin also hates pop-music. She enjoys going to the movies with Tiny, whom she smuggles into the theatre in her handbag, and they sometimes get evicted from cinemas for Tiny's snoring.

With best wishes

Tess Caddigh

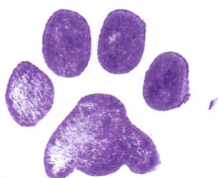

Tiny

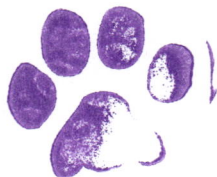

rike

Two Dogs and a Journalist

A British Pekingese and a American Shihtzu Travel the World

by

Tess, Tiny and Mike Crebbin

Photographs by Philip Crebbin
Captions by Malcolm Jones

Protea Publishing
ATLANTA

Title: Two Dogs and a Journalist
Subtitle: A British Pekingese and a American Shihtzu Travel the World
Authors: Tess, Tiny and Mike Crebbin
Photographs: Philip Crebbin
Captions: Malcolm Jones

ISBN 1-883707-92-7

Publisher: Protea Publishing Company
          Atlanta, Georgia, USA

email: kaolink@msn.com
web site: www.proteapublishing.com

For Tiny
(1987 - 2001)

THANK YOU:

I would like to thank the countless people around the world who made Tiny and Mike's adventurous lives possible: Lufthansa Airlines for letting them fly in the cabin, their vets in Canada, the USA, Germany and England who kept them healthy well into old age, the kind people who babysat them for me and who are mentioned by name in this book, the many celebrities who indulged their whims, and also my family who looked after them when I was on the road and couldn't take them with me, especially my husband Phil and my grandparents Ernst and Steffi.

I should especially like to thank the vets Fielding & Cumber, and Medivet in England, especially Martin Fielding, and Thomas. Also their veterinary nurses, especially Jill at Fielding & Cumber. Also thank you to Hailey, Sam, Chloe and Malcolm Jones, who became an important part of Tiny and Mike's lives after they arrived in England. Malcolm Jones also helped with selecting the photographs to illustrate this book, and always made sure that Tiny had his vitamin supplements, even if they had to be imported from Switzerland. Thank you also to Dr Wallace Sife, for support given.

Thank you also to Sean Tucker, Leo Loudenslager and Patty Wagstaff, who made Mike's experience of the airshow world such a fascinating one, and to Wayne of CBS television who allowed him to become a national celebrity.

Also to Mr. Derek Bhoumik-Shepherd for his kindness, and to Elliot Anderson who understood that Tiny was family. Another big thank you to my husband Phil, who edited and transcribed parts of this manuscript and who always ferried the little canine adventurers around the country, or around the world.

A big thanks also to Ryan of Photomall, for swift processing of the interior images in this book. A special thank you to veterinarian Dr. Lisa Newell of Malibu, CA, for her kind help and advice.

Finally, thank you to Mrs. Peggy Winston, Tiny's breeder, for such a delightful creature and the many good years we spent together.

INDEX

Part 1: Early Beginnings, or: how we got them

Part 2: Mike joins the family at the Equestrian Center, or: Tiny, Mike and the horses

Funny antics of the two little dogs at the stable. They meet the horses, getting to know the equines' personalities, and special friendships and hate-relationships develop between horses and dogs. Mike herds the horses in the paddocks at night. Tiny, naturally, owns the stable, and feeds "his" horses.

Mike almost dies after he is stepped on by a horse that does not like him. A little Pekingese, Tiny's "wife" and new addition to the family, is bought from a shady breeder, and dies. Tiny almost succumbs to a heat stroke in Quebec's hottest summer yet.

Part 3: Tiny and Mike go to Texas

Tess goes to Texas to work on death row. She teams up with a famous American attorney who has been the subject of a movie by the name of "The thin blue line". Description of death row. Despite an exciting time with the death row appeals investigations, Tess misses the dogs, who stayed behind in Canada.

Tess and her little dogs, all three of them young and naïve Euro-Quebec hicks (even Mike, who is from Texas), discover poverty in America. They feed the homeless with

Vietnamese frogs legs in coconut curry sauce, and buy Christmas presents for the men and women who live rough in the city streets of Houston.

Tess and her dogs deliver Christmas presents to the worst neighborhoods of Houston. They encounter danger and joy in places good girls and pedigree dogs should never go to.

Ignoring warnings from "Texas white racists", Tess and the dogs rent a house and open their doors to a member of the "Black Power" movement. He moves in with his entourage and kicks Tess and her dogs out of their own house, shouting "only black is beautiful". He hates white people and purebred dogs like Tiny and Mike.

Tess is given the task of taking over an appeals process in a capital murder case, and of turning a notorious death row inmate and gang member from a problem prisoner into a well-behaved human being. The problem is easily solved: Tess "gives" Mike to the convict to teach him responsibility. The convict is responsible for paying Mike's vet and grooming bills. Tiny and Mike take over the worst wing of Texas death row and charm their pants off. Hardened convicts request photos of Tiny and Mike, paint oil paintings of the dogs and worry about Tiny's health. The guards on death row think the world has gone nuts.

Tess goes to work for the prestigious German news magazine
"Der Spiegel ", but only if the dogs get hired, too.
Adventures on the job, all three of them.

A glamorous Houston socialite looks after Tiny and Mike
while the Tess goes to Hollywood to interview film stars.
Tess interrupts dinner-interviews with movie stars to "call
home" and check up on "the kids".

Debbie is the wife of a Houston cop. She believes justice
has not been done in the capital murder case the author is
working on, and that the prisoner may be innocent. Tess,
who volunteers her time on the case as an investigator, is
appreciative when Debbie contributes to the legal expenses
in her own way, grooming and boarding Tiny and Mike at
half price, and providing free day care for the little dogs.

Tiny, as a British Pekingese, is conscious of status symbols.
Quirks include sleeping under the covers, growling when
being treated like a dog, eating human food, going to
the movies, demanding to be served at the restaurant,
walking "alone" while giving the appearance that one is not
associated with any human in the park.

Both little dogs are almost killed in separate incidents.
Their guardian angels are working overtime to protect the
death-defying canines. A black man appears out of nowhere
to save Tiny's life and tells his shocking experiences with
racism.

Part 4 Back to Canada:

Tearful good-byes from favorite places and people in Texas. Despite having to leave friends behind, Tess and the dogs are glad to turn their backs on Texas, where Tiny is being made fun of for his flat nose.

Tess quits journalism and becomes the North American representative and writer for a European literary agency. First client: a writer with Aids who owns a Pekingese.

Tiny and Mike engage in impromptu pet therapy with the dying writer and his family: outings in the park, regular afternoon visits.

Tiny is smuggled into the Aids floor of Montreal General hospital and continues with pet therapy until the writer dies. Tess ends up becoming something of a good angel to this troubles family, not by choice of her own, but by choice of her Pekingese. This earns her the reputation of Mother Theresa of journalism.

Tiny and Mike ask for and get a cat. The cat's acquisition involves a beautiful Mafia girl, a cancer patient, the glamorous Cote d'Azur in France, and the ill-fated SPCA in Montreal.

Part 5: Tiny, Mike and zoo in Newport

Narragansett. Mike cheers up the family of a victim, who lives two streets from their summer home. Hurricanes, a Polish dog and the author discovers that a Texas acquaintance was on board TWA.

A visit to an airshow results in Tess having to work on three different book projects. Mike and Tess travel with the air show crowd, and when they visit an airshow in Nashville, Mike becomes the star of the show. Fan sessions with a famous pilot are part of their daily routine, as are waving to the crowds from the passenger seat. Photo sessions with pilots result in Mike's photo being posted on the Internet: on the website of a famous woman pilot!

Tiny and Mike prepare to move to Europe, where new adventures await them. They will take "their" animals: the cat and horse. They may have become a little older and slower, but they are still as determined as ever to live up to their motto: life is short, so you might as well live it while you can!

PART 1

EARLY BEGINNINGS

OR: HOW WE GOT THEM

Chapter 1

Everything Was Really Roger Daltrey's Fault ...

It was a typical foggy day in London, England. My husband, Phil, and I had been to an interview with Roger Daltrey, the lead singer of the legendary rock band "The Who." The interview had been on the occasion of the release of Roger's new solo album. It was supposed to be one of those press junkets, where they shove assorted journalists by the star in question, each journalist being given between ten minutes and half an hour to ask what often turns out to be the same questions of the tired, bored musician. As it happened, I was the last journalist slotted to interview Daltrey that day.

When I walked through the door, Roger offered me a sandwich, looked at his watch, and stated: "We can talk while I am having lunch. Fifteen minutes max, and then I'm out of here."

Four hours later, we were still talking. His press secretary had long since given up on sticking her head through the door and asking if he "was all right," meaning in star-press secretary code: "do you want me to get rid of this impertinent journalist?" Roger told her that he was just fine, that we would be here for some time yet and that she could go home.

Phil had dropped by, taken the photos, and given up on us. He headed for home after the first thirty minutes....

I was barely twenty years old; Roger had just passed the other side of forty. Despite the fact that I was working as British correspondent for a well-known Swiss music magazine, I couldn't care less about rock music, but I was deep into social causes. My first question to him had been: "Do you ever, in the midst of your stardom, think of the poor, the people who are starving on the other side of the world? Or is it easy for you to forget about them, because your position in society allows you to do so, because you live in a golden palace?"

As it happened, Roger cared very much. And so he shared with me the wisdom of his forty something years, his views about the injustice of the world, about the recent Band Aid effort of Bob Geldof...

"You are the first person to ask me that question, you know," he told me. "Usually, people only want to know about my music. They couldn't care less what I think of world affairs."

As for me, I couldn't care less about the music. Dutifully, I at some stage threw in the obligatory questions about the album release, but soon we were back to talking serious stuff. The walls between journalist and rock star ceased to exist. We were talking, one human being to the next, living in an insecure and suffering world, trying to find ways to deal with it responsibly. I discovered that Roger Daltrey was much more than a rock musician who could hop around the stage and croon some lyrics to the sound of heavy drums. He was a highly intelligent man, a seeker, a deep thinker. He captivated me with his ideas and theories, and the hours flew by unnoticed.

"Roger, let's do something," I eventually told him. "Let's put our heads together and make a difference. We are in a position to: you as a singer, me as a journalist."

He agreed. We discussed the possibility of a second band aid. He said he would talk to Geldof. If Geldof said no, we would do it without him. We exchanged phone numbers, vowing to meet again before the month was over, to discuss the matter further.

Before I left, I asked him: "Hey Roger, do you ever wonder whether people want to be your friend because you are famous, and if they really care for you as a person, or whether it is your limelight which attracts them?"

"Sometimes," he replied. "But I can usually tell. You learn to after a while, you know."

"I see," I replied. "I never listened to the "Who." I like opera in my private life. I came here because the magazine sent me, and I will probably never listen to another song of yours after I walk out of here. Though I must admit, for a rock singer, I mean, if you like this kind of music, you are really good."

He smiled. "Thank you."

"Anyway, what I was going to say is: I don't care too much about the music you make, but I do care about what you have to say. I think you are really smart and I think it's great you care, when so many people don't. My heart is not yet hardened to the pain of others, and I hope it never will be. But so many people I meet have already become cynics. All they can tell me is "you have to learn not to care" and that I will see things their way once I grow up. But you didn't do that. You said: great idea, let's make a difference together. That meant a lot to me. I would like for us to be friends while I am stationed here, talk on the phone from time to time. Maybe Phil and I could come and visit you and your wife, or the other way around. Is that okay?"

He replied that he would like that very much. He said he had a trout farm somewhere up in the English countryside, and since Phil enjoyed fishing, why didn't we come up and visit them some time soon.

"You will like my wife, she is a terrific person," he told me proudly. "And I know she will be very enthused about our new project..."

As I walked to the underground, past the famous wax museum of Madame Tussaud's, I thought about the new friend I had just made. I looked at the grey, London streets and reflected on the words he had told me when I had asked him if he was truly happy.

"I think none of us are ever truly happy," he told me. "Not the pioneers of the mind, because we always strive to go to the very end of our thoughts. We are always searching for something. Perfection, I suppose. We are searching for justice, for perfection not just in our own souls, but in humankind. And we never find it. And yet, we will never stop searching..."

23

"Roger, I think I am like that, too," I replied. "I have everything: I am only 20 and I have a journalism job as an overseas correspondent. I get to meet anyone I want to. I have a fiancé who adores me. But just like you said, you know: I am almost happy, but not totally. There is something missing, and I think it is what you were talking about: the expectation for justice and compassion in those I meet, which is never being fulfilled. So, tell me, you have lived with this longer than me: how do you deal with it?"

He said that you had to care, but you could not allow yourself to carry the world upon your shoulders. "You have to build a circle of sunshine around yourself, where you can retreat to and find happiness. It's not fame or the glamour that we both have in our respective jobs. It's the people who love us: my wife, your husband ... It's sitting quietly by a lake and watching a beautiful sunset. It's walking lush green fields with your dog...."

When I got home, it was dark.

"So, what did you two talk about all this time?" Phil greeted me.

"Ethiopia," I told him, "Morocco, South Africa. Bob Geldof. The poor who line the streets of London, whom rich people like us would rather not see. Growing up. Being a rock star. Trout. Marriage. Lakes. Dogs..."

Phil laughed. "That's a lot all at once, isn't it?"

"Yes," I told him, "but it was worth every minute of it. He is a great guy, and we will see more of him while we are here. In fact, Roger and I have decided to put another band aid together. Also, we were thinking of ways to get the surplus food which is being destroyed here day by day over to the starving in Africa and India. We are thinking of hiring a truck convoy, and some planes..."

Phil knew me well by now, and he was not surprised. Spontaneous help actions were as common for me as were instant friendships with my interview partners. None of what I

24

said seemed in any way unusual to him.

He did, however, drop his fork with surprise when, an hour later, while we were having dinner and my mind was wandering, I suddenly announced: "We are going to have to buy a Pekingese tomorrow!"

"Excuse me?" Phil asked. "Did you just say we are going to have to buy a Pekingese?"

"Yes," I replied. "See, Roger said that I have to try to find happiness in little things, because I'll never get the global justice and universal love of all mankind which I crave for. He said I have to get down to basics, make a list of the simple things which bring me joy. And I have reflected on that and found out that one of the things which always brought me great delight, no matter how bad things were around me, was having a Pekingese in the house."

Chapter 2

To Tell The Whole Story, You Have To Go Back To The Very Start...

Phil was aware that I came from a family that had a long history of owning Pekingeses. While growing up, my mother had brought a succession of them into our house: Pekingeses of all colors and sizes, starting with a young female whom we named Snoopy, when I was merely 7 years old. I had come to love the flat-faced, minute dogs with their big hearts and royally arrogant dispositions. Pekingeses are born with the delusion that they own the world, and they are somehow able to convince everyone around within a matter of hours that this is indeed true.

I had, in fact, lost my last Pekingese, a grey miniature male by the name of Herbert, not so long ago. Herbert had been my first "own" Pekingese, meaning that I had bought him for myself after moving to Australia.

Before making it as a journalist there, I was so desperately poor - having moved out of home at age sixteen, ten days after arriving in this foreign continent - that I barely had enough money to buy myself food, pay for the bus fare to school and purchase my school books. Still, I had to have a Pekingese. So I saved up every week, from the small allowance of $35 which my mother gave me. Although we were not speaking to each other, my mother - who was a rather wealthy woman from money she had made as a top model when young and then wisely invested in real estate - allowed me to live in the annex of one of her spare houses in Australia, rent-free. She also picked up my electricity and basic phone bill.

The $35 which she gave me in addition to live on were a purposefully low, impossible-to-get-by-on amount. She was hoping that the desperate poverty I had fallen into after moving out of the wealthy environment I had been raised in would

27

drive me back to her world of 12 bedroom homes and caviar for breakfast.

She was wrong: having been raised rich, I indeed struggled desperately to adjust to instant poverty, at the same time as having to get used to a new country with its new culture and people. But I did not turn back and run to the safety of wealth. Instead, I lived off spaghetti and tomato sauce, week after week. Luckily, at sixteen, I was still young enough that spaghetti was my favorite food. Being able, finally, to eat as much as I wanted of my preferred dish - without some adult restricting me to one helping per week for "nutritional reasons" - actually felt like a treat instead of a hardship.

Spaghetti only cost 50 cents for half a pound, and I paid $1 for a can of whole, peeled tomatoes. I only needed 3 pounds of spaghetti a week, and a can of tomatoes could last to make sauce for 3 days. Thanks to careful budgeting, I was able to lay aside $5 per week into a little box, marked "Pekingese money." For in the midst of all the upheaval of losing my roots and the financial safety of my family environment, I had decided that the worst thing about my current situation was not the poverty or finding myself in a country whose culture and people were truly alien to me, but that I was suddenly living all alone.

I was new to Australia, and had no friends or even acquaintances. I was sixteen, attending high school. While all the other kids went home after school to their mothers who waited for them with a hot meal and would curiously ask them how school was, I went home to an empty house. My neighbors were two rather strange men, not ideal candidates for friendship. One of them worked at the local prison as a guard; the other one was involved in somewhat shady business dealings. Willie, the shady one, had gotten himself a German shepherd pup from the pound and later taken it out into the bush and shot it, when the puppy grew into a big dog that needed a lot of food. Willie wanted to spend the money on booze rather than dog food, so the dog had to go. These were not exactly the kind of people I wanted to socialize with.

The people across the street were not much better. There was really nobody to talk to. I found it difficult to relate to the other kids at school. They were still living in their secure environments, while I was out on my own. When I wanted to talk about how to make ends meet on $35 a week, they spoke of boy problems or their parents' 9pm curfew. I, on the other hand, could stay out all night if I pleased. If I would have had someone to stay out with, that is. My biggest problem was that I knew nobody.

I had no car, and buses in Australia run sporadically and rarely on schedule. This precluded me from getting around to social events - even if I had known where they were - to meet people. I was not the kind who would turn to drugs or other destructive habits to while away the time.

I decided I needed someone to move in with me. Someone to greet me when I came home from school. Someone to at least show some interest when I had gotten an A on an exam paper.

That "someone," I decided, would have to be a Pekingese. Hence the box....

Many months later, just as I had finished high school with a straight A's and one B, making it possible for me to go on to university, I had $120 in the Pekingese box. One bright Sunday morning, I got on my bicycle and cycled the two blocks down to my neighborhood's only supermarket. I bought the Sunday edition of the "West Australian" and - to celebrate the occasion - a ham and cheese croissant. I went back home, made myself a cup of coffee and - as I had learned some years earlier from a friend in Monte Carlo - opened up the ham and cheese croissant, poured some strawberry jam into it, and closed it again.

Between bites of sweet-sour croissant and sips of coffee,

I opened up the paper and turned to the classified section. I found the "dogs and cats" section and went down the column to P for Pekingese. Three breeders were advertising Pekingese puppies. I called the first two. No good. They only had females left. I wanted a male. I called the third one.

"Yes, I still have one male left," the lady told me over the phone.

"What color is it?" I asked.

"It's a grey," she informed me.

I wanted a fawn, the typical Pekingese color. But this was the last male Pekingese left in the city of Perth. These were the only three breeders, and none of them would have puppies again until the middle of next year. I didn't want to wait that long.

"How much do you want for him?" I asked her. She wanted $100 precisely. Great!

"All right, I'll take him," I told her. "Now, there is one problem: I am new here, and I don't have a car. Do you suppose you could bring the dog to me?"

She supposed that she could. I hung up the phone cycled back to the shopping center, where the bank and cash machine was. I withdrew $115, clearing my account of all but the last $5. Next, I went to the supermarket and bought a dog leash, a feeding bowl, water bowl and a collar. When I returned home, I prepared for the new arrival as well as I could. The house had barely any furniture in it, and I was too poor to buy a dog basket. For a couch, I had a mattress on the floor of the small hallway, which doubled as my living room. I cleared away one side of the "couch," put a few folded towels on it and designated it to be the "dog area."

No sooner did I finish than Herbert arrived on the arm of his breeder. He was so adorable that I instantly fell in love with him. His face resembled that of the cute Gremlins in the Spielberg movie and he looked at the world with large, wondrous puppy eyes.

Proudly, I counted ten ten-dollar bills into the lady's hand. She handed over the small Pekingese, some baby food (this is what Pekingeses eat when they are puppies), instructions on how much to feed it and said: "This is your dog now."

In Australia, school ends in November and starts again in February. Because Australia is located in the Southern Hemisphere, our winter is their summer. Christmas, thus, is at the height of summer. University did not start until February, and I had all of the summer holidays to get acquainted with Herbert, the new Pekingese.

Soon, Herbert followed me around the house, having come to see me as his surrogate mother. With the help of my cute dog, I began to make friends and go out in the evenings. They were not druggies or otherwise bad company, but we lived a wild and free life. I took the dog with me wherever I went: dance halls, outdoor music concerts, little cafes, the beach. Soon, people grew accustomed to the little grey Pekingese on the streets of Fremantle, a chic seaport outside Perth, which would achieve worldwide fame a few years hence as the site of the 1986/7 America's Cup.

True to his breed, Herbert was afraid of nothing. He once threw himself into the waves with a death defiant look on his face after I called out to him while I was standing in knee deep water and he had been sitting on the beach. When I began to make money on the side as a model, Herbert came to the photo shoots and ended up in a shoot of designer sweaters.

During our modeling time, Herbert and I were booked - as a team - by a jewelry seller to attract customers to his store. It was the most stupid job in the world, really: we were to walk up and down outside the store, then stop and look interestedly at the jewelry on display. The idea was that people would see me stop and stop themselves.

Soon, Herbert became the star of the show. When I

stopped, people would stop, too. Not to look at the jewelry, but to exclaim: "Oh my, what a cute little dog this is." They would come over, bend down to pet Herbert, asking "what breed is he?" I would tell them, then involve them in conversation, saying, "we are from overseas, just visiting. My, you have some nice jewelry in Australia." It worked. They bought.

Word spread and I got a lot of bookings. But the agent always came to me with the specification: "Not without the Pekingese, they want the dog."

This was how Herbert and I passed an interesting and what would turn out to be rather lucrative summer. We traveled everywhere by bus, since I still did not have a driving license. Buses in Australia did not allow pets, so I transported Herbert in a big, brown shoulder bag. I put Herbert inside, until we passed the driver. Once on the seat, I would let the dog out of the bag. When our stop came up, the dog went back into the bag and we got out of the bus without the driver ever finding out that he had transported a Pekingese. It helped that Herbert was a miniature Pekingese and so he was small enough to fit even into regular size shoulder bags.

University started in autumn. I couldn't make up my mind whether to become a journalist or a psychologist, so I enrolled in both, opting for a double major.

"Are you sure you can handle the work load?" the director asked me when I filled in my forms. "That is a lot of classes you have there."

"Sure, I can," I assured him. "No problem."

There was, however, one problem. I had so many classes to attend that I was often away from home from 8 am until 9 p.m. No way that I could leave the little dog alone in the house for such a large amount of time. So I solved the problem by taking him to school. Herbert attended lectures, tutorials and canteen lunches. As the only dog in school, it was not hard for him to score from my fellow students, bites of roast beef and whatever else was at the menu at this particular university, which was known for its gourmet canteen food.

Australia is a very laid back country, and initially nobody objected to Herbert coming to school or taking up a seat in the lecture theaters, until, one day, I encountered one of those people who are a nightmare and exist in every society: the copycats. She was a girl in journalism school.

One morning, she decided to bring her huge, untrained German Shepherd puppy. The puppy barked and peed on the floor of the lecture theatre. Now, when Herbert attended class, you never knew he was there. He usually went to sleep on the chair next to me, and when the class was over, he dutifully followed me across the lawn to the next building, the next class. He was perfectly housebroken, and he never barked.

The shepherd puppy, on the other hand, was a nuisance. The girl was told to remove it. She told the teacher: "Why? If Tess can bring her dog to school, so can I." The hassle had begun. Afraid that the school would soon turn into a kennel if others followed suit, the dean issued an order that no dogs were allowed on campus.

As soon as the rule had come down, I marched straight into the dean's office. "Look, you have to allow my dog to school," I told him. "I am all alone on this continent. I am an immigrant. I put myself through school by working after hours as a model. I study hard. But unlike that girl who brought her stupid, uneducated puppy to school, when she needn't have done so because she has a mother and brothers at home to look after it, I don't. When I come home, there is nobody there. When I leave the house in the morning, there is nobody to check on it. I have no friends, only acquaintances. I barely have enough money to feed myself and the dog, so there is not a cent to spare, after I have paid my school bills as well, to hire someone to come in. Now, I have taken on responsibility for that dog, and I cannot leave him alone all these hours. I am not bringing him here to be eccentric, but because there is no other way. If you don't allow Herbert here, I will have to quit school.

Which would be a real shame, considering I am getting straight A's in journalism (I didn't want to mention psychology, as I was barely scraping by with 51% in the statistics and anatomy classes)."

That did it. Herbert got special permission and stayed. He attended journalism and psychology lectures and - as I made more money and could afford it - spent the lunch breaks with me and some acquaintances from school at an outdoor cafe in Fremantle.

Things began to happen. My situation changed. I landed a job as Australian correspondent for a major European music magazine before I was even half way through my first year of journalism at university. Soon, I began to date one of Australia's biggest sports stars. Herbert did not object to the sports star, probably because he never stayed overnight at our house. Not so with Colin, my high school biology teacher. In between the sports star, with whom I broke off frequently only to have a passionate reunion a few months later, I briefly dated Colin. More out of principle than because I liked him. While I was at high school, all the girls had a crush on Colin. He was 26, blond, blue-eyed and considered handsome. He never gave a schoolgirl a second look. Colin dated girls in their mid-twenties. I was sure he would make an exception for me.

So I called him, some five months after I finished high school. He came over, he took me out. We saw each other for a week or two. Then came the big night: Colin was going to stay over. Herbert growled when I kicked him off his usual spot on the bed to make room for Colin. I put Herbert on the floor. Being a miniature Pekingese, he was too small to jump back up on the bed. He needed to be lifted up, which I refused to do.

I explained to Herbert that he would sleep on the floor that night. Colin awoke at 5 am to go to the bathroom. I woke up, too, and opened my eyes to see Colin stepping into a pile of dog turd which Herbert had deposited neatly in front of the bed, just in the stepping range. I just about killed myself with laughter as I watched Colin hobble to the bathroom on one foot, grab a towel to wipe the other clean and start swearing.

He was not amused and when he came back, he put on his clothes.

"You will never see me again," he threatened. "How disgusting."

"That's cool, Colin," I told him, "I wouldn't have been able to see you again anyway, because my dog doesn't like you, judging from the gift he left for you. And if my dog doesn't approve, too bad..."

Colin left, muttering something about crazy foreigners and that he hated Pekingeses. True to his word, I never saw him again.

Then came the America's cup. By then, Herbert and I had been together for several years. I had become a "proper" journalist, having branched out from music into sports, general interest and occasionally politics. It was only natural that I was asked to report on the sailing event for some magazines in Europe.

The dog came with me to the media center and sat at my press desk as I wrote my stories. Because Europe had a time difference with Australia, I often wrote all night to meet a deadline. Herbert and I became a fixture in the media center after hours, when all good journalists were asleep in their beds and the Pekingese sat beside me on a chair as I slaved at the computer.

One of these nights, I met Phil. I was trying to work out how to explain to the German readers, some 10,000 miles away across the water, that I had been backing the wrong boat.

Phil, who was a big shot with one of the boats and a sailing expert, offered to help me out. One thing led to another and - after a brief battle between Phil and the sports star, when I took both men out to dinner with me - Phil won and we decided to get engaged. I thought it would be best if I

35

were to transfer to London, where Phil was based, rather than have him come to Australia.

Just as we were about to work out how to get Herbert past the stringent quarantine laws in the United Kingdom, the little Pekingese died in the middle of the night, at age five, of a heart attack...

So this brings me back to the present time. I was in London, without Pekingese. Phil himself had never owned animals. The first thing I had done when moving into his apartment in London had been to acquire, while Phil was away on a two-day business trip, a cream colored Persian cat whom we named Mortimer. Mortimer, as is customary for Persian cats, spent his time eating and sleeping. He treated Phil and me with disdain and considered us to be lower life forms, barely worthy of emptying his litter box. It wasn't really like having a pet at all. It was more for the principle of it.

Now, when Roger had mentioned "walks with the dog" on his list of "little things" to cling to for happiness, I became painfully aware how much I missed having a Pekingese around. In fact, the time in London was the longest I had ever gone in my life without having a Pekingese as part of the family. I was about to make some changes....

Chapter 3

He Was Royalty From The Very Start
Or: Tiny - Keeping The British Stiff Upper Lip

It had to be a grey Pekingese. Absolutely. And a miniature. I wanted an exact copy of Herbert. Or as close to it as I could get. What I didn't know was that Herbert had been the most expensive kind of Pekingese you could get. They had not cared in Australia, where nobody cared much about anything and hence all Pekingeses were priced at the same, low level.

Here in England, things were different. England was the Pekingese capital of the western world. The finest Pekingeses were born and bred here and exported into countries around the globe.

To get started, we called the United Kingdom Pekingese Breeders Association.

"Ah, you want a miniature," the man at the association remarked. "We call them "sleeves" here, because they fit into a jacket sleeve. That will cost you, especially a male sleeve. Sleeves are very hard to come by. There is usually only one per litter. Especially the male sleeves, they are very much in demand as breeding dogs. You can't breed with a female sleeve, because they are too small to have puppies. But a male, that is a different matter. Are you sure you don't want a female? That will be cheaper for you?"

"No, I told him, "it has to be a male."

He gave recommendations, and numbers of registered breeders to call. "Try your luck with those, maybe one of them has a sleeve in their recent litters."

When I added that I was looking for a grey, he point-blank told me that I probably wouldn't be able to pay for it.

"Grey is the rarest color among Pekingeses, and highly sought after. To find a miniature grey male will be real lucky, even if you could afford to pay the price they'll charge, provided they'll let him go in the first place..."

I had no idea that Herbert had been such a specialized and obviously valuable Pekingese! The man from the association gave me one final bit of advice:

"Now, watch out for the breeders," he cautioned. "Your not being a Pekingese expert, they may try to sell you a grey puppy which turns fawn later on. Many pups are born with a grey overcoat, but they lose it after six months. The way you can tell if a pup is a genuine grey is to check out its undercoat. Only buy the pup if the undercoat is grey, too. If the undercoat is fawn, he will grow up to be a fawn. If they do have a genuine grey, make sure it is really a sleeve. Ask to see the mother and father. If the father is not a sleeve, forget it. Compare the puppy in size to its siblings. If he is not considerably smaller, don't go for it."

He then told me the usual: make sure I buy a flat nosed puppy, as puppies with protruding noses often have breathing problems later in life and are not considered well-bred.

Phil and I called every breeder on the list. Many of them were miles away from where we lived, clear on the other side of the country. We didn't care. We were desperate. Most breeders had no sleeves. Those that did, had no greys. When we finally found a breeder that had a grey Pekingese, it was not a sleeve. Then we found a grey female sleeve.

When we had just about given up, we located three breeders, one near the border with Scotland, one in Yorkshire and one in the West country, all of whom professed to have a grey miniature male Pekingese in their recent litters - at a price, of course. The cheapest price we were quoted was £400, which converts to more than $800 U.S., a far cry from what I had paid for Herbert a few years earlier in the land down under.

Over the next week, photographs of the little Pekingeses arrived in the mail. One of the breeders, to prove to us that the Pekingese was truly a sleeve, had photographed the pup next to a cigarette packet. The puppy was smaller than the upright pack of Marlboros....

"Oh, we have to go to see this one," I told Phil. "He is gorgeous."

So were the others, though none of them arrived in our mailbox next to a cigarette packet...

Thankfully, we had a fast car, a Lotus, which ate up the miles as we drove across England to visit the breeders. I was in Pekingese heaven as I sat on their living room floors and played with assorted puppies and their parents.

The first one was a genuine grey, but his parents were both normal sizes. Although he was cute as can be, we passed it by.

The pup beside the cigarette packet was a fawn with a grey overcoat. But he was a miniature. He was mischievous and curious. He came to nibble at my shoes. Although he was the smallest, he dominated the entire litter. I was tempted to go for him, although he did not have the right color.

"We have come this far, we might as well go up to the west country and look at the last one," Phil suggested. "You said you wanted a grey, so let's go and see if the other one is a grey."

"But this one is so adorable," I said to Phil. "I think we should make a deal on it right now, before it goes."

Phil didn't. He told the old couple, who were the breeders, and who were trying to pressure us by saying "there is someone coming to look at him tomorrow morning" by way of the usual sales tactic, that they would have to wait until we called them at the end of the week to let them know.

The following day, he took me to the West country. That's where we met Tiny for the first time. Tiny was a genuine miniature grey sleeve. He also was the most expensive of them all, as he had champion bloodlines. His face was perfectly squashed in, as a well-bred Pekingese's should be, and he was friendly to all humans, including us.

He was incredibly bossy with his mother and father and his siblings, but we wrongly assumed that was a puppyhood trait he would grow out of. Being the finest and most precious of the litter, Tiny was already royally spoilt and used to getting his own way.

There was a line-up of people who were coming to see Tiny, but - because the breeders were so far away - most of them had to wait for the weekend. Tiny was not yet ready to leave his mother anyway, and would not be for sale for another three weeks.

"Tell you what," Phil and I offered. "We are going to buy the puppy right now, and we will leave him with you for another three weeks. We'll pay you, of course, and we'll give you a little extra for you to deliver him to us when he is ready to go."

The breeders agreed. "I suppose in that case we could register him straight away in your name and wouldn't even have to transfer ownership later on," the lady mused. This was what we decided on.

We celebrated the deal with the obligatory British cup of tea and forked out a ridiculously high amount of money for the minute grey creature that frolicked about on those people's living room carpet. Then we sipped the last of our tea and left, minus the dog and the money, with a sales contract in hand and the promise that they would bring him to us before the month was over.

It was a drab, grey January afternoon when we drove to pick Tiny up from Paddington station. The breeder who brought him had him wrapped in his jacket.

"Now, it's cold outside," he warned us. "Keep him well wrapped, or he'll catch a chill. A Pekingese baby is just like a human baby and requires the same caution and care. They are not like ordinary little dogs. You can send me the jacket back by mail."

He handed over the dog, the baby food and the feeding instructions. The latter I already knew from the experience with Herbert. Having done so, he hopped back on the train and was gone. Phil and I headed for our car, with a jacket containing a little Pekingese on my arms.

A few days later, I left for a one-month trip to Australia, where I had some urgent business to attend. Phil remained in London with Tiny, Mortimer and an entire hallway covered with old newspapers, transformed into Tiny's playroom and toilet.

It was Phil's job to house train Tiny while I was gone and also to get him better acquainted with Mortimer, who so far was not taking the slightest notice of the puppy.

When I returned, Tiny had grown visibly. He now had the run of the house and stomped about as if he owned the place. He was perfectly toilet trained, thanks to Phil's efforts. The attempt to get going a friendship between Mortimer and Tiny had failed miserably. Instead, the cat was completely under Tiny's thumb. Although Tiny was still eating his baby food and did not even like the cat food, he would growl at the cat to chase him away from his food, then leave it unattended. But the moment the cat came back, Tiny would shoot back to the cat's feeding bowl and chase him off again.

Eventually, we resorted to feeding the cat on the kitchen counter, where Tiny couldn't reach him.

It was now time to introduce our little grey terror to the world. During Tiny's first three outings, we learned some important facts about our new family member. The first one was that he loved playground slides, the second that he was highly adventurous and the third that he was extremely partial to vanilla ice cream. Although he is now a dignified dog in his 9th year, none of these three facts have changed.

Tiny's first big outing was to the children's playground around the corner from where we lived in Richmond. It was

41

here that we discovered Tiny's love for slides. We put him on top of the slide, called "Tiny, slide," and he went into sliding position and zoom down to where Phil or I stood to catch him. When he was finished, he would ask to be lifted up on the slide for seconds.

We tried him on the swings as well, but these he did not like at all. Slides, however, were to become Tiny's great love....

He especially liked being admired by passers-by, which stopped at the unusual sight of a fluffy, minute grey creature on four legs using the children's playground slide with obvious enthusiasm.

Tiny loved being the center of attention and would - after a successful slide - walk over and greet his audience. In his early puppy days, Tiny was still at a stage where he considered all people to be equal and was generally nice to everyone. This was soon to change, but for now anyone who cared to stop and come over was treated to a tail wag from Tiny.

Tiny's second outing was by accident. He had been playing in our back garden and somehow found a way out of it. From there, he had crossed the street in front of our house, gotten to the other side and walked into a neighbor's garden. The neighbor, who had on previous occasions seen us out walking with Tiny, was aware that the dog had wandered off alone, scooped him up and rang our doorbell with a very frightened Tiny on his arm. Tiny's tongue had gone all white with fear, and he was shaking all over.

The little Pekingese had been curious enough to venture beyond his boundaries, and then had become intimidated by the big, wide world out there, away from the safety of his "people." He was very glad to be back home and we learned early on a valuable lesson: Tiny will always look for the other side of the fence, no matter how big his playground, and it was of utmost importance to check even for the smallest holes in the fencing which he would try to squeeze through...

We also learned that Tiny's tongue was an indicator for

42

his state of mind. Tongue all the way out, stuck way out between the teeth meant: grin. Tongue white and only a small patch showing meant: fear. Tongue loosely sticking out half way, pointing downward meant: relaxation. Tongue half way, pointed straight meant: indifference. Tongue stuck between teeth, pointing upward, teeth showing: highest jubilation. Because of his unique way of communication by way of positioning his tongue, Tiny became known as "Tiny and the tongue."

On his third outing, we took Tiny to Richmond Park to get him used to the leash. Later in life, Tiny would object to walking on a leash. But at this stage, he was still young and somewhat obedient. When we told him to walk on a leash, he did it. Oh, blessed early days...

By now it was spring and the sun shone. Birds sang in the trees and the population of London had come out of winter hibernation to enjoy the first days of warm weather. Tiny, who still had his puppy fluff and was not yet fully grown, was a hit in the park with children and adults alike. He still did not consider himself a big enough star to be arrogant, and so everyone who cared to got to pat and admire him.

Phil and I rented a boat and took Tiny rowing down the river. Before we went out on the water, I had gotten myself a cone of vanilla ice cream. Now, as Phil was rowing and I sat watching him, sun warming my face, ice cream slowly dripping, I became aware that Tiny stared at my ice cream cone with a look of intense concentration and greed.

"Do you want to try some?" I asked him.

A tail wag. He stuck his tongue out between his front teeth in a Pekingese grin. I handed him the cone. Tiny tried a little bit, then some more...then he couldn't stop. He gulped up the ice cream with increasing greediness and eventually stuck his entire face way down into the ice cream cone. When he re-surfaced, he had ice cream dripping off his chin and all over his black face. He had just discovered his first love...

43

As time went by, we acquired some additional family members. A horse, another Persian cat, a grey, whom we named Mushroom for no particular reason, other that we couldn't think of a name. A black house cat named "Cat Nigger," who arrived thus named from the local pet store. We tried to call the cat by a different name, but he would not listen. Call him "Nigger" and he would come running...

The two Persian cats stuck together and wanted nothing to do with either Tiny or Nigger or Phil and I. Tiny delighted in walking over them when they were sleeping, waking them up. The cats would give a yawn, walk away and go back to sleep at another spot. Tiny and Nigger bonded quickly and would wrestle together late into the night.

Nigger proceeded to become an embarrassment due to his offensive name. When our TV had broken down one day, we called the repair man. He was a dark-skinned man from India. The repairman and Nigger were both in the living room. I was in the kitchen, preparing the food for our entire animal family. Not wanting to walk all the way to the living room, I called the cat when his meal was ready. "Hey, Nigger come here." To my utter horror, the TV repairman appeared in the doorframe.

"Yes?" he asked.

"Oh geez," I stammered. "I am terribly sorry. I was calling the cat. Did you think that.... Oh God, how awful, I would never..."

The poor man did his best to calm me down again and I did my utmost to explain about the cat's name that came from the pet shop. Eventually, we both laughed, the cat appeared to claim his food and I decided to call him "cat" from now on...

Tiny was great at making friends in his early days, even if he did not meet them in person. This was how we turned the photolab girls into pet sitters.

44

We took heaps of photos in those days, since our animals were all extremely photogenic. The girls at the photo lab, a pair of young sisters who had come to London from Iran, were so intrigued with the pictures they developed week by week that one day they asked if they could get to meet "that cute grey dog," and would we mind bringing him to the store next time we came by. We did. They fell in love. Soon, Nasreen and Nazir went in and out of our home and took care of our private zoo when we were on the road, travelling for business.

As Tiny grew out of his puppy stage, he also grew more aloof to people around him. Indeed, he became a true Brit. Tiny socialized from then on only with a few select chosen people, in whom the Iranian girls were included as they had known him from his puppyhood. As far as new people went, Tiny treated them the way a star would treat his fans: with polite distance. When they came too close without his permission, he growled. When the growling did not keep them away and they exclaimed, "oh, how cute, this little thing is growling," Tiny said "ra,ra,ra," a variation on the bark, and bit them. With his little teeth, he never did any damage, but it scared the offenders into submission and the next time, they treated the Pekingese with respect.

Tiny soon developed his own set of rules: "what Tiny says goes," and it was considered wise to stick by them. He also developed into a great guard dog. Because he is a little dog, Tiny learned to modify his bark. To scare away imaginary intruders after they rang the doorbell, he would lower his voice and bark "rau, rau," making you think - if you didn't see the dog - that the bark came from a very large canine. When he wanted something from us, he raised his voice and said "waff, waff" until he got what he was after: being lifted up or down from the bed, or getting to go with us when we went out and intended to leave him behind....

The following winter, we gave Mortimer, who had never

cared much for us anyway, to our neighbors. We then packed Tiny, Mushroom, the Cat Nigger and assorted members of our increasingly growing equine family on a plane and moved to an equestrian center in Canada.

Tiny had no problems with the flight. Being a world traveller came naturally to him. He had, after all, already spent one year of his life in England. Clearly, it was now about time to see the world. The small, grey Pekingese arrived in Canada in his special pet carrier, without a trace of jet lag, waffed his way through customs, and took possession of the horse farm the following day...

Chapter 4

How To Acquire A Puppy In Ten Easy Steps
Or: And Mike Makes Two...

From the very beginning, Mike was not an ordinary dog. Mike was a dog who came to us under a rather absurd set of circumstances. It involved the death penalty in Texas, a race-car driving cop and the movie "Mississippi Burning..." I was on assignment in Houston, Texas, doing a story about a death penalty case. The inmate in question, James David Autry, had been dead some 5 years and there was reason to believe that he had been innocent. Together with a photographer, I was to dig up the facts of the case, interview Autry's family as well as death row inmates still alive who had known him ... it was a tough story.

My photographer, a sensitive young man, had lost his nerve when asked to walk into the death chamber and photograph the gurney on which the state of Texas executed its condemned inmates. With shaking hands, he had tried to change his film in the death chamber and dropped his camera on the floor. The following day, he took the first plane home to Montreal, mumbling that he wasn't cut out for this job.

Six hours later, my replacement photographer, Bastian, arrived at the same airport. The flight from Montreal to Houston is quite tiring, often requiring one or more changes of plane. When Bastian arrived at Houston's Hobby Airport in the early evening, he was exhausted.

" I've got great news for you," I greeted him, trying to sound as casual as possible. "We have to drive straight on to Colorado. We are expected there in the morning for an interview with Autry's brother. Sorry about that."

Autry's younger brother was in prison in Colorado Springs on minor charges. The interview with him had been arranged and fitted into a tight schedule prior to the photographers' change. There was no way it could be rescheduled.

The photographer always had to do the driving, as I frequently typed up interview notes and impressions while in motion. With a long story such as this one, otherwise the information could easily get lost.

On the way out of Houston, I felt sorry for Bastian. He looked rather green from his flight, lack of food and sleep.

"Okay, listen, I think we may have a few hours to spare, if we race afterward to make up the time. Come on, let's pull off and go to a movie," I suggested, indicating the nearby Greenspoint mall just North of Houston, off the I45.

Bastian was all too happy to get a break and exited the I45 to pull into the mall, which had a big, multi-screen cinema. As it happened, they were showing "Mississippi Burning," a movie I had always wanted to see.

"Let's go for it, shall we?" I asked Bastian.

"Fine with me," he replied and we bought our tickets for the 7pm show. It was only 6:30. What to do next?

"What shall we do for the next half an hour?" I asked Bastian.

"How about we look around the mall a little," he suggested.

I did not have to look far before I spotted IT: A giant pet store, right next to the cinema.

"Doctors Pet Center" it read in big pink letters, and underneath, a black banner with hearts: GIANT PUPPY SALE

"Oh come on, let's have a look," I said to Bastian and dragged him with me.

You are not thinking of buying a dog, are you?" the horrified photographer asked me. "We are on assignment, we are living in hotels and we have to be out of here in three weeks," he pointed out. "That would be impossible."

" No, of course not," I replied. "What do you think I

am? Nuts? I just miss my dog back home (I meant Tiny) and I would just like to see if they have a little Pekingese. Just to look at."

The pet store was full of people. Little dogs of all shapes and sizes could be seen in cages behind giant glass windows. They looked happy and healthy. All of them tried to look their cutest: little Dalmatians chow chows, Labradors, poodles.... There was not a single Pekingese.

There was, however, one Shihtzu left. A few months earlier, Phil and I had seen a little Shihtzu on one of our travels through the US. Its owner had taken it for a walk outside the motel where we stayed. We had sworn there and then that our next dog would be a Shihtzu. Now would be as good a time as any to find out more about the breed, for future knowledge, when we could consider adding another dog to the family...

It was not long before the trained eye of one of the sellers spotted my interest in the small black and white Shihtzu puppy.

"She is a cutie, isn't she?" the girl remarked, joining me casually.

"Yes, she is quite nice," I replied, trying to sound indifferent, so as not to encourage her.

"To tell you the truth, we have had some trouble selling her, because she is hyperactive and behaves like a male dog. That's why she is reduced more than the other dogs," she remarked, indicating the price tag outside the cage. "If you look here, you will see that all the other pups are 25% off, this one is actually only half price. A great buy, if you ask me. She has champion bloodlines. And the behavior problem she will soon grow out of, if you ask me."

"Very interesting," I remarked, trying to look bored.

"I've got an idea," the salesgirl said. "Would you like to play with her?"

We still had 20 minutes before the movie started. There was nothing else to do. I might as well spend the time playing

49

with a Shihtzu...

"Yes, sure," I told the girl and before I could think about the implications of my action, I found myself in a small room with the sign "Puppy play room" on its door. With me were Bastian and the Shihtzu.

The dog ran around the room in circles, danced, wagged her tail, was very cute and ... very active.

"Cute dog, eh?" I remarked to Bastian.

"Yes, she is. But you can't consider it."

"Yes, I know, I am not."

The salesgirl came back.

"So, do you like her?" she asked.

"Yes, I do, but quite frankly, I think you are still asking too much money for her." Mike had been reduced from $800 to $400.

"How much would you be willing to pay?" she asked.

"Not more than $250," I bluffed, knowing that with this ridiculous offer, I would soon be off the hook.

To my utter horror, the salesgirl smiled and said "just a minute, I'll talk to the manager."

Bastian and I swallowed hard and looked at each other, wordlessly. This was not going the way we had planned. Not at all!

The girl came back.

"Congratulations, you got yourself a dog," she beamed. "The manager says it is okay."

"What do we do now?" I asked Bastian.

"Let's flip a coin," he suggested. "Heads it's yes, tails it's no. We'll flip three times, two out of three wins."

He flicked the first one. Tails. Just as well. It would have been impossible to have a dog and take it with us ... Second time: heads. Where would I even keep it? At the hotels? What would we do with the dog while we were at interviews? Take him, or rather: her? Maybe ... But at the Colorado Springs Jail? Impossible ... they would never let a dog in.

Third flick: heads! That meant yes. We had a dog!

I went to the register to pay for the dog.

"Listen," I said to the girl who had served us, "we have a bit of a problem. We are journalists from Canada, and we are here on assignment. We are on our way to the prison in Colorado Springs, and we can't take a dog there. But we'll be in Houston again next week, and we could pick her up then. Would you look after her for us?"

First, the girl's jaw dropped open. Then she started laughing. Then she remarked how great it was to meet real life foreign journalists. She said it would also be a great honor to look after a foreign journalist's dog. She said yes.

In the five minutes that remained before the movie started, we sat down by the side of the mall's indoor pond and played with our new dog.

"What are you going to call him?" Bastian asked.

"I think since she wants to be a he, we should do her the favor and call her Mike." I had always wanted a dog named Mike, and now was as good a time as any to seize the opportunity...

Mike went off to charm some of the mall's shoppers ... an urge that would never leave her. Whenever a stranger passes, Mike still runs up to them, wagging her tail, wanting to be patted.

"Mike," I called out. "Mike, come here."

The dog turned and came to us.

"Clear case of a Mike," I said to Bastian. "That's her name from now on, and she will be a he."

Name and gender problem settled, we walked back inside, handed Mike over to the girl and took her phone number. Then we left the store, shaking hands with everyone and giving the dog one final pat on the head.

The staff there must have thought we were crazy, buying a dog and leaving him behind! The look on their faces, as we left the store, indicated that they did not know what had hit them. Not that I could blame them...

"Mississippi Burning" was interesting, but more interesting was the cop's reaction who stopped us just outside Huntsville when we were speeding by at some 100 plus mph.

"Officer, there is a perfectly valid explanation for this," I began. "You see, we are journalists from Canada, on our way to Colorado, and we stopped and bought a dog..."

The cop was unimpressed by the dog story. I don't think he believed us. Who would? However, he seemed delighted to meet foreign journalists. "I am a bit newsworthy myself," he boasted and then showed us his car, a specially adapted race-car version of an ordinary patrol car. It looked like something out of "supercop" crossed with "Highway to Hell." The cop, a frustrated race-car driver, had taken advantage of not being restricted to speed limits. Bit by bit, he explained, he had adapted his car to turn it into a true racing machine.

While Bastian and he talked cars and I looked on, the cop explained that he had been featured in several nationwide magazines for his racecar style vehicle and his superior driving skills.

"I am afraid I will still have to give you a ticket, though," he mused. "Since you are out of towners, you will have to follow me to the nearest grocery store and pay it with your credit card. That will be $120."

Somehow, we talked him down to 90$, trading the discount for a mention of his car in our story.

"Do you know your way around here?" our new friend asked.

"No," Bastian said, "I only got here this afternoon."

"...and already you have a dog and a speeding ticket? Fast start isn't it?" the cop remarked.

"All right, follow me, let's see what you can do with this baby," the cop said, indicating our small, rented car.

The cop made a U-turn on the freeway, then went straight down a steep embankment and raced along the I45

52

to exit for the nearest convenience store. Bastian bravely followed.

When we got there, the cop grinned approval at Bastian: "I am impressed, I didn't think you'd make it down that embankment."

Having concluded that we were crazy enough to buy a dog while going to the movies, he obviously wanted to see if we were crazy enough to race down the freeway with a cop.

When we returned from Colorado, we picked up Mike from the girl at the pet store. After this, Mike came on several interviews with us and stayed with us in motels - all of which, I may point out, did not permit animals. Not a problem for Mike.

At the tender age of 3 months, he/she had already worked out how to charm anyone who crossed out path. A typical motel check-in scene would go like this:

1) We would drive up to the motel, leaving Mike in the car. Bastian would fill out the forms while I waited.

2) We would drive to the rooms and settle in.

3) Mike and I would take a walk around the motel gardens. Mike, well behaved, on a leash.

4) Someone from the motel would spot us and shout, "Excuse me."

5) I would pretend not to hear. Mike would pretend not to hear.

6) The motel person would walk over to us and say "Excuse me, Ma'am, but animals are not allowed here. You are going to have to leave. You cannot stay here with that dog. I am sorry."

7) Whereupon Mike would pretend to tear the leash out of my hand (of course, I was clued up, this was pure show) run up to the motel representative, wag his/her tail wildly and dance in front of him/her on two legs, pretending this person was the greatest human being this little dog had ever met.

8) The person would hold out as long as possible, trying to look the other way, trying to ignore the dog.

9) The person would finally break. He or she would bend down, pat the dog, who would keep dancing and smiling.

10) When the person came up again after being bathed in Mike's affections, he/she would typically say something like "My, that is a cute dog you have there. All right, just this once, but don't let the other guests see you."

I am pleased to report that we were only kicked out of two motels in all the time we spent in Texas.

The rest of our assignment (I like to divide our time in Texas as pre-Mike and post-Mike) was spent driving to interviews with the dog's face hanging out of the car, enjoying the wind, conducting interviews with the dog lying quietly on the carpeted floor in the interviewee's office or - on special occasions - even on their lap, going through the motel check-in routines, brushing the dog, bathing the dog, writing reports and stories with the dog looking on and, finally, working out a way to get the dog back home to Canada.

It was easier than we had anticipated. We found a vet to give Mike her shots. We bought her a plane ticket. We drove into Houston Hobby Airport, got rid of the rental car, put baggage and dog on a baggage cart and drove to check-in, accompanied by exclamations such as "Look, what a cute dog" and "Mammy, look at that dog," all of which Mike thoroughly enjoyed.

We stopped several times on the way to the counter, for Mike to give a tail wag here, and receive a pat there. The dog was clearly holding court in the airport lobby...

Finally, we watched as Mike was being stuffed by ground personnel into a dog carrier box and then the dog carrier and Mike's nose - looking out through the airholes - were left behind as we went to board our plane.

It is impossible to describe the look on Phil's face when he picked us up at the airport in Montreal and the first thing I said to him after Hello was "Oh, by the way, there is someone we have to pick up at cargo..."

PART 2

MIKE JOINS THE FAMILY AT THE EQUESTRIAN CENTER,

OR: TINY, MIKE AND THE HORSES....

Chapter 5

The Stable Owner And The Herding Dog

In the early Nineties, Phil and I owned a private equestrian center in the southern part of Quebec. Until I found out that journalism and equestrianism do not mix, since both require an equally exclusive dedication.

We had bought the equestrian center when moving from England, with its own indoor riding arena, outdoor jumping course and outdoor three-day event course. The barn had 36 box stalls. We filled up a number of them with some of the finest jumping horses from Germany: Holsteiners and Hanoveraners of proven competition bloodlines. There were some 40 acres of paddocks and fields to go with the farm, as well as its own small, private forest.

As soon as we had bought the horse farm, Phil and I decided that we needed a somewhat larger dog than Tiny to guard the farm. For Christmas of that year, I gave Phil a little sheep-dog mix puppy that he named Sheba. Sheba soon grew into a good-size dog, and would sleep at night in the barn with the horses. She was kind to Tiny, but the two of them only mixed occasionally, as Tiny tended to stay with us in the restaurant which we had converted into our living quarters.

When we bought the stable, our finances had not been quite enough to buy a house as well as the riding stable. So we took all the chairs and tables out of the adjacent restaurant which had big windows looking out into the indoor riding arena. We put a bed and our furniture in there, so Phil could now watch me ride at night from the bedside window, which looked out into the arena. This happened quite frequently, as I would often ride at 1 am in the morning, after having finished my journalism assignments for the day.

Journalism is a tough job, where often you spend the afternoons chasing down a story, doing interviews, and the entire evening writing the story to send it to a magazine or radio station the next morning. I usually was not done with my work until 11pm. By the time I had eaten, tacked up my horse and made it into the arena for a jumping session, it was usually well past midnight. When good citizens were asleep in their beds, I rode my horse over hurdles. Phil and Tiny, both sleepy eyed, would many nights watch me through the window: Phil in his pajamas, Tiny struggling to keep his eyes open.

During the day, Tiny was the stable owner. He would often walk the long corridor of the stable in his small, red, hooded raincoat, head proudly thrown back, little bowed legs swinging out to either side. From time to time, he would give a gracious tail wag to a horse as he passed its stall.

At feeding time, Tiny sat high on top of the hay bales, which we stacked on the cart in front of the grain drums as we passed the stalls, dishing out to each horse their ration of grain and two flakes of hay. When a horse was all too eager to get its food, pacing impatiently up and down in its stall, Tiny growled at it. The horses never took much notice, but the little Pekingese felt in charge all the same.

His favorite horse was the fat horse, a large Belgian warmblood that had once been provincial jumping champion. His official name was "Baladin," but we usually called him "the fat horse," because he only had to look at food and he put on weight. The fat horse tried to be tough and distant, but when he felt that none of the other horses were looking, he would blow gently into Tiny's face, and even accept a lick on the nose from the little Pekingese. The moment the other horses were around, however, he would act indifferent and pretend that he neither cared about me nor the little dog.

It was very important for the fat horse to keep up his macho image with the other horses. He considered himself to be something special and was the leader of the herd. He tried his best to come across as a tough, independent horse, who needed nothing and nobody. With me, he would even go as far as sighing and turning his face to the wall when I tried to pet him. When the others were not around, he would put his head in my lap and wait for me to scratch him behind the ears.

The fat horse and Tiny both delighted in being treated with special privileges. Because it made Tiny so happy, we allowed him the illusion that he owned the stable. When visitors came, it was in all essence the dog and not us who showed them around. As for the horse, we allowed him some special privileges, too: all our other horses spent their day outside in the large paddock beside the jumping field. The fat horse was the only horse whose stable door was open day and night and who was allowed to roam free around the farm as he pleased.

Like Tiny, the horse liked being reasoned with, rather than commanded. When I took him out for a ride one day, without saddle or bridle, just with a halter and two ropes attached to its sides, the fat horse tried to bolt. It would have been useless to try to pull back under control such a powerful animal with nothing but a flimsy halter and two ropes. Instead, I leaned forward on the horse's neck and - as he was bolting - told him "Bad fat horse, that's not very nice. I thought the fat horse was a responsible horse"! The fat horse thought about it for a few strides, then he slowed down to a trot and eventually allowed me to pull him into a walk.

Tiny would jump up at my leg when we were in the stable together, begging me to hold him up to the fat horse's head so the two of them could sniff each other. When other horses were around, the fat horse sighed and turned away, pretending not to know the little dog. Tiny was delighted that more often than not, there was an opportunity to be alone with his equine friend.

Sheba fulfilled the duties of a normal barn dog, such as guarding the riding center, rounding up the horses when it was time to come in from the paddock, playing rough guy games with Phil and the stable hands. Tiny treated Sheba with the arrogant disdain that a nouveau riche stable owner has for the helping hands. He was nice to Sheba, but clearly acted superior. Sheba, who was three times the size of Tiny, retreated respectfully when Tiny wanted access to her feeding bowl. It was not unusual to see Sheba standing by, peacefully wagging her tail, as Tiny stood over her bowl and ate her food. Sheba fully accepted that Tiny owned the place and everything in it, including her.

Into this "family" arrived Mike. At first, Tiny was not amused, to say the least. Unlike Sheba, Mike came to share the house/restaurant with us. Unlike Sheba, Mike did not sleep in the main barn. To Tiny's utter horror, Mike slept on the bed. Tiny reacted by making himself as large as possible, leaving little room for either myself or Phil, much less another dog. He proceeded to lie, fully spread out, right bang in the middle of the bed. This left a very small corridor for both Phil and myself on either side of Tiny.

If we tried to move him, he growled and - when necessary - bit. Mike was wiser than us and did not even try. He modestly curled up at the foot-end of the bed.

Mike was very friendly and tried everything, from tail wagging to dancing to gently initiating a wrestling match to win Tiny over. To no avail. Tiny stayed distant. For three days, he would have nothing to do with Mike, Phil or myself. Whenever we came near him, he growled. The only contact we had with Tiny during that time was when he demanded his food, demanded to be let out to do his business, or came to the barn at feeding time to feed "his" horses and socialize with the fat horse. Even during his worst moments, Tiny did not neglect his duty as a stable owner.

Finally, Mike's sunny personality won out and Mike and Tiny slowly began to make friends with each other. Once Tiny had been reassured that he would still stay the "kid" of the family, and Mike would just be our dog, everything was settled. Mike accepted that he would not eat until Tiny said so, and would stay in the background until Tiny told him it was okay to come forth. Mike also accepted that Tiny called the shots: he decided when it was time to play, time to eat, sleep and socialize with the humans.

Before too long, the little dogs stuck together like glue. There were a few things we soon learned about Mike. The first was that Mike was a kind, happy-go-lucky dog. He never growled and never was in a bad mood. We also learned that Mike had been given two stomachs and no brain. Mike ate everything, from raw garlic bulbs to apples, cucumbers and lettuce.

When Mike was disciplined for his boisterous activity, for running off and getting too close to the road, he forgot it the moment he was released, would bounce around wagging his tail and often do the precise same thing again. It was impossible to get through to Mike. Mike would not come when called, unless he felt like it. When let out in the morning, Mike would frequently run round in circles, saying 'ra,ra' as he passed, and literally have his brain go out of gear until he had run off excess steam and then plumped down somewhere in the grass to relax.

Mike turned out to be very charming. He would walk up to strangers, dance for them on his hind feet, in hopes of food or a pat on the head. Mike is a dog who truly enjoys meeting new people, a trait that became apparent very early in his life. Because Tiny had developed into a rather aloof dog, Mike's boisterous personality was better suited to that of Sheba. Although Mike's first loyalty was always to Tiny, Mike delighted in rough wrestling matches with Sheba during the many times of the day when Tiny wished to be left alone.

Mike soon was initiated by Sheba into the art of rounding up the horses in the evening to bring them in from the paddocks. Because they both loved eating, I thought Mike would bond with the fat horse. But the fat horse, like Tiny, decided to stay aloof and kept to himself. Mike soon learned that the deal with the fat horse was the same as with Tiny: he owned the place, or at least part of it, and was not to be messed with. Mike accepted that the fat horse stood above him in rank order and left him alone. As for the other horses, they were inferior to dogs and had to be kept in check.

The horses accepted Mike as Sheba's sidekick and listened to the dogs' authority when it was time to be rounded up for feeding time. All except one horse, which resented Mike immensely. It was a black former dressage horse whose name I cannot recall. The horse was not even truly our horse. It had been given to us when we bought the farm by the farm's former owner. The horse was suffering from an asthmatic breathing condition known as heaves, and was unsuited for all but the lightest work. The owner had wanted it to be destroyed, unwilling to feed an animal which was no longer of use to him. The horse, due to its condition, required special feed that had to be bought at a high price. We took him over anyway, saving his life.

Its life consisted of sleeping, eating and whiling his time away in the lush, green pastures of our farm with the other horses. But that was not enough for him. He wanted to compete. He wanted to be ridden in the advanced dressage movements, like one or two of our other horses. He wanted to wear a double bridle and dance under the rider. He wanted to compete. It was not possible. The horse did not know that. He stood at the gate and watched as I put the other horses through their paces. He grew depressed and irritable.

We "gave" him to the stable groom, so he would be ridden around the wide, open fields by his own, special person who looked after him. To no avail. The horse did not want to go out on rides. He wanted dressage. He wanted to perform. Whenever I was able to do so timewise, I put a double bridle on the horse and rode him. He arched his neck and proudly danced under me: half-passes, even the difficult movements of piaffe and pirouette. I never rode him more than 15 minutes.

It was all his condition allowed.

He wanted more. He wanted to dance in front of an audience, wanted to soak up their admiration, which was still stored away somewhere in his memory. Memory of another life. Before he became ill. He wanted his past back. His horse's brain did not understand that the past cannot be re-created, no matter how hard we try. He did not understand that our dreams die harder than the past in which they lie buried, that we hold them in our hands (or hooves in that instance) long after they turn to dust....

For that horse, the humiliation of being bossed about by a little dog like Mike was too much to take. He accepted Sheba as a necessary evil, but greatly resented being told what to do by this new, minute Shihtzu. He refused to act on Mike's command, breaking out of the herd, and would only be brought in the stable once Sheba came to Mike's aid.

As much as Mike bonded with Sheba out in the fields, after working hours the little dogs stuck together. When we let them out to play, we called them back at dinnertime. There was no need to use their names. We simply called "little dogs," and they knew who we meant. Sheba listened either to her own name, or to "big dog." When we called: "little dogs, big dog," all three of them came running, knowing it was time for a cookie or other treat.

Among the horses, Mike bonded with an Arab named Smartie. Everyone at the farm was amazed at this particular friendship, since we did not at the time consider Mike to be a very intelligent dog. Nice, yes. Funny, yes. But smart? No...

Smartie, on the other hand, carried his name because the diminutive Arab gelding was able to outsmart anyone on the farm, including the humans. One could almost see his brain ticking away as he was working in the ring.... Smartie was only 14.1 hands, but he could jump hurdles well over 5 feet. He did so by a combination of athletic ability, ambition and incredible

65

intelligence.

Smartie did not need a rider to tell him the right jump off points. He worked it out himself, during the free-jumping sessions. This was when we let the horse in the ring, without rider, wearing nothing but his halter. He went up to the jump, sized it up for good measure, cantered around the outside of the arena and took it. He did so until he got it right.

As mischievous as Smartie was with everyone else, he did whatever Mike demanded. When Mike wanted Smartie to come inside, the horse allowed himself to be rounded up and ran ahead of the dog to the stable. When we gave Mike the lead chain, Smartie followed him - until, that is, Mike dropped the lead chain, not keeping in mind that he could not lead the horse and bark at the same time. As I said, Mike was not very smart then...

Smartie prided himself in getting every rider off his back at least once. With me, he had not succeeded thus far. One day, I took him out for a ride. He had been acting up throughout the ride, rearing and bucking, refusing to go forward, trying to turn on his haunches to gallop back to the stable. To his dismay, I kept him under control. When he reared, I stuck like glue to the saddle. When he bucked, I went into half-seat and let him buck under me, not even being affected by his efforts.

Finally, the horse settled down. He pricked his ears forward and relaxed into a nice, even walk. I relaxed a little, too, and gave him more rein, to see what would happen. Nothing. The horse walked, as calm and peaceful as can be. We walked for a long time, and eventually came to a cornfield. There was a small path alongside the field, which we had to take to get to the next patch of forest.

No sooner had I entered that path than Smartie took off, without any warning, at a full gallop, cutting a right angle into the cornfield. The corn stood high at that time of year and the stalks whipped my legs back in the saddle, almost throwing me off over the horse's back. I knew how dangerous this situation was. If I were thrown over the back of the horse, my feet would get stuck in the stirrups and I could be dragged to death. The horse would not stop. There was no way I could ride him into a circle, as the corn stalks were too high. I had only one chance: I had to try to get my feet out of the stirrups and jump off.

Somehow, I succeeded. I jumped off at a full gallop, not even trying to hold on to the reins. I landed in the cornfield, luckily without getting hurt. Although my head hit the ground, I was wearing my helmet and came to no harm. I watched Smartie disappear at an alarming speed into the corn.

I picked myself off the ground and made my way toward home. After 10 minutes, I was met by a couple walking, holding Smartie by his reins. I swear the horse was grinning all over his freckled, equine face....

"Is this your horse?" they asked me.

"He sure is," I replied. "He threw me in the cornfield."

"Are you hurt?" they asked me, alarmed. "We caught the horse just as he was about to make for the road. He was going at an incredible speed."

"No, I'm okay," I told them. "I was lucky enough to be able to jump off. I don't even want to think what would have happened to me had I stayed on board...," I said, pointing to the horse, whose chest was badly cut by the cornstalks. One stirrup was completely missing. I concluded that it must have been torn off by the powerful cornstalks as the horse zoomed through them at a full gallop. No telling what would have become of me, had my foot still been in the stirrup when this happened.

"Yes," they agreed. "He jumped the huge trench coming out of the field, at full speed. We saw it and thought he was going to fall. You're lucky you were not on him."

"Anyway, thanks for bringing him back," I told them. "Could you be so kind and hold him for me as I get back on?"

"You are not going to ride him?" they asked.

"Sure am," I replied. "Don't worry, he won't do anything

now. He just wanted to get me off his back once. He succeeded. Now it's over. He'll be quiet as a lamb..."

They looked at each other, then at me. They clearly did not believe me. But I was right. Smartie walked home without as much as one wrong move. I never had a problem with him thereafter. He had had his day. He had proven that he was able to outsmart me. That was all he needed to know.

I could have sworn that I saw Mike and Smartie fraternizing in the paddock that evening, laughing their heads off...

Chapter 6

A Summer Of Veterinary Emergencies, And We Finally Find Out That Mike Is A Tough Guy

We had had Tiny and Mike for a while, when it became evident that, although they were male and female, they had not the slightest interest in each other in a romantic way. We had hoped that eventually they would produce offspring, having heard that a cross between Pekingese and Shihtzu is a most delightful little dog. They wrestled, they slept curled up to each other, they went everywhere together.

But when Mike was in heat, she tried - convinced that she was a male dog - to hump Sheba. Mike also lifted her leg when she went to the toilet. This she had learned from observing Tiny. Mike was tough like a guy dog, Mike marked his territory like a guy dog. In all essence, Mike was a guy dog.

Mike and Tiny were not so much like brother and sister as they were like brother and brother. Two guys enjoying a special friendship of male bonding. It was not until many years later that Mike discovered she was a girl and began to feel attraction for other, male dogs. But that is another story.

For now, we had to give up on the idea of ever seeing offspring between Tiny and Mike.

"Let's get another little Pekingese then," I suggested to Phil. "A little girl, and when she grows up, she and Tiny can have puppies..."

We made a few phone calls and finally drove somewhere out in the sticks the Quebec countryside, down an abandoned farm road and to a small, dirty house that seemed to be nearly falling down.

"Are you sure this is it?" I asked Phil.

"This is the address they gave us," he told me. "So we may as well go and knock at the door."

"Do you think they are a reputable breeder, though?" I

asked him, concerned. "It doesn't look too inspiring, does it?"

"We'll soon be able to tell if they have pure-bred dogs or not. And if they do, it should not matter whether they are licensed by the kennel club or not. What difference can that make, so long as the dogs are pure bred?"

"Guess you're right," I replied. "Okay then, let's go on in."

Little did we know that it made a big difference indeed whether a breeder was licensed by the kennel club, guaranteeing his integrity and the health and well-being of his dogs.

The inside of the house was as dirty as the outside. The woman who opened the door was unkempt and wore a soiled shirt.

"What do you want?" she asked, not too friendly.

"We are the people who called about the Pekingese puppy," Phil explained.

"Ah yes, come in," she gruffed, with the faintest hint of a smile. She led us through a dirty kitchen into the living room. "The dogs are in there," she informed us, pointing to a makeshift kennel in the middle of the living-room carpet. In the fencing were a Pekingese bitch and her five puppies. They looked well enough. One of them, a small cream-colored female, was very pretty. She also was friendly and came up to us instantly when we called out to her.

"We'll take this one," we both informed the breeder simultaneously and grinned at each other because we had had the same thought. As we had suspected, there were no papers.

We could tell the puppy was purebred, though, and thus we did not worry too much about the papers. We paid $300 cash, as the lady would not accept checks. She gave us a receipt. No health guarantees or warranty. Once she had the money, she handed us the puppy and shoved us out the door.

The puppy, which we named Amber, stayed with us for three days. During those three days, she bonded with Mike, who discovered, to everyone's amazement, her mother instinct.

Tiny, as could be predicted, remained alienated and wanted nothing to do with the puppy. The puppy was playful and followed us around the house.

On the third morning, she collapsed in her pen, just after she had gotten up. We called the vet and took her there. She looked to have died on the way, in our car, ravaged by intestinal parasites. The vet gave her CPR and revived her, and put the small creature on a drip and a ventilator.

"I don't know if she'll pull through," the vet told us. "Leave her with me for the day, and I'll see what I can do. I will call you this evening."

At 5pm, the vet called. "I am sorry, but your puppy has died," she informed us. "I tried everything I could to save her, but she was too far gone. I don't know where you got her from, but she had been ill for weeks."

When I told her, the vet cautioned us against ever again buying from shady "breeders." "They run puppy mills and keep the dogs in horrible conditions. They are often left without adequate food or water. When people come to see the puppies, the dogs are brought inside the house for the duration of the visit. Then they are shoved back outside into the overcrowded kennels or boxes where they are kept."

Not only did we lose $300 for our ignorance, but we also lost an adorable potential new family member that sad afternoon.

The summer of 1990 was not a lucky one as far as our dogs went. Only three weeks after the incident with Amber, we almost lost Tiny. Tiny had been out walking the farm grounds, as was his habit, on a particularly hot summer's day. He had fallen asleep in the sun and failed to wake up, suffering from severe heatstroke. When we discovered Tiny, he was listlessly lying on his side, his tongue hanging out of his mouth. He did not react to us calling to him, and was unable to stand up or even turn over.

We called the vet immediately. "This is serious," she cautioned us. "Your dog has gone into shock and could die. You must immerse him in cold water immediately and try to give him some ice cubes. Keep him wrapped in cold towels and come here immediately."

So we did. We spent five agonizing hours until we got the relieving call from the vet that Tiny, though still very weak and on drips, was going to be all right. It scared the hell out of us. We had no idea what we would do without him...

Happily, we forked out our first $400 in veterinary bills for Tiny. Little did we know that this was only a small amount of the total payment we would make to vets for Tiny over the next eight years. But even if we had known, it would not have mattered. Tiny was an expensive dog, but worth every cent of it!

This summer also marked the first and only veterinary emergency we would have for Mike in the seven years he/she has now been with us. It happened one nice summer evening. The horses were in the paddock, waiting to be brought in for their evening meal. That day, we had a herd of ten in the field. As they could not all be brought in at once, I took Sheba and Mike out into the field with me, and had them each herd 5 horses.

I then took Sheba and her herd inside, instructing Mike to stay with his herd in the paddock, until I could come back for them. Among Mike's herd was the black ex-dressage horse that was suffering from heaves.

Just as I had reached the gate of our 10 acre field, I looked back to see the black horse break out of the circle. Mike went after him, to try to get him back to the others. The horse turned around and came after Mike, rearing and bringing his hooves down on the little dog. Mike went down into the grass and did not get up again. The horse stepped on him once again, for good measure and then cantered off.

I left Sheba and the horses to find their own way into the stable and ran back out into the field to retrieve Mike. Mike was conscious, but unable to move. I picked up Mike's limp body and carried it inside on my two hands. Inside the house/ restaurant, I found Phil and briefly explained to him what had happened.

We instantly got into the car and raced to the vet. Mike was drifting in and out of consciousness, and I kept talking to him to keep him with us. Somehow, I sensed that if Mike lost consciousness now, we would lose him for good.

The vet rushed Mike off to the emergency room and once again we were sent home and told to wait for her call. Incredibly, when she called us back, she said that the X-rays showed no internal injuries of fractures. "That's a truly tough dog you have there," she told us. "Not a scratch. The dog is suffering from what could have been potentially fatal shock, but you did the right thing keeping her conscious while coming here. She is going to be all right, but I will keep her for the night, for observation."

This is how we found out Mike was truly a tough guy. As for the horse, I called the horse butcher and asked him to pick the black horse up that very afternoon. A creature that would step on a small dog not once, but twice, out of spite, was not something I wanted in my stable. As far as I was concerned, this was not a life worth saving.

The horse was saved by one of our stable grooms. "Can I have him?" she asked, "or is this an automatic death sentence?"

"If you can have that stupid beast off my property by 6pm and make sure he goes somewhere far from here where I'll never have to lay eyes on him again, you can have him."

"How much do you want for him?" she asked me. "Is the meat price okay?

"You know what?" I told her. "You can have that thing for free. That horse is not worth a dime."

As for Mike, he recovered completely. Except that his attitude toward horses totally changed. He now hated horses with a passion, including Smartie, and never went near one again without the safety of a fence between him and the horse. From the safety of the other side of a fence, Mike to this day feels compelled to charge at every horse he sees, barking wildly.

PART 3

TINY AND MIKE GO TO TEXAS

76

Chapter 7

At First, I Went Alone

It happened suddenly, without warning. It was 1am as I was riding the fat horse over some huge combination jumps in the indoor arena. Phil was asleep as I tried to jump higher and higher.

I had been back from Texas for some six months. There was a death penalty case down there which, try as I might, I had been unable to forget. I had come across it while researching the Autry story. The man I had interviewed had claimed that he was innocent. In Texas, even the most guilty killers would look you straight in the eye and swear to the fact that they didn't do it. Usually, there was nothing to it. In this case, I mused that there just might be.

The prisoner had pointed Bastian and me to his trial transcript to prove the validity of what he was saying. We had subsequently checked it out at the courthouse and found what we considered to be some outrageous facts: that he didn't fit the description of the killer, that eye witnesses who had seen the killers leave the scene of the crime positively said that he had not been there at the time of the crime. That deals had been cut with co-defendants, who lied on the stand to escape prosecution, that they had admitted this afterward and the admission had been recorded.

What I did not know at the time was that occurrences of this sort were not unusual in Texas death penalty cases. The state that holds the highest record of innocent convictions in the country had recently released two death row inmates after they had been proven innocent. Both had spent more than a decade on death row. Both of them had come within hours of being executed. Both had been saved only because people who either had or were able to raise a lot of money put themselves behind their cases. I had no idea that in Texas, you buy justice.

In the case of one death row inmate, the Supreme Court even ruled that there was no constitutional bar to executing a factually innocent man, so long as due process at trial had been followed.

This book is not about the death penalty or the justice system or lack thereof in the toughest state of the U.S. This book is about Tiny and Mike, but it needs to be explained how we got to Texas in the first place...

I had been unable to forget this particular case. To me, who had been brought up in a system where justice still means what the word stands for, it was a bother. In Canada or Europe, there is no death penalty. Further, we would never put a man in prison on such "evidence," or lack thereof, as had happened in this case.

To re-open this case on appeal, there were some witnesses, including alibi witnesses, who would need to be interviewed. The case would need the combination of a good lawyer and a good investigator just to have a chance of being heard. For six months I had been haunted by thoughts that if there was even a doubt about that man's guilt, he should not be killed. Now I was thinking of it again, in the quiet of the big, indoor riding arena as my horse cantered rhythmically toward the next hurdle...

I stopped my horse immediately after clearing a big triple combination. "What am I doing here?" I asked myself. "A man in Texas is going to die for a crime he may have never committed, only because he has no money for a lawyer. And I am putting my money into horses, my biggest concern is to jump over hurdles faster and better than anyone else and maybe one day chase after a stupid medal! This is wrong. I am trained as an investigative journalist. I have enough money to hire a lawyer for the case. I am going to Texas to work on it!"

I got off the fat horse and led him to his stable. As usual, I left the door open, so he could wander about freely and show off to the other horses. I brought him a late night snack of hay, patted him good night and went inside the house to wake up Phil.

"I have to return to Texas," I told him. "It shouldn't take more than a few months. I'll be back by April, I hope..."

"You are doing what?" Phil asked, slowly coming to from his sleep. Mike did not even wake up. He blinked lazily and rolled over. Tiny kept snoring... While Phil and I discussed a decision that would greatly impact their lives as well, the little dogs were dwelling somewhere in dreamland. As usual when he is dreaming, Mike was giving a few yaps, his feet were moving back and forth as he was pursuing an imaginary enemy in his sleep.

I told Phil of my reflections when clearing the last jump. He and I talked it through. Having been brought up in Western Europe and Canada, where the death penalty itself was considered a brutal and outdated punishment, I had great moral problems not just with the issue itself, but all the more with even the ever-so-remote possibility that an innocent man might go to his death. In the case at stake here, the possibility was not even a remote one.

"Okay, I suppose we have to do it, then," Phil sighed. "When will you go?"

"Next week" I told him. It was initially decided that I would go on my own, and Phil, the dogs, the horses and the cat would stay behind. It was, after all, a trip to last but a few months. I would try to find pro bono representation for the inmate and then work with the lawyer on a full investigation on the case. With my training as an investigative journalist, we concluded that even a major criminal investigation should not be a problem for me, once I had familiarized myself with the local laws.

"Three months tops," I told Phil. "I go down there, crack the case wide open with whatever attorney I'll find, come up with new evidence needed to re-open the case, then they can file the proof that the witnesses lied at the guy's trial, and I am out of there..."

"Okay, let's do it," Phil agreed. Little did we know that the months would turn into years, that the jaded lawyers in Texas were unwilling or unable to take any further cases pro bono, that the really good, hot shot criminal attorneys did not even consider taking a pro bono case, whether the person was innocent or not.

Nor did we know that, no matter the new evidence, the courts would go out of their way to ignore it. Killing a man on death row was a political sport in Texas, whether or not he deserved it. It had nothing to do with guilt or innocence.

Phil and I were under the mistaken impression that I would go down there, show to the courts that there had been a mistake, and they would say: "Thank you, Tess from Canada, for showing us this mistake and saving us from a potential miscarriage of justice. You are hereby awarded the honorary medal of the State of Texas."

Little did we know that the courts, on the contrary, would close their eyes and ears, saying: "If a mistake has been made, then we don't want to know about it. Let's kill him fast, before anyone finds out." Little did we know...

Nor were we aware of the fact that Houston is not the most pleasant place on earth if you are not used to it. Temperatures soar in summer to more than 100 degrees on average, and flooding occurs in winter. There are hurricanes and tornadoes. The Texas courts and politicians are corrupt. Many white Houstonians have a reputation for being unkind, brutal and racist. Due to poverty, injustice and one of the highest rates of prison and police brutality in the country, the crime rate soars. Entire parts of the city are unsafe to venture into after - and sometimes even before - dark. People live virtually imprisoned in their houses, with burglar bars on the windows and doors...

In the five years I was there, I met some nice people in Texas, but not too many... Aside from the Hispanics, who

80

were almost all nice, I can count them on one hand: there was Robert Mosbacher Jr, the only honest politician I met who ran for office in the governor's elections of 1991 and who - of course - never made it. There was Jim Granberry, the dentist turned chairman of The Board of Pardons and Paroles who rather resigned from office than continue its corrupt practices which had nothing to do with justice, only later to be discredited and defamed in the papers.

There was Willie Nelson, a country singer with a big heart, who repeatedly invited Tiny, Mike and myself to his farm near Austin. There were Willie's friends. There were the courageous men and women of the EMT system in Houston, and a few good cops. There were the astronauts at NASA, and two guards on death row in Huntsville who had human qualities and - the rarest possession of all - a heart. There was Debbie the dog aunt, and the people at the Doctor Pet Center in Houston who gave Tiny huge discounts...

The rest of them are best forgotten ...

But, first things first: I went to Texas. Phil and the assorted animal family stayed behind. I tried to find a lawyer and couldn't. I found out that many death row inmates did not have representation on appeal and that the pro bono centers did not give special treatment to cases where there were doubts as to someone's guilt. The inmates were taken on a first come, first served basis, guilty or not. There was such a long waiting list that most inmates were likely to be dead by the time it was their turn...

Like almost all Western Europeans and most Canadians, I am against the death penalty. Yet, I still believe that an innocent man, or potentially innocent man, deserves more help than one who is guilty. This attitude put me at odds with the liberals and conservatives alike. The conservatives, because they were for the death penalty and thought it was better to kill a potentially innocent guy than to let a guilty one live.

81

The liberals, because they were against the death penalty for anybody, guilty or innocent, did not think that an innocent man deserved more help than a guilty one.

I met with longhaired, liberal lawyers living in shabby apartments and representing as many inmates as they could. I met with lawyers who had gone insane with ... who knows? I met with hot shot lawyers in suits and ties and prime location city offices who told me "innocent or not, if he doesn't have $50,000 up front, I won't even look at the case."

I kept extending my trip. After four months, I still did not have a lawyer on the case. Meanwhile, in Florida, the showjumping circuit went on its way. No chance that I was going to be able to compete. My whole focus in life had gone from trying to make it to the Olympics to trying to obtain justice for a Texas death row inmate.

Phil and I decided to sell the horse farm. This would be best, as I would have to stay in Texas much longer than anticipated and, the fewer animals we had, the easier it would be for him to travel to see me. With heavy hearts, we gave Sheba to friends. The cats both opted to stay with the horse farm.

Phil, Tiny and Mike moved into a house by the lake. Finally, we decided that there was no option but to fork out $20,000 of our own money which allowed me to talk one of the Houston hot shot lawyers into representing the case for such a "bargain" price. The "bargain" did not include monthly expenses, court filing fees or his work after the initial appeal. The subsequent appeal would run another $10,000, followed by another $5,000 later on, followed by... What did I care?

For now, I had a lawyer and the work on the case could begin.

"If you want to work on the case as an investigator," the lawyer explained, "this will take years. It will be a good experience, and you'll get more than one book out of it in the long run. Further, you'll become totally trained as a criminal investigator and you'll have excellent references, having worked with one of the top law firms in the country. Afterward, you'll be able to work in the field if you wish. You'll have an intimate knowledge of criminal law in Texas, as well as national death penalty law. You'll understand the Supreme Court as well as the Fifth Circuit and the local courts.

"You will learn about depositions, affidavits and the sensitive practice of interviewing witnesses. I'll throw all this training in because you are paying the bills and I'm willing to take you on as an investigator in the case. But I need a commitment from you to stay here as long as I need you. If you don't want to do it, I'll hire someone else. Make up your mind."

I asked him to let me think about it for a night or two. I went back to the shabby little motel where I was staying to save money, so that I would have more available to put into the case. I thought it through: it was the opportunity of a lifetime. Not just for the training I would get or for the many things I would see there and could later use in books or stories ... no, it was also the chance to do something worthwhile with my life.

I had always felt a little guilty about being a journalist; you reported, yes, but you never actually did anything to help anyone, to truly be useful. I had always admired the teachers, social workers and nurses ... those who were blessed to truly make a difference in other people's lives. This was my chance to do the same, for once.

Already I could see that it would be a long, tough road ... But I knew I had to do it. I called the lawyer the next morning.

"Yes," I said, "yes, I'll do it."

"Good," he replied. "I thought that you would. I am putting you in touch with Jane, my assistant lawyer (hot shots always work with assistants). The two of you will work on the appeal together. When can you meet with us to go over the trial transcript?"

83

That settled it. I was moving to Texas. Because I was not getting paid for my work on the death penalty case, on the contrary, would have to pay for the privilege of working there, I still needed my journalism work. I informed Phil of my decision, hoping he would not be too angry with me.

"If this is what you have to do, you have to do it," he said, understanding as ever. It once again occurred to me how lucky I was to have such a great husband. "I'll come to visit you as often as I can," he promised. "After all, Texas is not the end of the world."

I transferred, through my press agency, to Houston. I moved out of the motel and looked to move in with someone. I needed every spare cent for the investigation of "my" case from now on. In Canada, people move in together for companionship, or for splitting the bills. In Houston, single people lived alone or with their families. Only weirdos or the desperately poor put ads in the papers for roommates. Only drifters or poor people answered them. Little did I know...

I thought it would be nice, being in Houston on my own, to have someone to fix my car when it broke down, and to have dinner with in the evenings. So I answered an ad for someone to share a house in the Galleria area. The next day, I moved in with three men: one was a traveller/adventurer from Great Britain by the name of Tony. Another was a quiet man by the name of Jay who laid bricks for a living. The third man talked to himself while doing the dishes and thought that was normal. They were not exactly my kind of crowd...

But I was too busy to worry about immediately moving again. For now, my days were spent between studying at the law library, combing through the trial transcript and driving to death row to meet with the inmate we were representing. I worked, ate and slept. It got awful lonely. Despite the fact that I had moved in with someone to avoid this, I always ate alone.

I had no idea that Texas, and the US in general, was

a country of lonely people. People could live with you, be around you, and still everyone minded their own business and lived for themselves. It was a world of isolation, marked by an absence of true, in-depth friendships. It was not what I was used to from Canada. Much later, I learned that many people in the US literally die from loneliness - either because they seek a friend in drugs or alcohol, or because they eventually kill themselves.

I came to hate the American saying "good for you," because it implied - though meant in a friendly manner - "there is division between your life and mine." I was used to friends saying "good for both of us, I am happy this works for you because I am your friend and we are in this together." Texas was so different!

As always, there were willing males to ease the loneliness. They started out as saying that they wanted to be friends. I believed them. But soon - from investigators to lawyers to police officers - they all tried it on. When I said "Excuse me, please, but I am married, no way," they would typically reply: "But this is America. Here, everyone cheats on their spouses. It's okay. He doesn't have to know..." I was appalled and decided to spend my time alone rather than with male "friends" who always wanted more.

To me, Texan men seemed like leeches: they saw a woman alone, and decided she was fair game. Whether or not she had a husband. Luckily, I later found out that not all Texans were like this. After a year or two, I even made some genuine friends. But the first 11 months were a rocky road.

To top it off, Phil called from Montreal to say Tiny had escaped from the garden and was lose somewhere in the city.

I have long since come to believe that Tiny and Mike each have a special guardian angel, and this time I once again found a reason to renew that belief. While I sat in Texas, worrying about Tiny's safety, the little Pekingese strolled the streets, unharmed by cars, until he was found and picked up by a woman quite a few blocks away. She checked Tiny's collar and found his rabies vaccination with the phone number of the vet on it. She called the vet, who called our number at the horse farm, only to find that it had been disconnected. But one of her assistants happened to know a friend of Phil and said "He knows someone from a horse farm. Let me ask him: maybe they are the same people."

She called the house and asked if a little, grey Pekingese was missing. So, finally, we got Tiny back safely.

A few weeks later, the same happened to Mike.

"Look, this isn't going to work," I told Phil when he explained the latest mishap to me over the phone. Luckily, Mike had been found again and returned to him a few days later, but it was just a worry I didn't need. "You had better bring them down here when you come next," I told him. The last few times, Phil had come without the dogs to visit me. Now, it was getting close to Christmas and we were getting ready to spend the holidays together in Houston. Not that we wanted to, but the case kept me so occupied that I could not get away for more than a few days. Phil, on the other hand, was able to do some work for the company in Texas and Florida and would be able to stay with me in Houston from Christmas time until March the following year.

During the months I spent alone in Texas, I had acquired a large ginger cat named "Kittykat" from a lady who worked at the local Kinko's. She was transferring from Houston to Austin. The cat had been a stray and she did not want to take him. She left him with me, and the cat came on walks with me, slept in my bed and even followed me under the shower.

At night, the cat sat up with me to read the transcript of the trial and find out discrepancies between witness and police testimonies. In other words: the cat was my partner in work and life. I had no idea how he would react to the dogs or vice versa. We would have to wait and see...

Chapter 8

Then They Arrived, And We Were Headed Straight For The Slums...

The week before Christmas, Phil arrived in Houston in our Quebec registered car, crammed full to the roof with clothes and other luggage he needed for the three months to come. Tiny and Mike sat in the back, proudly acting as though they were on a throne on top of a suitcase.

The little dogs marched inside the house, and then inspected and dutifully marked the back yard, both of them by lifting their legs. When growing up, Mike only had Tiny as a role model, and so lifting her leg comes natural to her. This leads many people to think that I am kidding when I tell them that Mike is a girl...

The yard passed inspection and was declared official dog territory. That was precisely when the cat arrived from one of his nightly excursions. He spotted the dogs and immediately wore a look on his face that read: "Hey, what is that? Are they fluffy cats or what?" The Kittykat advanced to investigate; the three sniffed each other on the back porch. The dogs were delighted at the idea of having a cat once more. They love cats, as they are so easy to control. Cats can be swept aside when you walk by them, they can be glared at to intimidate them and they can be chased about the house for exercise. Cats are wonderful...

The cat did not agree. Once he had checked out Tiny and Mike he determined that, though they looked like fluffy cats, their smell indicated that they were dogs. The cat walked away and wanted nothing to do with any of us.

Over the next few days, the cat became increasingly withdrawn. He spent most of his time outdoors and rarely came for long walks with me anymore, as had been his custom. He was clearly not amused by the idea of living with two little creatures who smelled like dogs, made a lot of noise and were by far not sophisticated enough for a cat to hang out with.

It soon became evident that the living arrangement was not going to work out. There were too many people in the house now. The men, who were still complete strangers despite the fact that I had been staying at the house for some time, did not like the dogs. They treated the little animals with complete indifference, complained about them being bathed in the tub and on several occasions carelessly left the front door open, allowing Tiny and Mike to venture outside and take a walk around the neighbourhood.

Luckily, on the three occasions this happened, I was able to find them each time within minutes, but this was not how I wished to spend my time, nor did I wish to be surrounded by these kind of people for any longer. They simply did not care: neither about themselves, nor anyone around them, nor the finer things in life, including little dogs.

Once I quit being buried in my work, I realized at once that these people were not the right environment for either Phil or myself, nor the little dogs. Phil and I decided to move for the 1st of January. We could only find either executive apartments on short-term leases or houses on a one-year lease. This did not suit us, as Phil did not want me to live on my own after he was gone the following March. The executive apartments we ruled out, since they did not have fenced yards for the dogs.

Finally, we were referred by friends to a lawyer, who said he had a big house and offered that we could share it with him. It had a dog-size yard. There were four bedrooms and two baths. A move on the first of January would be fine, though he was happy if we wanted to move in before then. On the 26th, immediately after Christmas? No problem...

First though, there was Christmas to contend with at the other house. It was so depressing ... Phil and I were far from family and friends, on a shoe string budget, in what we considered to be a hostile city, living in a fine house with run-down people. There was not even a putting up of a Christmas tree. The other three men in the house were going to celebrate Christmas by "getting drunk and getting laid" - rather crude and basic!

"This is hell," I told myself. "It's got to be. What am I doing here? How did I get myself into this situation in the first place?"

It is astonishing what positions once can manoeuvre oneself into when jumping headfirst into the water without testing it for temperature or depth. Here I was, with Phil and the dogs, stranded in a big crime city, in a US death penalty state number one with its hang-them-high mentality, and Christmas Eve was just one day away. It was going to be the worst Christmas of my life! Unless...

"Hey, let's dress the dogs up in Christmas dresses and take some photos," I told Phil. "If we don't have the Christmas spirit around us, let's create it!"

Phil initially looked at me as if I was crazy, but then followed me to Pharmor, the now defunct, number one Discount store of Houston. Here, we loaded up our cart with a Father Christmas hat, assorted bowties, plenty of gift-wrap and anything else that looked Christmassy.

"What do you want the gift wrap for?" Phil asked me. "To wrap the dogs?"

"Sure," I replied. "And why not? Nobody here to give us any gifts, so we might as well have some fun..."

No sooner had I spoken the words "Nobody here to give us any gifts" than I had another idea. I had heard of the homeless, abandoned people of Houston, and I had seen them a few times when driving by their downtown hangouts. Most of them were black, many mentally ill. Houston had recently passed a law that allowed mental hospitals to discard non-dangerous patients after medicating them for three days. These hospitals would drive truckloads of mental patients into downtown Houston and abandon them there, with a further five-day supply of pills.

Many of these men walked around in a daze. A great number suffered from schizophrenia, and were unable to orient themselves, much less find work. All of them were in urgent need of help, which they were not getting. Often, they did not have enough money for food and went hungry.

The mental patients lived in one part of downtown. In other parts, under the bridges, in dim side alleys, on the abandoned main streets of downtown after midnight were the remainder of the Houston Homeless: Vietnam veterans who had been unable to find their way back into society after the war. Ex-Convicts who had been turned out into the streets by the Texas department of criminal justice after more than a decade behind bars, with $200 in their pockets and nowhere to go. People who had been orphaned and had grown up on the streets. Runaways who preferred the tough life on the streets to the abuse they experienced at home.

They were all out there, and none of them were being treated like human beings. They were being spat on, overlooked, despised. They were written about derogatorily in the papers; they were being made fun of. Good citizens of Houston were cautioned against going near them, because they were deemed to be dangerous.

For many of them, Christmas was just another day when they would go hungry. The Salvation Army put on meals for the homeless at Christmas, but the schizophrenics could never find their way there. "They just stay out on the streets," a Salvation Army officer explained to me. "We have our hands full, just feeding those that can make it to the missions. We can't go after the other ones."

I decided that I would. I had always prayed, as a little girl, that if God were to grant me one wish, he might send me to hell and allow me to comfort the poor souls there. It looked like my wish had finally been granted. The indifference, the lack of love, the degradation of human beings to a level less than animals ... if it wasn't hell, then I didn't know what was. My own sense of isolation of being stranded here, in a shabby environment ... it was all straight out of Dante. But even hell is not dark enough a place that it cannot be shattered by love....

"We are going to give them Christmas presents," I announced to my husband while wheeling the cart through Pharmor.

"Who is them?" Phil wanted to know. I had just blurted out my final thought, and had forgotten to fill him in on what came before. I quickly related my thought process to him. He was not surprised at all. He knew that I would have liked to be a nun when I was a little girl. In my single days, I had often eyed the possibility of entering the order of Mother Theresa. After marriage, I forever stayed a borderline nun, taking my greatest inspiration not from people like Tony Robbins and Dale Carnegie, but from the humble, loving work of that old Armenian woman who, I am convinced, was a saint living among us.

We were operating on a strict budget, but we still managed to fill the shopping cart with Christmas cookies, assorted candy, canned food and whatever else we thought the Homeless might enjoy. Summer sausages found their way into the cart, canned tamales at 3 for one dollar, Danish ham in a can, herring imported from Germany, rice-a-roonies, spaghetti...

At the house, we stored away the gifts we had bought, to be wrapped the following day. For now, we dressed up Tiny and Mike. Mike wore a Father Christmas hat as his prime dress, while we stuffed Tiny in his little red and white striped sweater. The dogs enjoyed the dressing up session as much as we did, and kept wagging their tails and bouncing around. Finally, we decorated them with gift bows which we stuck on their heads, backs and anywhere else we could fit them.

The cat sat and watched, and ran away with a shocked

"Miau" when it came to be his turn. "So much for the cat," I sighed, and shrugged my shoulders.

Never mind. We had plenty of work still ahead: we took the Christmas cards we had bought at the store, put them up around the table, on empty shelves and anywhere else where we could find room. The three strangers who lived in the house came by from time to time, clearly thought we were nuts, shook their heads and left again. We didn't mind. We were bringing the Christmas spirit right into their impersonal, cold home, whether they liked it or not.

Once we had the cards in place, we positioned Tiny and Mike between them, on the table. They walked around, wagging their tails. Mike jumped off the table.

"No, Mike, we need Mike to stay, please. We want to send the photos home to our families, as a Christmas greeting." I told Mike, addressing him as "the responsible dog of the two."

I explained the same to Tiny, switching languages as I did, since Tiny only speaks German and does not understand a word of English. This is due to the fact that, having been brought up in Germany until I was a teenager, I was convinced until age 20 that all animals spoke only German. When we got Tiny, it was only natural that he would be raised in German. Even the fat horse "spoke" German, as did Smartie. Mike was our first English-speaking animal, mainly because it would have seemed a sacrilege to address a Texan in anything but English...

We had since long found out that it was fairly easy to guilt our dogs into almost anything, from going swimming to not chasing after a squirrel, so long as you used the right tone of voice. With Mike, the moment you say, "Mike is a responsible dog, so we need Mike to...," Mike will do almost anything to prove that he is indeed responsible. Using the keyword "responsible," I have been able to guilt Mike into sitting the house, walking slowly by Tiny's side instead of running away, even getting on a swing in a kiddy's playground...

It worked this time, too, and - I could swear that it was for the sole reason of doing us a favor - Tiny and Mike began to pose. As if they knew what was going on, they looked straight into the camera, Tiny grinning his characteristic Pekingese grin, Mike putting on a cute face.

They posed on the table, among the shelves, on the floor. Surrounded by Christmas cards. With silly bowties on their heads and wrapped in stupid Father Christmas suits.

We had them instantly developed the following day, pasted them in Christmas cards and sent them home by express mail, with a message: "Merry Christmas from Texas. Phil, Tess, and the "kids." Our signatures were followed by paw prints of Tiny and Mike and - reluctantly - of the kittykat.

Paw prints are very easy, for anyone who wants to try. You buy some ink, you take the dog paw, dip it in the ink and press the paw on the paper. Careful to wipe the paw off afterward, so the carpet does not end up in a mess....

Paw prints and Christmas cards done, Phil and I sat down at the kitchen table and began to wrap the presents for the homeless. Everybody got two lollipops, some Christmas cookies, a can of staple food, and a can of delicatessen food such as a summer sausage. By the time we finished, we had some 30 little packets, neatly wrapped in Christmas paper and sporting - just like the dogs the day before - a little bow.

"I don't want to boast, but I know I am rather beautiful." Tiny in England, 1988, at less than 1 year old. Being a miniature (sleeve) true grey Pekingese dog, Tiny is one of the rarest dogs in the world. More than a decade later, his breeder still remembered him for being a "True Grey."

"Looks like we're sleeping on the bench tonight..." Tiny and Mike enjoy a walk in Herman Park, Houston/Texas in 1990.

"Is that all, just three Christmas cards?" Tiny and Mike prepare for their Christmas Charity Drive, 1990, Texas.

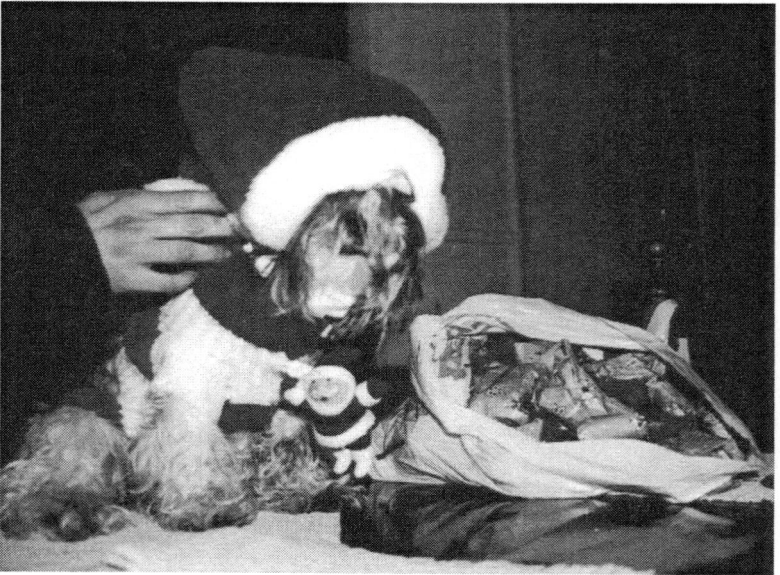

"Hoh, hoh, hoh. Here we go again, off to give the prezzies." Mike dressed up as Santa Clause, prior to venturing into the Streets of Houston, Christmas 1990.

"Any more papers you want me to read to you?" Tiny and Mike's Cat in Houston, who has put on funny glasses just to do them a favor.

"This way, silly." Tiny and Mike take each other for a walk in Houston, and wrap themselves around a post. As usual, Tiny wins the tug of war.

Tiny, Mike and their Rhode Island Cat attend most business meetings. Here they have dinner with Graham Walker, British Admiral's Cup Team Skipper and backer of the 1986-87 British America's Cup Challenge.

"Huh, private beach! So where's the sand?" Tiny goes for one of his beloved walks on his private beach at Castle Rock, Rhode Island, Summer 1996. He truly enjoys the breeze picking up his long ears and making them flow in the wind.

"Hey, Mike, do you realize they are going to train us to go down to the Titanic." Tiny, Mike and David Gallo of Woods Hole Oceanographic Institute in Cape Cod, Massachusetts. They insisted on coming along, and participating in the meeting. Gallo was smitten.

"You carry the bags - no you." Tiny and Mike as a middle-aged dog couple, resting at a mountain lake in the Bavarian Alps, Germany, 1997.

Chapter 9

... And It Became One Of The Best Christmases We Ever Had

It was decided that Phil and Tiny would stay behind while Mike and myself ventured out into the city of Houston on Christmas Eve in search of homeless people to give our Christmas presents to.

Mike was a tough dog, much better suited to the cruel streets of Houston after dark than Tiny would be. As for Phil, he was not as good as me when it came to walking up to total strangers and greeting them as if they were family. He finds it somewhat embarrassing, which I don't, since I subscribe to the Catholic theory that we are all brothers and sisters. Either way, somebody had to stay behind and make our Christmas dinner.

We dressed Mike up once more in his father Christmas hat, bow ties and all attached, put the wrapped gifts into a plastic bag, and at around 10:30pm we set out into the streets of Houston in my old white Audi, named Farley after actor Farley Granger. Because I was still somewhat new to Houston and unsure of how to get to the bad parts of town, I stopped a cop and asked.

"Excuse me, officer," I said through my open window to a tough looking Houston cop who was parked at a downtown curb. "I am looking for some homeless people. Could you tell me where they are, please? Could you direct me to the roughest part of town?"

The cop looked at me as if I had lost my mind. He put a piece of chewing tobacco into his mouth, chewed a few times before shifting the tobacco under his upper lip, where it left a prominent bulge, then he asked: "what do you want the homeless for, lady? Don't you know it's dangerous to be out alone downtown after dark?"

"I want to give them Christmas presents," I explained

to the cop, whose jaw dropped. "I am from Quebec, and it is tradition there to seek out the less fortunate on Christmas Eve and give them a little something. So I've got about 30 Christmas gifts with me..." I said, holding up the bag to show to the cop, whose jaw was still hinged wide open, "and now I need to go where they are to give it to them."

"That's the darndest thing I ever heard," the cop remarked, finally closing his jaw. "You people crazy up there or what?"

"Maybe," I replied, shrugging. Now the cop spotted Mike in his red Father Christmas hat.

"What the hell...." he began.

"That's Mike," I told him and added proudly: "Mike is a Texan. I got him here last year when I came to Houston on a business trip." Mike, hearing his name mentioned, climbed on my lap and stuck his head through the open window to look at the cop.

"You people really must be crazy up there," the officer remarked, shaking his head. But then he allowed himself a brief "Hello Mike," addressing my dog, before he became a tough cop once more.

Finally, he gave me directions to get into the worst part of town. "But you better be careful," he cautioned me. "Those people are dangerous. If anything happens to you, don't say I didn't warn you, lady."

Mike gave the cop a final grin, I waved at him and we drove off. As the cop had indicated, we drove all the way down Main Street, clear through downtown, past the courthouse and out the other side. We crossed some railroad tracks. On the other side of the tracks were factories. The streets were eerie and quiet. Not a sound could be heard. We were the only car on the road. The cop was right: it was scary.

Finally, under a bridge, I spotted some black men huddled together. I drove up to them, wound my window down and honked the horn. "Excuse me..." I shouted across to them.

One of the men rose to approach my window. "My name is Tess, and this is my dog Mike. We are from Canada and in Houston for a while on business. We have come to wish you a Merry Christmas and give you a little something."

The man could not believe his ears. "Oh man, really?" he exclaimed when I showed him the bag with the gifts. "That's incredible..."

He shouted over to his friends, who all came up to the car. Soon, the car was surrounded by eight black men, some of whom had very tough faces; others just looked weary and spent.

I gave them each a present. Then I asked: "are you guys hungry?"

"Oh yes," one of them replied. "We don't have any transportation to get into downtown or none. We don't see too many of them do-goodin' folks come into our part of town, you know. Them white folks are scared of comin' here. So we don't get to no soup kitchens and none..."

"Well, I got some canned food," I told them. "I can give you a can each, if you like. What does everyone want?"

And then I began rattling off the list of canned food I had with me: "Who wants corn, beans, tamales, ravioli...?" The men shouted out their preferences and I did my best to accommodate them.

Then they asked about Mike, who tailwagged his way through the entire group. I explained to them that Mike was a Shihtzu and told them what little I knew about the breed. In their part of town, the only dogs were mongrels, and they fell all over themselves trying to get Mike's attention and patting him. As the officer had advised me, I did not leave the car, and so Mike held audience through the window.

Between playing with Mike and asking questions about Canada, the men began to unwrap their presents. "The last time I had Christmas cookies was when I was a little boy," one of them exclaimed with tears in his eyes. They told me that many of them had been in prison before, one of them even for an armed robbery.

"The prison system here is tough, you know," one of the more hardened men told me. He informed me about abuse at the hands of the system that he had suffered. I told them that I was here to work on a death penalty case of a man who might be innocent. They asked if he was black. I said no, that he was white and that even white people end up in Texas jails when they shouldn't.

Then the hardened ex-convict, who had been branded a violent repeat offender by Texas Department of Corrections, unwrapped his present and stuck a cherry flavored lollipop into his mouth while patting my Christmassy dog who was wrapped in bowties. I truly wished his parole officer could have seen him...

Then I tried to leave. One of the men stuck his hands through the window and grabbed the wheel. "Hey, lady, don't you have some more food?" he wanted to know. "Give me some."

Some of the others followed suit. It became clear that they had decided not to let me leave until I had handed over everything I had. I was not going to do it.

"Listen, I would really like to give you some more," I explained to them, "But I can't. I have heard that there is a group of mental patients in downtown who are worse off than you and who have no food. This is where I am headed next. If I give it all to you, I won't have any for them. Remember what we had said about kindness and sharing?"

They withdrew their hands from the car window, suddenly ashamed. Finally, they directed me to the part of downtown where the mental patients were and patted Mike good-bye. They warned me to be careful:

"Them white folks probably warned you about us," one of the men said, "but this is different. Those people are really dangerous, they are crazy. You got them schizophrenics out there, and psychotics ... all them patients that the mental institutions dump on the streets. There's been a lot of killings over there."

"Yeah," I told him, "and some cop warned me there had been a lot of killings in your part of town and not to go here either."

The homeless men said exactly what the cop had said: "Don't say we didn't warn you." I drove off in search of the dangerous mental patients whom I was sure would appreciate being touched by the Christmas spirit just like anyone else.

The cop may have been wrong about the homeless men in the factory district, but boy, was I wrong about the mental patients. I drove in the direction indicated with a la-di-dah attitude, a smile on my face and my dressed up Shihtzu dog dangling his face out the window to catch the muggy Houston breeze.

Behind a derelict old hotel, just before entering the main part of downtown, I found them. Like a pack of dogs, a group of men were huddled in the darkness. All the men were black. There must have been about 20 of them. Not being used to violent crime from the small Quebec country town where I am from, I saw nothing bad in them. They were people, and all people were basically nice! Thus was my attitude...

I wound down the driver's window, dog's head out first, followed by mine. "Excuse me..." They came to the car. All of them. At once. In their eyes I read mistrust and fear, mingled with real insanity. I got really scared. But I was here, and I was going to give them the Christmas presents, because I was determined to bring the Christmas spirit to the most forgotten of Houston society.

"I came to bring you some Christmas presents and some food," I blurted out quickly into the many menacing faces that peered into my car. Hands stretched out as I hurried to put a present into each of them. The hands invaded my car, pushed my dog aside and tried to make their way into the bag, to grab a handful of presents at the same time. I tried to fight the hands off. There were too many of them. They started shouting and screaming at each other, fighting for a space at the window of my car.

Mike, as usual, was unaware of the danger of the situation. He kept wagging his tail and tried to get as many pats by the greedy hands as he could. "Wait a minute, I've got food," I screamed at them, trying to get their hands out of the Christmas bag and trying to get them away from my car.

"Stand back," I yelled, "so I can get to it." I got out the bag of the food cans from under the passenger's seat. The moment the food appeared, the hands came back in. I found myself surrounded by a sea of black hands: grabbing, tugging, pushing. They were everywhere. I put the cans of food into the hands before me. A fight broke out over a can of beans. I started throwing the food cans on the street beside the car, and a pack of men descended on the can, still fighting over it.

In an attempt to get inside the car, at the food, the men started pushing the car from one side to the other. I was afraid that they were going to roll Farley over on its side. With horror I realized that these men were desperately hungry and willing to do anything to get at the food.

I tried to wind the windows up, but it was impossible. There were too many strong, black arms stuck through them. I did manage to free my hands for a split second and turn the key in the ignition. The engine turned over, and the re-assuring sound of the motor filled the silent Houston night air. I took the entire bag of canned food, and wrenching it free from the greedy hands that were still in my car, I threw it all through the window and out on the street. The men let go of my car and began to fight over the food.

I drove off, shaken at the thought of what could have happened to me and my blissfully unaware dog at the hands of these desperate, mentally ill men. I was even more shaken by the thought that the city of Houston would leave the mentally ill to their own devices, to fend for themselves on its streets. As I would soon learn, Houston was one mean, cruel city...

For now, I was headed to another part of downtown where I suspected there would be more homeless. Following a tip from the cop, who had told me "look under the bridges downtown, that's where they usually are," I did just that and was lucky. I found a group of five men, three black and two Hispanic. I stopped and gave them the presents I had been able to save from the mental patients.

They were delighted. "I would have given you some food," I told them, "but the guys downtown behind the hotel took it all from me. They were so hungry..."

The men could not believe that I had driven in there, stopped and lived to tell about it. It was from them that I got my first idea that downtown Houston was a war zone after dark. It was as dangerous as a third world country in the midst of a civil war, complete with shoot-outs, stabbings and the like.

"We don't even go in there," one of the men said. "You're Mother Theresa or something?" he asked.

"Something like that," I grinned. "Trying for it anyway."

"You're doing good," he said.

These men were delighted to pat Mike and find out about him. They said that people usually drive past them and did not even see them. "You treat us like human beings" a Hispanic man said. "That feels really good."

They unwrapped their presents, telling me that this was the first time in more than a decade that they had had a Christmas present. We talked for about 20 minutes. They shared their life stories with me and I told them about Mike, Tiny, who had to stay at home, and what brought us to Houston.

One of the men kindly offered to break the death row inmate out of prison in case that the legal defense failed. "Hey, you know, the system here's real corrupt," he told me. "You can get all the evidence, and the courts won't look at it. So, if you think there's even a chance that the guy could be innocent, he shouldn't die. If you find they turn the appeals down, come and see me. I am always here. I have friends. You give me his name and what cell block he's in, ask him for a drawing where he's at, and we'll do the rest. We'll get him out of state and take care of the matter..."

I laughed. "Why...thank you, that's real nice of you to offer, but I think I'll try the legal system first."

"I am serious," the guy said with a straight face. "You don't know the system here yet, being from Canada and all... Death penalty is no easy conviction to overturn here, whether you got evidence or not. You'll think of me one day, a few years down the track."

I looked at my watch. It was 10 minutes to midnight.

"Gentlemen, Mike and I have to go," I informed them. "We are going to midnight mass. But listen, if you guys are here tomorrow, we are making a Christmas goose for lunch. There's only two of us, so we'll have plenty left over. I'll bring each of you a plate, if you like. It's going to be a German recipe, with dumplings and red cabbage. You'll love it."

They confirmed that they would be there the next day and would very much like to have some goose. They had never tried it, much less had they ever had a taste of German dumplings. They were in for a big treat.

Mike and I drove on to midnight mass at Houston's St Vincent de Paul church. For the years I would spend in Houston, this church would become one of the places I spent a lot of time in, so impressed was I with the midnight mass during my first Christmas there.

Mike had to stay in the car and I went inside to listen

108

to a beautiful sermon, some of its contents not unlike what I had just told the homeless men in the factory district: love, brotherhood and kinship of all men. Though I was Catholic, I had in the past often been put off from going to mass, finding in the faces of priests and congregation alike no real faith and joy in a life that pleases God, but a sense of duty and often harshness.

For a long time I had stayed away from church completely, going only during Christmas for a sense of tradition rather than religion. And so it was during this Christmas in Houston.

But the mass was so beautiful, the priest so genuine, the faith in the hearts of the people so real that I kept coming back over and over again and for the first time in years finally began to attend Sunday masses. The church often drew me back during the afternoons for silent reflections and prayer, when I stopped over while on the way to the courthouse or to the prison.

After mass, the chorus lined up outside church and sang Christmas carols. Despite being so far away from home, in a city I considered hostile and like something out of George Orwell, I felt a sense of belonging and joy flood through me. I was stranded in Texas, and yet, in my heart I knew that I was home, and would always be home, wherever there was Christmas.

I drove home with Mike, realizing also that there was work for us to do here. In this city, so cold and unkind and racist, divided by hatred and greed, Tiny, Mike and I would make a difference by setting our love against their cruelty. I had the love in my heart, and I had two very cute little dogs - together, we would try to affect Houston and make it even a little bit of a better place by the time we left. This was something I swore that night as I drove back.

Sometimes, these things are easier said than done. It was 1:30am as I headed for home. There was nobody on the streets as I stopped at a red traffic light and a truck with two men in it pulled up beside me. The men looked at me with a lecherous expression. I rolled my window down and smiled at them:

"Merry Christmas" I shouted to them.

"Merry Christmas," they shouted back. The light changed. I drove on. The truck overtook me. Then it turned and began to follow me. There was nothing nice about it anymore. There was a smell of danger in the air. The men were not smiling any longer. I turned Farley around on the deserted road and raced into a motel I had spotted on the side of the freeway.

"Two men are following us," I explained to the motel clerk as I walked into the reception area with Mike. "Can we stay here until they are gone?"

I was lucky that this was one of the few motels that did have an all-night reception. Most of the cheap motels, fearful of the high crime rate, operated after hours only through a small window of double glazed glass. This motel, of the more expensive variety, kept its doors open.

The motel clerk laughed at Mike's appearance and then bent down to greet the dog. He asked where we had been, and I told him. He warned me, like everyone else had done. He also thought I was crazy.

This was when I found out that kindness in Houston was not an asset; it was something that made people look at you as if you had lost your marbles. A city where kindness was considered a bad and stupid thing would have done hell proud....

It was the first of many times when I would have to defend myself for an act of humanity. With time, I got used to it and stopped judging the city of Houston by normal, civilized standards. If I did, I constantly got disappointed, angry and sad. Once I began judging Houston by the standards of a third world country, the constant violence, human rights violations by authorities, corruption in politics and the judicial system

110

no longer phased me. I had come to expect them and was pleasantly surprised when occasionally I found someone in Houston who operated by first world standards.

In general I had come to consider it as a battle zone, which is exactly what the motel clerk told me it was.

"You really shouldn't be out alone at this time of night," he warned me. "It wouldn't be the first time someone got raped and murdered on Christmas Eve. You don't want to make the paper's headline tomorrow, do you? We have 5 murders a day in Houston, and they don't stop just because it's Christmas Eve. Now you have a cute dog here, and you have a nice life. Stay in your part of town and don't get yourself involved with the bad stuff while you are here. Enjoy your time in Houston, and don't venture out after dark. Then nothing is gonna happen to you."

I hid at the motel for half an hour and finally ventured outside to drive home. This time, somewhat unsettled by the talks I had had with the motel clerk and some of the homeless people, as well as my experience with the truck, I was not quite as carefree. I began to see the streets of Houston as menacing and dangerous and vowed to leave the "kids" at home after dark in future. Houston's streets after dark were no place to be for a self-respecting, purebred little dog. As for me, well, that was another matter...

Christmas with Tiny and Mike is always great fun. The dogs really get into unwrapping their Christmas presents and they always know something is up when presents lie on the floor. Mike usually runs around the presents excited, wiping his hind feet and giving a few waffs. Tiny wags his little tail and sniffs at them, snoring excitedly when he smells something which he thinks is for him.

Typically, the dogs get for Christmas one big box of dog cookies each, a few cans of assorted flavors of mighty dog, some dog chews and - if they need it - some sweaters or shoes or raincoats to venture outside when the weather is not nice.

Usually, we unwrap presents on Christmas Eve, as I was used to from my childhood in Germany. But because I had come back too late from my outing into the city on Christmas Eve, we decided to do it on Christmas Day this time.

Without a tree, we sat around the living room floor and piled up the gifts in their colored wrappings in our midst. Tiny and Mike unwrapped their presents with a lot of joy, and stuck their noses right into the paper as Phil and I unwrapped ours. When we showed them what we had got, they wagged their tails politely, giving an excited "waff" now and again to indicate that they could really understand and appreciate the Christmas spirit. They probably couldn't, but did not want to let on...

Mike sniffed out a box of dog cookies and began to "unwrap" it by chewing its side. Finally, he got in and extracted a cookie that he gulped down. They turned out to be Tiny's cookies, but we let him have some anyway after having gone through the effort. Tiny needed some help unwrapping his can of Mighty Dog "Beef fillet and peas." We shared the can between the two little dogs and finally helped them unwrap all their gifts and piled them up for them:

Tiny had 3 cans of Mighty Dog, which he would eat over the next week, a packet of Iams lamb and rice dog biscuits, a packet of Lucky Dog dry dog food, which we usually do not feed them because it is considered the "hamburger" junk food equivalent of dog foods, but which they both love. Then he shared, together with Mike, a packet of dog chews.

Mike had done well for himself, too. He had received the same amount of Mighty Dog as Tiny, a packet of Mother Hubbard's peanut dog biscuits which he preferred to the Iams lamb and rice variety, and also an assortment of dog food trial size packets.

The cat, who spent his first Christmas with us, received some cans of gourmet cat food and a pair of Mardi-Gras sunglasses that we all thought were wonderful but the cat was not amused about. In fact the cat still had a lot to learn about Christmas. He sat apart and looked like he had no idea what this was all about, nor did he make any attempt to participate in the unwrapping of the presents. He looked at the four of us in an aloof, cat-like manner and clearly thought we were idiotic, sitting on the floor and umming and aahing as we unwrapped presents of various shapes and forms. When it came to eating his gifts of gourmet cat food of the salmon and trout variety however, the cat was as excited as everyone else.

While all of this went on, the goose browned in the oven. Just as we had finished unwrapping, the goose was done and Phil and I sat down to a wonderful meal. Not forgetting those I had left behind downtown the night before, or the promise Mike and I had made to them, I made up five paper plates with goose, dumpling and red cabbage, put some foil around them and got ready to leave.

"I have to go now," I explained to Phil, apologetically, "so I can get it to them while it is still warm."

And so five homeless people in Houston came to have the Christmas meal of their life that day, delivered by me and one small, bouncy little Shihtzu dog. As for me, their joy warmed my heart right to the core, making my first Christmas in Houston one of the best...

Chapter 10

We Move, And Get The Short End Of The Stick In Texas Racism

A few days before the New Year, we moved into the house of Steve Frankoff. Steve was the attorney whom I had been introduced to through one of the death penalty attorneys. He had a civil law practice on Main Street downtown. He lived alone in his sizeable four-bedroom house off Willowbend Road, in one of Houston's less affluent suburbs. The house itself was in a wealthy subdivision, that boasted carefully kept lawns, a swimming pool and a private garden only a walk way, but the area was surrounded by poor housing, and mainly black housing projects. The contrast between this subdivision and the black housing subdivision immediately outside its walls was frightening, but not unusual for Houston.

Steven Frankoff was handicapped with partially crippled legs, but was still able to walk with a pronounced limp. He made up for this by being kind to other people. He had a big heart and found it difficult to say no. When he heard that we were looking for a place to live while I was working on the death penalty case, he had immediately offered his home to us, dogs and kittykat included.

We arrived on a dark, cold Texas winter's night, to be greeted by Stephen on the front door step. He led us inside the house, where we were met by an odd looking dog who seemed to be a mix between a spaniel and a dachshund. Tiny and Mike immediately went to take possession of the house, marching by Stephen without even acknowledging him, and briefly sniffed at the dog. Tiny snarled at the dog once and it retreated under the sofa, though it was about twice as large. While the dogs inspected the house, sniffing a lamp here, a chair there, jumping on the sofa, off again, on another sofa, Stephen showed us to our room and the private bathroom that came

115

with it.

"What's with the dog?" I asked him. "I thought you mentioned that you did not have any animals?"

"That's Simon," Stephen replied. "It's a long story. You see, Simon and his owner will be staying with us for a few days."

After we had let the cat out of his carrier and he had settled into our bedroom, Stephen told us the story of Simon and his owner over a cup of coffee. Stephen had been driving home from work one evening, just before Christmas, when he saw a girl by the side of the road, trying to hitch a ride. Stephen stopped to pick her up.

The girl had just spilt up with her boyfriend. They were both heavily into drinking and had drunk away all of their money. She did not have a cent to her name and nowhere to go. She also had a dog named Simon. The trouble was that Simon had been dropped off at the dog pound by her boyfriend, who thought that the dog ate too much and that the money would be better spent on booze. The girl, I will call her Sue, had not enough money to rescue her dog from the pound and was terrified that it would be put down.

"So I drove to the pound, got the dog out and, of course, I told Sue that she could stay here until she her brother can pick her up from Austin. Trouble is, her brother is away until January 6th, so she'll be with us until then. She's been sleeping on the couch."

So she had given him a sob story and he had bought it. Sounded just like the kind of stuff I would have done. I decided that I liked Stephen very much....

As for Simon, he was a different story. Simon had the pathetic dog act worked to perfection. Tiny and Mike did not like him at all. Neither did I. Whenever I fed Tiny and Mike a little treat, I would give one to Simon first. Then it was Tiny's and Mike's turn, and Simon stood by, with a look on his face that read "I am starving, and this mean person did not give me any. But I won't say anything. I am just a poor, abused dog whom nobody loves." Whoever saw Simon sit there like that would soon guilt me into giving him a second dog treat.

The following morning, we met Sue. Sue was a nice enough girl, who could have been pretty if she put half an effort into it. But she did not. Instead, she spent much of her energy trying to work out how to get enough money to get another drink. It was tragic...

Mike greeted Sue with his typical Shihtzu dance, and Sue fell in love. Tiny was a little more stand-offish at first, but eventually came to like Sue enough to allow her to pet him and even lift him up on the sofa to sit next to her. Inspired by the dogs, Sue began to come home earlier in the evenings. Before Tiny and Mike arrived in her life, she usually had someone come to pick her up around 9pm to go drinking with and she wouldn't come back until the early hours of the morning.

Now, Sue began to divide her evenings between playing with Tiny, Mike and Simon in the small fenced back yard and accompanying me on walks around the subdivision's landscaped gardens. Then she would go out, return drunk around 1am and - when she found me still working at the computer - come to sit with me. I did not get much work done these nights, but Sue confided her life story to me, which was one of sexual abuse and rejection. She told me of her dream to become a singer, and sang some of her self-written songs to me while Phil and Stephen slept peacefully and Tiny snored under my chair. Mike and Simon could be softly heard arguing in the background, and the living room was filled with her beautiful voice. Sue was a walking example of a could-have-been with a capital C. She was enormously talented as a songwriter and she could have been a singer. She had a nice face and pretty eyes. She could have been beautiful.

There were many things that this young woman, who was only in her early 30ties, could have been. But alcohol had grabbed hold of her and driven her to the edge of despair. She lived from one drink to the next. She was scared of life, scared of people, scared of herself. Not that I could blame her; the USA can be a very scary place if you have no money and no family to go to. She had none. As she confided to me, the story about the brother in Austin had been a lie. There was no brother. There was an ex-boyfriend, a drug-addict. She thought that maybe she could stay with him. She had made up the story of the brother so that Stephen would let her stay in the first place.

Eventually, Stephen paid for Sue's car repair. Once she had her car back, Sue drove everywhere, drunk. January 6th came and went. Sue stayed. Sue played with Tiny and Mike. Contact with the little dogs seemed to give her joy, and it was the only time I saw her smile. Simon never took part in these games. He sat off to one side, wearing a poor-me expression on his face while Mike ran around Sue in circles, saying "ra, ra" and Tiny put in an occasional waff and threw himself in front of Sue to have his stomach patted. Simon was invited to participate, but he did not wish to - unless he was the only one to grab all the attention.

One night, Sue came home drunk and drove into the wall of Stephen's brick garage. She somehow managed to hit one of the supporting posts and the entire wall came down. Stephen, whose patience had been truly tried and tested by Sue's drunken escapades, crying spells and unwillingness to get help, drew the line. With a $5,000 repair bill in his hand, caused by Sue's negligence, even he had had enough. He threw her out. Sue packed her belongings into her car and went to Austin. We never saw her again.

She left Simon behind, without telling us. We came back from work one evening and Sue was gone. Simon was still there. Stephen asked me if I wanted him.

"No way," I told him, "he's your dog now, Stephen, have fun."

118

Stephen sighed and resigned himself to the fact that he had a dog....

Outside the boundaries of our subdivision, in the "bad" part of town, was a small convenience store, a "Stop 'n Go." They are common to Houston and have well-stocked grocery departments. They are also notorious for crimes. Stop 'n Gos, because they are open 24 hours a day and thus make easy targets, are routinely robbed and often the storekeeper is shot during the course of the robbery. The worse the neighbourhood, the more dangerous it was to work in a Stop 'n Go.

Because our Stop 'n Go was in a poor neighbourhood which bordered the more wealthy, white subdivision Steven's house was in, it was considered dangerous after dark. Mike and I were not deterred by warnings we heard and we often ventured on our own, by foot, into the Stop 'n Go - admittedly only in daylight - walking the few feet from where our subdivision stopped, through the gate, across the street. I was always the only white person on the streets, and Mike was the only non-mongrel dog. But we did not mind being oddities. I had never believed in racism and greeted people as I came across them. They greeted me back and often stopped to pet Mike. Mike danced for a few black kids who lived in neighbourhood housing projects and for whom Mike soon became the highlight of their afternoon.

The kids often came from poor, abusive families. They had little self-esteem and not much to look forward to. At age 12, many of them already were addicted to cigarettes, and possibly worse... Mike represented a sane world, which they had previously only read about. The little dog was friendly to everyone, free of prejudice and always had a smile on his face. The kids often would hang out in front of the store all afternoon, waiting for Mike and me to appear to get our daily ice cream. They asked questions about his breed and listened with wonder as I told them that dogs like Mike came from a far away place in Asia.

Sometimes, I gave one of the kids Mike's leash, and they would run with Mike across the field behind the Stop 'n Go, calling out to the little dog, who would run with them, jumping up and down with joy. When the kid came back, his eyes shone with happiness and he was grinning all over.

Soon, I grew to love the kids in the neighbourhood, and black people in general. White Texans circulated so many bad stories about black people, painting pictures of them as winos, racists and dangerous criminals. Black people smelled, they were "niggers," they didn't want to work, they all took drugs...

The stories I heard were awful, and I was disgusted by the prejudice in Texas society. "Skin color does not matter," I told those who made racist remarks over and over. "If you are nice, you're nice. If you are mean, you're mean. Both times, it doesn't make any difference what color you are."

The white attorneys I worked with were shocked when I told them that I took Mike out to play with the kids in the black neighbourhood, and they prophesied that one day I was going to get killed.

"Take it from me," one attorney said. "I've been a criminal defense lawyer in this city for over 10 years. I've seen what these blacks do to people. Stay away from these neighborhoods."

To me, the entire concept of racism was ridiculous, so I paid no attention to these remarks. I also paid no attention when some attorney told me that black people were racist towards white people in Houston, too. Racism worked both ways in Texas, I was told. Naturally, I didn't believe it.

"Ridiculous," I told him. "That is something you white people make up to justify your bad treatment of the blacks."

Little did I know that this one time, I had been told the truth. I found out soon enough, as did Tiny and Mike.

It began with a crucial event in Steven's life. Steven had

gone to a party one evening and met a lovely lady by the name of Phyllis. Phyllis owned a sandwich store and was quite wealthy. She took one look at Steve and fell in love. Steven fell in love as well. Steve came home one evening with Phyllis in tow. He presented her to Phil and me.

"You two are my best friends," he told us. "I said to Phyllis that I wanted you to meet her and see what you think of us together, because we got engaged and want to get married next week."

It was all a little fast, but Phyllis was a lovely woman and obviously very smitten with Steve. Over coffee, we found out that Phyllis was a really warm lady with a marvelous sense of humour. They held hands. They looked deep into each other's eyes. They were on cloud nine. Phyllis had even brought some roast beef for Tiny, Mike and Simon from her sandwich store. No need to mention that she got the dogs' vote of approval. Mike jumped on her lap and kissed her cheek in gratitude and, possibly, calculation, hoping to get another roast beef treat out of her next time she came.

Not that there would be a next time. Steve gathered all his clothes and moved into Phyllis's house. We got an invitation to the wedding ten days later, which we could not attend because I was away on assignment at the time and Phil came with me.

Steve called us a few days after his wedding.

"Now that I've moved out, you are going to have to decide whether you want to rent the entire house or get someone to share it with you. I need $1,000 rent for the house, so see if you can get someone to move in with you and pick up the other $500."

"I think that will be better," I told him. "I don't want to live alone in such a big house, and Phil is going to leave two weeks from now."

We set out in search of someone to share the house with. I had been undercover for a while to investigate psychiatric hospital fraud in Houston. One of the psychologists I worked with was a young, black man by the name of Andy.

Andy talked with a bourgeois accent and described himself as an "upper class black professional." He claimed to be from Minnesota, where he had allegedly received his psychology degree. He now worked for several private mental hospitals in Houston. Andy came complete with beeper, suede leather briefcase and Jaguar sports car.

Andy was a lot of fun to be with. He, a girl called Jenny, who worked in juvenile hall and was half way through her Masters, and I often hung out together after our classes at the CADAC school finished (I had subscribed to a course to study for my Certified Alcohol and Drug Abuse Counseling degree, a field where a lot of the more "shady" professionals can be encountered). We went to movies together, had dinner now and again, or drove to the beach in Galveston. I thought that I knew Andy fairly well.

When I mentioned that I was looking for someone to share my house with, Andy said that he might be interested. He said that he lived in an "Upper class" apartment complex but that it was getting a little small. Could he have a look at the house? He could and he did. He decided that he would like to move in, if that was all right with Phil and me.

We consulted Tiny and Mike. They liked him. He was kind to them. As for Simon, who was also with us at the house, he loved the idea of someone else moving in. He had tried his "poor me" routine on Andy, and Andy fell for it hook, line and sinker. Andy indicated his willingness to adopt Simon if he moved in.

The first three weeks went well. Andy, Jenny and myself kept going out together, even after Phil had gone. Andy took part in a photo session with Tiny and Mike, where we put the silly Mardi Gras glasses that the cat got for Christmas on Tiny and then on Mike. Andy took photos of Mike, and me and then of Tiny and me. Then he held Tiny so I could take photos.

Finally, we put the glasses on the cat, who - just to do me a favor - sat still and kept them on his nose, pretending to read. The cat looked into the camera with an expression that said "what a silly idea, but if you really want to..." We had a lot of fun.

Then odd things began to happen. Andy tried to recruit me for an alcohol and drug abuse facility that was privately run by a woman who had a lot of money. With money, you can "buy" facilities, and the courts will send the drug and alcohol related criminals there as part of their probation once they come out of prison and are released from the halfway house.

It turned out that for every patient who had private insurance, if we referred him to a "private mental institution," we would get $700 commission. It was the same if we could find neighbors who could justify a forceful confinement. For this, we only had to prove they would be a danger to themselves and others. This was easy, whether they were indeed a danger or not. Had the person expressed sadness? Great, that meant he was depressed and suicidal. All we needed was a family member or friend to say so, or to talk that person into officially asking us for help.

I listened, took notes, attended "therapy" sessions at the halfway house and kept my mouth shut. I went with Andy to "work" at his private "practice" where he saw clients while operating under the license of a local psychologist. He offered that I could do the same. The psychologist vouched for you and referred you part of his caseload, so the patients never got to see your qualifications. You did not need any. The psychologist took a cut between 10% and 30%. I never saw any patients, but I went with Andy a few times to see him do it. It was common practice in Houston, though I am not sure it was legal. It certainly cured me forever from any temptation to see a therapist in the United States. No matter how bad it got, I would rather handle it alone than be shoved into shady practices or - heaven help me - be referred to a private mental institution for a head hunter fee.

Andy had a reason why he worked under someone else's license, he told me. The degree from Minnesota, though acknowledged there, did not include Texas board certification. He was going for his certification now, but in the meantime, he had to work for someone else. It sounded odd, but within the far bounds of the reasonable. I decided to believe it.

Then Andy's mother allegedly bought a house just a few streets up from where we were, in the black neighbourhood. She moved in there with Andy's younger brother. She claimed to be in possession of a Ph.D., and took over the running of the halfway house facility, which happened to be in one of Houston's worst neighborhoods. She came over one evening, wearing a "Black Power" T shirt, boasted how much money she made at the facility and how she was milking the system. She said that if I was nice to her, she might let me be part of it.

Soon, the "Black Power" upwardly mobile, black community virtually moved into the house. Andy's mother brought her son, who brought his friends. They did not acknowledge me in conversation, and frequently took up the living room all evening. They treated both me and the dogs as third class citizens while they discussed Martin Luther King, Mandela, the bad white people and how great it was they had found a way to milk the system. The referred to white people as "pigs" and told me, when I said that I was not a racist, that a white person was still a white person. Even Tiny and Mike had something wrong with them: they were expensive, white people's dogs. Simon, on the other hand, was adored by Andy's overbearing mother, who seemed to run the entire "black power" show.

The reason why Simon was so great was because he was a mongrel "whom you white folks just throw away and dump in the pound, just because he does not have a pedigree, but he has more heart than those brainless purebreds there."

Simon came up and humbly licked Andy's mother's

naked feet, while I took my dogs to my room and concluded that there must be something very wrong with Andy's mother.

Finally, Andy convinced Steven that he had enough money to buy the house from him. He was going to give him a down payment the following week; he was just waiting for enormous sums of money to be sent from his bank in Minnesota to Texas. I came back from the courthouse one day to find Andy was changing the locks and evicting me.

"You are lucky you came back when you did," he greeted me. "A few hours later and you would not have been able to get in. I am leaving on vacation this evening, and I am changing the locks before I go."

I called Steven. He said there was nothing he could do, as Andy had bought the house and he had signed the deed over to him.

"Steve, don't do that," I warned him, "I think there is something very wrong with Andy and his family. Andy told me he had to leave Minnesota because he got a white girl pregnant and wanted nothing to do with it. They've been shouting black power slogans in our back yard. They just kicked me out on the street with no notice. I think they are out to ruin white people. They hate us."

Steve did not listen. As for me, I found myself, with Tiny and Mike, on the street in Houston, and my husband was 2000 miles away ... all that for not having listened to that attorney when he warned me about racism.

For me, it was not so bad. I found a place to stay within one hour and moved into a Hispanic neighbourhood with a nice girl who ran a dog grooming business. The only loss I had was the kittykat, who refused to move with us and decided to stay with the neighbor instead. The neighbor was happy to adopt him, and so I left him behind.

For Steve, the loss was worse. It turned out that Andy had no money at all. He kept telling Steve the money would come next week, next month. Steve, with his good heart, kept believing him. Meanwhile, the black power crowd partied in his house. Eventually, the roof of the house caved in from neglect and who-knows-what-they-did-to-it. Steve finally evicted Andy, and had a renovation bill of more than $10,000, not to mention the loss in rent.

Andy turned out never to have had a psychology degree. His mother was not a doctor. By the time anyone could sue them, they had packed up and left, with Simon, to go to another state, to run another scam, to cheat other mental patients who came to them for help.

As for Simon, I suppose that he became a criminal dog. His talent of conning people was only marginally less than Andy's. I suppose they say dogs are like their owners, so this was a match made in heaven. One day, Andy will end up in jail, and Simon will do his poor-abused-dog act and end up being taken in by some law official or the arresting officer.

For all I know, Simon at the time of writing might even be dining on roast beef and gourmet chicken fillet on silver plates, fed to him in bite size chunks by the wife of some federal judge somewhere....

Chapter 11

Mike Becomes A Convict's Dog
Or: How Tiny And Mike Charmed The Most Dangerous
Section Of Death Row

Our convict had come out of the tough California prison system. In San Quentin, where he had spent time on a break and enter charge, there were a few simple rules: if you were young, you could either be raped, become one of the rapists or join a gang. If you were white, you joined the white gang. For blacks, there was a black gang. Mexicans had two or three gangs.

He had been 19 when he entered San Quentin, a former runaway who had been incarcerated in California's controversial youth authority during a time when the system came under investigation for gross human rights abuses of the children there, such as beatings, sexual abuse and use of psychotropic drugs as a punishment. In went a soft young child who had run away from home, scared of the arguments between his parents. Out came a bewildered young man who, after years of severe abuse at the hands of a system that he trusted to help him, could no longer fit in. The only crowd he could fit in with was the "wrong" crowd, desperate people who had equally been abused once and turned to crime and drugs.

This led our death row inmate to San Quentin eventually, where he was introduced for the first time to the real prison system and - scared by an incident of attempted rape of his person - followed the advise of an older convict to join the white gang for protection.

In Houston, he was four years later arrested for a murder that we had reason to believe he had not committed. The prosecution used his gang history to convict him. Glossing over lack of evidence in his purely circumstantial case, the prosecution relied on justice Texas style, which has very little to do with actual justice. They tried to cut a deal with the other two parties involved, saying if they would testify that our man did it, they would get off. The first party said, "I won't do it, because he wasn't there" and, as a thanks for this honest statement, ended up on death row. The second party testified, and got off, while our man was indicted.

Based on a testimony that streaked with contradictions, and independent witnesses saying that the man was not guilty, they cited sudden police "evidence" from a police department known for its corrupt practices, which evidence even the most stupid juror would identify as having been planted. That is unless they came up with something to gloss over the entire facts of the case and confuse the jury. They did by using the gang aspect.

Trying to re-open the case, we began to gather new evidence, which would show beyond doubt the necessity for a new trial. We knew that legally, we had won. The law was clear on the new evidence that needed to be uncovered for a new trial to be granted.

We thought our biggest problem was that we would get a new hearing and the prosecution would argue once more about the dangerous nature of our convict, citing the white gang connection as well as his bad conduct in prison, in order to turn attention away from the facts of the case. These should have no bearing on the consideration of whether or not he was guilty of the crime he was incarcerated for, but in Texas, they did.

"We have to reform him," Jane said. "It's the only way. Otherwise, we'll get a new trial, the stuff goes to the papers and they will zoom in on his bad behaviour and nobody will care about the facts anymore. He has to become a model prisoner, that's the only way."

"But how?" I asked her.

"I don't know," she replied. "I'm the attorney. I take care of the legal side. You're my sidekick; you take care of everything else. Go, talk to him."

A day later I sat in the visiting room, on the other side of a glass partition from our death row inmate. His name was Mike, just like my dog. Mike was 35 now. He looked tough. His hair and beard were long and unkempt. He had frequent run-ins with the guards on his cellblock and was housed on wing J21, the wing reserved for the most dangerous inmates. In Texas, where beatings of inmates on death row are still an accepted means of discipline, he was used to being beaten and to fighting back. He had suffered fractured ribs, had spent time in prison hospital frequently after run-ins with the guards and was ... a mess!

In somewhat of a defense of our inmate, some of the guards and wardens on Texas death row were truly horrible people. Tobacco chewing, fat and brutal representatives of the lowers ranks of humanity, they delighted in the power they exercised over prisoners and visitors alike, even going as far as harassing journalists and attorneys. The Texas approved the practice of strip searching male prisoners by female guards did not help to make the prisoners feel human. Many reacted by behaving like the animals they were treated as - including, unfortunately, our inmate.

I had no idea how I could possibly reform someone who lived under such conditions, so I went straight to the point:

"Okay, Mike, you have to clean up your act, or we don't even have a chance to fight your conviction. You have to shave. You have to start grooming yourself, cut your hair. Start wearing decent, clean clothes. Leave the gang. Stop fighting with prison officials..."

The list was long. The hardened convict, who had spent more than a decade on death row and who had become increasingly bitter with each year that passed, laughed at me.

"I can't leave the gang, because they'll kill me," he explained.

"I don't care," I replied. "So they'll kill you. If you don't leave them, you can be sure that they'll kill you in that death chamber. How do you want to explain to the courts that you are a member of a gang? Go to whoever the gang leader is, explain that you have a real chance to get out and that your attorney has advised you to leave the gang."

Mike and I spoke for four hours. By the time we were through, he had a list of do's and don'ts. Over the next weeks, he cleaned up his act. He stoically went through the strip searches and thought of the day he might walk out of prison a free man.

There were a handful of really decent guards who were so impressed by this old convict's 110% effort to turn himself around that they gave him a much-needed gentle word of encouragement here and there. Sometimes there was just a kind snicker from the mailroom lady as Mike's new book reading list started arriving: instead of "Hacksaw - A Convict's Story" or "The Manifesto of the Aryan Resistance in the United States" now she delivered books like "The Little Prince" by St Exupery, "The Prophet" by Kahlil Gibran and "Jonathan Livingston Seagull" by Richard Bach.

Mike, who had survived on death row by building himself an image of a tough guy best not to be messed with, began to explore his softer side. First with children's books, then with books which were food for the soul. He wrote and asked for more books of Kahlil Gibran, having been so impressed with "The Prophet." Over the years, he devoured them all.

One day, he surprised Jane and me with the fact that he had applied for a grant to go to university (he had previously completed his GED while in prison). He was accepted and received all his reports back with straight As. Mike, who had suffered from undiagnosed dyslexia as a child and was told by his teachers that he was stupid, began to discover that he was highly intelligent. He started to write: first award winning poetry and then the first few chapters of a novel. He proudly framed the poetry award and hung it on his wall. The award carried a prize of $25, his first earned money in over a decade. He went on a journey of self-discovery and came out the other end as a changed man. He wrote to his family, who were thousands of miles away, and made up with them. He re-established contact with his 13-year-old daughter who promised to visit him for the first time since he was incarcerated.

But something was missing. Mike the death row inmate needed to have someone he could love and be responsible for. I thought about this for a few weeks and then came up with a brilliant idea: since they had the same name, I decided it was a wink of fate. Mike the inmate would from now on be responsible for Mike the Shihtzu and become his "owner."

"I have decided to give you a dog," I told Mike on one of the next prison visits. "His name is Mike and he is a Shihtzu. He has a best friend called Tiny, who is owned by me. I will look after Mike for you until you get out, if you do, then you can take him with you. Meanwhile, it is your responsibility to pay for his food from your allowance, for his vet bills and whatever else he might need."

Although they never met in person, Mike and Mike became good friends. Mike the inmate asked about Mike in letters to myself and his attorney and he even read several books on Shihtzus and Pekingeses, to familiarize himself with the two breeds. From our outings, I sent him photographs: Mike in the water, Tiny and Mike on a slide, Mike meeting some children on the beach in Galveston ...

Mike often proudly passed the photos around to other death row inmates in his wing, showing off "his" dog and sharing with them the latest adventures of Mike and Tiny.

Some of the death row guards could not help being impressed by the change in the death row inmates' attitudes on the toughest wing, brought on by the little dogs. Soon, something very rare emerged: little kindnesses towards the inmates. There was the mailroom lady who stopped now and then for a friendly chat, the nurse who was kind when one of them was feeling ill, the guard who brought an extra blanket, the guy at the tower who made sure that the visit request would be processed speedily.

The spirit of Tiny and Mike kept spreading through death row. They became phantoms of hope, a dream of a life in which beauty and laughter was still real. They did not need to be there in person to invade death row and turn a place that is by all definitions hell on earth into a patch of heaven. All Tiny and Mike had as their tools to make a difference to these desperate, imprisoned men were their photos and the stories I would write about them to Mike. But it was enough.

They were just little dogs. They did not judge. They did not care whether someone was guilty or innocent. Many of the men on death row opened their tattered hearts to allow Tiny and Mike inside. Death row changed because of them. Hardened convicts would wake up with a smile on their faces and count the hours until they met with Mike the inmate in recreation, only so they could find out from him what the little dogs had been up to today. They saved up their allowances, and sent them to me to buy the little dogs a treat.

One Christmas I received a beautiful oil painting of Mike from one of the inmates, a young boy of 24 who was on death row for a crime he had committed as a juvenile. Mike, our inmate, kept reporting in his letters that he had instructions from an ever-increasing number of prisoners to ask me how Tiny and Mike were doing, and that he shared with them whatever information I could send him about their escapades.

When the man who had painted Mike's picture was facing execution, we sent him a good-bye card with Mike's paw print on it. Rumour has it that he had Mike's photograph with him in his final hours, as he sat in the death cell, waiting to be killed.

As for Mike the inmate, he took part in decisions concerning "his" dog.

"Mike needs to go to the vet to get his claws clipped," I would tell him for instance, or "I think it is time again for Mike to go to the groomer for a bath, what do you say?"

We would then calculate the money it would cost to do so, and I would deduct this amount from Mike's the inmate's monthly allowance, in order to spend it on Mike, the dog. I would then send him the exact invoice, to let him know where his money had gone. Mike became a very responsible dog owner, and would even scold me for disciplining his dog on one or two "close calls" we had, when Mike almost ran in front of a truck.

Eventually, Mike's daughter Rene came to visit. She was 16, and living in very poor housing conditions with her mother and her little daughter. She was a lovely girl, although she had been deeply traumatized through years of sexual abuse by her mother's former boyfriend. She had very little self-confidence or opportunities. When she met with her father, whom she had not seen since she was two years old, tears of love and joy began to flow. Mike told her that he had finished his schooling from inside prison and inspired Rene to do the same.

Rene stayed with me for several days, during which she made close friends with Tiny and "her father's dog" Mike. We went to the park together, where the girl played with the dogs, laughing as if without cares, far removed from the environment of drugs and violence in Los Angeles where she was living. We took photos of her and the dogs, which she loved.

"I would like to be a vet," she confided, "but everyone always told me it was impossible for someone like me, because I am just white trash, a convict's child and no good."

" Of course you can be," I assured her. "And nobody is trash. That is an awful thing to say. You ought to be proud of yourself for having made it this far, and you can even be proud of your father, look how he has changed, despite everything that happened to him. And never forget that your father may have been a petty criminal, but he is not a killer. If he ever gets his chance in court, he will be able to prove that. There is no shame in your father being on death row. There is plenty of shame in the people who put him there, using lies and perjury to do so."

Rene was a lovely young woman, who left Texas filled with dreams and the vow to work to make them come true. The first was to get her GED. To go to university and become a vet. And - when her father got out of prison - to help him with establishing a home for run-away children, where the children could live in an atmosphere of love and acceptance and grow up to fulfil their potential.

At the time, her dreams were not too far out of reach. Already many celebrities had taken an interest in Mike's case. Some of them were willing to help him if he got out. A prominent author specializing in innocent convictions wanted to go public with the case. Edward Heath, former Prime Minister of Great Britain and a sailing colleague of Phil, had spoken to the owner of The Washington Post, who wanted to help with publicity when needed. But the attorney decided that publicity would be more damaging for the case than filing it quietly through the courts. For now, she said, all we could do was our best to amass the new evidence still needed because - obvious though it seemed to the casual observer - the existing evidence was not enough for the Texas judges. To keep our client mentally sane during this ever-longer period of waiting, we had, thankfully, two charming little dogs and their adventures in Texas to help us.

Chapter 12

How Tiny And Mike Came To Have Their First Stay At The Four Seasons Hotel And Why Germany's "Der Spiegel" Magazine Paid For Their Grooming Bills

Siegesmund von Ilsemann was bureau chief in Washington DC of Germany's prestigious newsmagazine "Der Spiegel." In this capacity Siegesmund runs the DC office of "Spiegel."

One nice, hot Texas summer's day, I called the DC office of "Der Spiegel" and Siegesmund happened to pick up the phone.

"I am a Canadian journalist," I told him in fluent German. "I am in Texas, working as investigator on a death penalty case. We need to generate some more funds for the case, and we have got some original letters from the inmate to offer for sale. Would you be interested in a book for the German market?"

Siegesmund was immediately intrigued, not only with my offer of the letters for publication, but also with the fact that I had decided to work on the case without being paid.

Siegesmund wanted to meet me. "Yes, we would be interested," he said. "As it happens, we are also planning a story on the death penalty. Since Texas is the main Death Penalty State, why don't I fly to Houston next week, you help me write the story - we'll pay you of course - and we can discuss the letters."

"Sounds good to me," I replied. "You might also be interested to know that there's solid circumstantial evidence the guy didn't do it, which the courts keep ignoring in favor of much less solid evidence."

"Yes, I want to see that," Siegesmund told me. "Can you arrange for me to visit the inmate together with you?"

"I think so," I replied. "I'll have to clear it with the

attorney first, but it should be all right."

"Okay, I'll book a flight for next Wednesday, I'll be in Houston Wednesday, Thursday and Friday. I'll probably arrive Wednesday early evening, so we would plan to go to death row on Thursday, if that is possible. Could you be so kind and book a good hotel somewhere downtown, in the name of Spiegel magazine. I'll call you back tomorrow to confirm the flight times."

There, done. It was as simple as that, and I was working for Spiegel and had their local bureau chief fly out to meet me. What he didn't know was that he was by no means flying out to meet me, the death row inmate and his attorney, nor was he booking my services as a journalist by myself. To be exact, he was booking my services along with Tiny and Mike and he was in actuality flying to Houston from DC to meet a Pekingese with a VIP complex and his Shihtzu side-kick with their owner. The death penalty story was just an added bonus. Little did he know...

It began with the fact that he had entrusted me with booking a hotel for him. I called the Sheraton. "Do you permit dogs?"

I asked. "No." "Okay, thanks, good bye." Next came the Hilton. Same response.

Then The Westin Galleria, Houston's finest. "Dogs?" the horrified receptionist answered. "Of course not." Then came a list of reasons, citing health regulations, the city's food and drug administration and other such bureaucracies.

The Four Seasons downtown was next. "Do you allow dogs?"

"Yes, Ma'am, we certainly do. We love dogs."

That sounded better. The receptionist went on. "We even provide extra services for the dogs. We walk them while you are at meetings, take them to grooming appointments and have your favorite dog food ready in your room upon check-in if you advise us in advance what they eat."

136

Thus began a long love affair between myself and The Four Seasons hotel chain... They were a hotel after my own heart!

"Great, for now I just need one room," I told the receptionist, "in the name of Spiegel magazine."

"And how many dogs will you be bringing?" he asked.

"None, so far," I replied. "But we may need a second room as the night wears on, and that would be for the dogs then."

"Oh, they can stay in the same room as the owner," the helpful receptionist volunteered, obviously thinking that we were going to book the dogs a separate hotel room if they were to stay overnight.

"Yes, I know. I am the owner. I need the room for an out of towner who is coming in for a meeting. I wish to bring my dogs along to a dinner meeting, and in case it gets too late, I will stay over and require a second room, with the dogs. If we finish early, I will be able to drive home."

Siegesmund arrived one week later, right on schedule. He took the shuttle bus from the airport to The Four Seasons and we met at 7:30pm Wednesday evening in the lobby.

I instantly liked Siegesmund, even though his first question, with a surprised frown on his face, was:

"And who are they?" looking at Tiny and Mike.

I held my head high and looked him straight in the eye. I could see that this was a conservative, serious businessman who had fought his way to the top of the ladder and who liked to come across as "correct," suit and tie included. Little dogs did not fit with this man's image at all.

"They are Tiny and Mike," I replied. "They are journalists, too. I am going to do a book about their life, and they travel with me wherever I go. They will sit in on our meeting, or there will be no meeting."

Siegesmund looked at me with frank amusement. He

did his best to keep from grinning (something that I sensed this man did not do very often) as he asked: "So, I take it they are coming to death row with us tomorrow, too?"

"As a matter of fact, no they are not," I replied prissily. "Because the Texas Department of Corrections won't let them in."

"I am sure you would have no problem convincing them," Siegesmund mused. "I don't usually allow dogs at meetings either."

"Yes, but the TDC are beyond any sense of humour, take my word for it. You'll see."

For now, it was time for us to go to dinner. Siegesmund and I took a seat in the posh basement restaurant, which served a wonderful buffet. To our right and left, respectively, were seated Tiny and Mike who looked on as Siegesmund and I talked about death row.

Mike had long since learned that by intense concentration on a piece of food, as it left the plate and made its way from the fork into the mouth of the eater, so long as he truly concentrated on the morsel throughout this entire process, the next morsel would usually, as if by magic, find its way into Mike's mouth. It was a trick Mike had been practicing for a long time, and even conservative Siegesmund was not immune to it.

As for Tiny, he does not lower himself to such practices. Tiny is a very assertive little dog. When he wants food, he says "raff raff" and he gets food. So it was this time, too. Siegesmund fed Mike, and I fed Tiny to shut him up. For all his conservative attire and manner, Siegesmund actually turned out to be very nice, once he thawed. He even took Mike on his lap once we went into the drawing room for some coffee and further talking.

We talked about death row, then about life in general. He had just lost a family member to cancer. I was about to lose a close friend to the same illness. "I am scared of losing him," I

138

confided, "and yet, there seems to be nothing I can do to stop the process."

"I know," Siegesmund replied. "Losing someone is the most heartbreaking, horrible thing that can happen to a person. There is nothing I can say to make this better for you. The process of loss is horrible, and once you have lost him, it will be even more horrible. It is something you have to live through. That's life, that's why it is important to cling to little things which give us joy, while we can."

"Like the dogs?" I asked, trying to make a joke.

Siegesmund cradled Mike in his arms. "Yes, for instance," he said. I was silently wondering what Spiegel would say if they saw their tough bureau chief right now, sitting in the lobby of The Four Seasons, cradling a slightly overweight Shihtzu dog. They probably wouldn't have believed it...

By the time we finished talking and had gone over the next day's schedule, it was very late, too late for me to drive home through the dangerous, deserted streets of downtown Houston.

"We'll need a second room," I said.

"Yes, good idea, that way we can set off from here together in the morning," Siegesmund replied and went to reception to book a second room for the dogs and me.

The funniest thing was expression on Tiny's face as he walked over the plush carpet into the richly decorated elevator, which reeked of elegance and money: he had his head thrown back, nose up, ears softly swaying as he walked and had, by all considerations, the air of royalty.

"Your Pekingese isn't half arrogant, isn't he?" Siegesmund remarked. "I don't think I have ever seen a dog like that."

Mike behaved as Mike always does, no matter the environment, like a friendly, nice dog. Tiny was a different matter. Before he had been at the hotel for more than six hours, he walked in and out of the elevators as if he owned the place. People remarked "what a cute pair of little dogs," as we met them in the elevators, going up and down to breakfast or for walks, Mike would go up to them, wag his tail and bask in the attention. Not Tiny. He gave a royal wag, not too much, and then bared his teeth if they tried to touch him. He was greatly offended whenever someone treated him like a mere dog or, worse still, like a commoner. It was those people who admired him from afar, keeping a respectful distance, who Tiny was most fond of.

"You must excuse him," I explained to the other guests in the elevator, shrugging. "He owns the place, and that can go to a guy's head a little, you understand?"

I make a fair guess that many of an out of town businessman, or film star or whatever else they were went about their work that day with the memory of a faint smile still written on their faces...

Siegesmund and I had breakfast on Thursday morning with Tiny and Mike sitting beside us on their own. They did not have their dog food, so I ordered them - courtesy of Spiegel magazine - a giant slice of ham each.

"So, are you ready for your first visit to death row?" I asked Siegesmund.

"I don't know," he replied. "I suppose so. You have done this before, right?"

"Yes, I do it all the time," I told him. "Seen a few of them go to their deaths, too. It is not as bad as it first seems. You grow used to death and dying. Human life matters little here, human emotions even less. Just think that the State of Texas is the last bit of true Wild West still left in the world, and you'll be okay."

"And them?" Siegesmund asked, patting Mike and carefully pointing to Tiny. He knew better than to get too close to Tiny or, worse still, make an attempt to touch him.

"I think we ought to drop them off at the groomers," I volunteered. "They both need a bath and a clip."

"Fine," he replied.

"Spiegel won't have a problem paying for it, will they?" I asked. "After all, I am on expense account while doing the story with you..."

"Wait a minute," Siegesmund said. "You want the magazine to pick up grooming bill for your dogs?"

"Yes."

"Impossible," he replied. "No way."

"Fine, I can't come then," I replied. "You'll have to go to death row on your own. We obviously don't have time to drop the dogs back to my house, and I am not going to let them languish in the Texas heat in my car. It is because of the magazine that I did not get home last night and the dogs had to stay overnight here with me."

Siegesmund sighed.

"So, you'll authorize it to be put on the magazine account then?" I asked.

"I am going to have to, won't I?" Siegesmund said and was clearly not as amused as I was.

It was the first time, ever, in the history of Spiegel magazine that they picked up the grooming bill for a pair of little dogs. Or big dogs. Or any dogs at all for that matter. A hundred bucks bets that it will also be the last time...

Chapter 13

Sushi, Sunny, Film Stars And Baby Language

Despite my best intentions to stay in Texas throughout the time of working on the death penalty case, this was not always possible. Frequently, my job took me across the United States, to Latin America or to Europe, often without the possibility to stop over in Texas in between trips. There were times I had to be away from Houston for four months or more...

One such time took me to Los Angeles, off and on, for the better half of 1990. I try not to fly, so I went back and forth by Amtrak train, Houston - Los Angeles - Houston - Los Angeles - Houston, and so on.

When my first leg of the Los Angeles trips came up, I was still at a loss what to do with Tiny and Mike. I couldn't very well take them with me on the train, as Amtrak did not allow dogs. I was not brave enough to drive across the States on my own in my beat-up white Audi, "Farley." The obvious solution would be to leave them in Houston until I returned, but where?

In a kennel? Not even an outside chance of that. The image of the little dogs caged and dispassionately given only minimal attention by the staff, being fed and watered out of a sense of duty rather than love by people who did this for money and not because they liked little dogs... no way! I did, however, look at a few kennels, and all of them, no matter what "luxuries" they advertised, were equally lonely for their canine occupants.

The solution arrived by itself, in a Houston Sushi bar, two days before I was to leave. I adore sushi and lived almost exclusively off the raw Japanese delicacy while in the lone star state. By the time I was in Houston for two months, I knew most of the city's sushi bars and their menus better than the locals. That lunchtime, I had ventured to try out a new sushi bar off Westheimer Street, which was supposed to be a valuable new addition to the sushi world of Houston.

Sushi bars are highly social places, where you are seated in close proximity to a total stranger. People who arrive at sushi bars alone have usually made some friends by the time they leave.

A typical sushi bar friendship begins something like this:

"Say, what is it you are eating there? Looks interesting."

"That's eel. And what do you have. What's that slimy yellow thing there on your plate?"

"Sea Urchin"

"Urgh"

"You should try it. Really, it's good."

"Really?"

"Yes, I promise."

"Okay. I'll give you one of my eels if you give me one of your sea urchins."

"Done."

Sushi orders usually come in pieces of two, so this kind of deal is easy to make. Two strangers-now-turned-sushi-friends will sit next to each other, each chewing the recommended piece of fish from the other. Whoever swallows his piece first will then ask:

"So, what do you think?"

"Wasn't bad."

"Told you."

"What do you think?"

"Yes, it was very good."

And then usually follows the inevitable American question, by which most friendships are being defined and most people judged:

"By the way, what do you do for a living?"

With that, the conversation is on its way. Depending

on how much the sushi eaters have in common aside the sushi, business cards are exchanged or, in absence of these, telephone numbers are swapped written on the napkins with a pen borrowed from the sushi chef. A considerable number of friendships, romances and serious business deals can be traced back to beginnings in a sushi bar somewhere or other.

On this particular afternoon, I traded what I believe was a piece of sweet shrimp or Amaebi for a piece of giant clam with a blonde Texas bombshell by the name of Sunny, who was lunching with her banker friend. Having exchanging the obligatory information about the taste of the sushi, Sunny inevitably asked what I did for a living.

"A journalist? Really? How interesting. How long have you been in Houston? It must be such an exciting life, meeting all these people..."

"Actually, it can be a pain in the butt," I told her. "For instance, right now I have to leave for Los Angeles, where I'll be for six weeks. I don't know anyone here, and I have two little dogs that I can't take with me. I still don't know what to do with them while I am gone."

"What kind of dogs are they?" Sunny asked, elegantly tossing back a curl of her golden, curly hair. Sunny was, by all standards, a true Southern beauty.

I had my business diary with me, which always contained a recent photo of Tiny and Mike who enjoy posing for pictures as much as any vain child would. This meant I was never short of supplies to stock my diary with. I shoved the photo past the sushi plates and the soy sauce dish, to Sunny.

"They are a Pekingese and a Shihtzu, see," I told her, handing her the photo. "Here, that's them."

"Oh my God, they are adorable," Sunny exclaimed when she saw the photograph. "I'll look after them for you if you don't have anyone else to do it."

After our sushi lunch, I followed Sunny to her elegant

145

home in the Houston suburbs, where she introduced me to her geologist husband. The husband and Sunny conferred for a few minutes, and then decided that they would be honored to look after Tiny and Mike. They promised to spoil them rotten.

They wanted me to make a list of do's and don'ts, what to feed them and when, and anything else they ought to know about the little creatures.

"Always keep Mike on a leash," I warned them. "When surrounded by houses as opposed to open country, Mike frequently starts running in circles and goes crazy. He was brought up on a horse farm, so he is not used to cars, and he just loves running. You can't let him off the leash, or he may run into the road before you are able to catch him."

I gave them a schedule for their bathtimes. To keep the notorious Texas fleas at bay, they were to be conducted once a week. There was the matter of grooming, too. Both were longhaired dogs and needed their fur thoroughly combed every other day.

"I'll do it with pleasure," Sunny beamed. "Right now, I am putting a business together with my banker friend, so I have plenty of spare time while he is sorting things out."

I took the dogs over to them the night before leaving for Los Angeles. Sunny and her husband were instantly taken with them. Mike ran around their house in circles, jumped on Sunny's lap and did what he could to be a nice Shihtzu. Tiny, who was predictably being adored because he was "so cute" actually wagged his tail and was on better behaviour than usual. I handed Sunny the little box which contained Tiny's eye drops (Pekingese eyes bulge and dry out easily. The vet recommended for Tiny's eyes to be moistened with sterile saline solution once a day), Tiny's ear medication (he is prone to ear infection, and thus the dog box always contains an anti-biotic, anti-fungal ointment, for instant treatment in case the infection flares up again), the grooming equipment for the dogs, one bottle of flea shampoo, one bottle of Tiny's medicated anti-flake, anti-itch shampoo with coconut scent, one bottle of silky-hair dog shampoo with almond scent and their leashes.

"They sleep on the bed," I informed Sunny, explaining the absence of a dog bed. "Hope you guys don't mind. They think they are human, and they would be offended if anyone suggested to them that they sleep on the floor like dogs. In fact, Tiny doesn't even like it when you mention the D word."

Sunny and her husband laughed and said the dogs would be welcome at the foot end of their bed. While we talked, Tiny and Mike started wrestling on the floor. Tiny growled at Mike who pretended to be wrestled to the ground by the smaller dog. With a lot of "rrr" "rr"s and barking at each other, they rolled around on the floor, until Mike got up, grabbed Tiny by the tail and pulled him across the living room.

"What the hell...?" Sunny's husband asked.

"Oh, they have a whole show worked out, which they put on to entertain people. They have met you for the first time, so you'll be treated to the entire show. You are expected to watch in awe and give it your full attention."

"Ah," Sunny and her husband exclaimed and dutifully watched as Mike let go of Tiny's tail and threw himself down in front of him, looking up at the Pekingese and barking. Tiny grabbed hold of Mike's upper leg, bit into it and then Mike got up and patted Tiny on the head a few times, which caused Tiny to jump up on the sofa. There was a playful mocking fight for the sofa, and then Mike grabbed Tiny by the ear and pulled him off. One final wrestle on the ground and the show came to its conclusion. Sunny and her husband clapped, impressed. Both dogs came over, wagging their tails expectantly.

Sunny patted them on the head. "Well done, guys, very entertaining." The dogs did not go away. "Now what?" she asked. "What do I have to do now?"

"Now they want a cookie," I explained. "It's always the same show, they have their routine worked out, and they expect the audience, in lieu of entry fee, to "pay" with a dog biscuit. I handed Sunny the box of dog biscuits that I always carry hidden with me. We use Milky Bone dog biscuits, which come in assorted colors and flavors.

"Tiny first," I instructed her. "You have to hold the two different flavors up to his nose, so he can smell them both and take his pick first. Mike gets the flavor that is left over."

Sunny almost killed herself with laughter as Tiny marched up to the cookies, smelled first the green, then the brown one, and finally decided to go for the green one. Making choices, I explained to Sunny, is very important to Tiny. It confirms his illusion that unlike Mike he is not a dog, because he has the power of choice.

We were all set now, except for the fact that there was still somewhat of a language problem. Mike was no problem; he was a Texan and spoke only English anyway. But Tiny spoke German and some French, not a word of English.

"Try telling him to come here," I told Sunny. Sunny said "Tiny, come here." Nothing happened.

Tiny started rubbing his ears on the floor. "He's not allowed to do that," I informed Sunny. "Tell him to stop."

Sunny said: "Tiny, stop." Nothing.

I said "Tiny, arret-ca la, ne fais pas ca." He stopped.

I said "Tiny, herkommeln" and he came over.

We tried this a few times, any which language, until Sunny suggested: "You better write us down some of the most important commands for Tiny, so we can communicate with him."

I sat down at the kitchen table and wrote a list of Tiny's most pertinent vocabulary, most of which consists of German baby language:

Herkommeln = Come here

Aufhoereln = Stop that

Schnell scheisseln = Go quick and do number two

Pippi macheln = Go and do number one

Muss der Hund jetzt rausgeheln? = Do you have to go outside?

Ein schmeckel = Food (this usually sends Tiny running to the kitchen from wherever he is and is the perfect way to get him to come in from the garden

Jetzt gehn wir wohin = Time for a walk

"How do you pronounce that stuff?" Sunny asked. We practiced it together, in the bedroom, outside of Tiny's earshot. When she was well versed in German baby language, Sunny tried her luck. She called from where we were: "Tiny, herkommeln." A few seconds later, Tiny appeared in the doorframe.

"I can't believe it. This really works!" she exclaimed.

I left Tiny with Sunny for nine weeks, as my trip to Los Angeles kept dragging out. In between meetings with directors and interviews with assorted film stars, I excused myself and walked to the public phone of the "Petit Four" cafe in Hollywood to call Sunny.

"How are my dogs?" I would ask.

"They are doing great," she assured me. "We are having lots of fun together. I gave them a bath yesterday, and now they smell heavenly."

We exchanged dog talk for a few minutes, and I told her "give them a hug from me" each time before I hung up. When I got back to my table, people would frequently ask: "Is everything all right?"

"Yes," I replied. "I just had to call Houston to check on the kids."

"How many you got?"

"Two, a Pekingese and a Shihtzu," I replied, and added: "Would you like to see a photo?" With this I shoved the photo from the business diary in front of a rather amazed film star's nose.

Chapter 14

How We Came To Meet Debby, The "Good Aunt"

When I finally returned from Los Angeles, I had stayed much longer than initially intended, due to the triple work load of interviewing witnesses for our death penalty case (our prisoner was initially from Los Angeles and I had been sent to interview his home boys on the streets of the rougher neighborhoods of the city of angels), doing journalism work and researching a documentary for a Canadian film producer. This meant literally hundreds of interviews, meetings, dinners, and parties to attend. When the train finally pulled into Houston station, I was exhausted and looked forward to seeing the dogs again.

" Do I really have to give them back?" Sunny asked me. "I have so much fallen in love with them. Could I not pay you whatever money you ask for, and you let me keep these two and go get yourself some new ones?"

After talking with her husband about the matter, Sunny finally conceded to give up the dogs. She brought them to meet me outside Houston's Myako Sushi bar, where we met for a quick bite and she told me her adventures with the two little creatures. "We went walking together every day," she recounted, " Tiny became so affectionate once he got to know me. You have such lovely dogs, I really wouldn't have given them back, if my husband hadn't appealed to my conscience..."

I am sure she was joking, but I resolved nonetheless to seek someone else to look after the dogs in future. I watched Sunny hug Tiny and Mike good-bye before she handed them over to me, wiping a tear from the corner of her eye. If nothing else, it would do her no good to grow even more attached to them in the years to come only to give them up each time I came back from a trip. Not to mention what would happen if there had been even a trace of seriousness in her flippant remark.

"I'll be happy to look after them again," Sunny offered as she handed me the various brushes, creams and ointments which went with the dogs. I politely said thank you and must confess that I never called her again. Instead, I set out to search for a new dog sitter.

We came to meet Debby because her house was right off the I 45 freeway, a little to the North of Houston. When I drove from Houston to Huntsville for my weekly visits to death row, I passed a sign by the freeway that read Debby's grooming. One day, I decided to stop there on the way home.

An attractive brunette in her early thirties came to the counter, followed by dogs of all shapes and sizes. She was extremely friendly and had an engaging smile. I liked her instantly and told her a rather long story:

"Hi, my name is Tess. I am from Canada and I have two little dogs travelling with me. I saw your convenient location here and I wondered whether it would be possible for me to drop them off when I pass here once a week on my way to Huntsville in the morning, and leave them with you to groom. I would then come and pick them up in the late afternoon, on my way home."

"You certainly can," Debbie said. "That will be no problem at all. I'll feed them lunch and let them out in the yard on nice days. I have a huge fenced yard in the back, and they could play there until your return."

I turned to the walls and admired huge, framed photos of Debbie at a dog show with a prize-winning Labrador. She looked glamorous and so did the dog in the picture with her. "Wow, is that what you do, dog shows?" I asked her. "You must get around a lot."

"Yes, that was my prize winning bitch," she replied. "She died a few years ago, of old age. As you can see, I don't believe in putting my dogs to sleep when they grow old," she added, indicating a few white-haired canine ladies and Gentlemen who walked around her side of the counter, some of them coughing, some of them limping slightly on their arthritic legs, but all of them happy.

"I know what it is like, I travel a lot, too," she informed me. "Just a few months ago, a guy from Uruguay ordered two dogs from me and paid for them by money transfer. I actually flew out to Uruguay with the dogs and delivered them in person, as he had requested."

"Sounds like you have a great job," I told her. "Do you run the dog grooming business on the side?" I asked.

"No, it's the other way around. I used to breed full-time, now the breeding is a side business and the dog grooming is my main living. How about you, what do you do? You said you go to Huntsville every week. Do you work in the prison there?"

Huntsville was known only for it's concentration of the larger part of Texas' penal institution and for it's Sam Houston University, which in turn was famous for its criminal justice center. Nobody ever went to Huntsville for its own sake, hence, and there is an old Texas rule: if you had business in Huntsville, you had business with the jails in some way or other.

I told her what I was doing in Huntsville.

"Great," she replied to my surprise. Usually, the reaction I had gotten from Houstonians was more along the lines of "Canadians go home, we don't need you to stick your noses into our justice system." I was suffering the full backlash of Errol Morris, a journalist and film maker from Canada, who had raised more than 1 million dollars to hire an attorney and proved, through his own investigation and an attorney's, a certain Texas death row inmate, Randall Dale Adams, innocent. To the embarrassment of TDC, Morris generated high publicity for the case and they had to let Adams go.

Not only was I Canadian and a journalist, but to top it off, I was also working with the same lawyer. Everything they could not do to Adams due to his enormous publicity, they did to me in the prison in terms of harassment. The courts were determined not to let another Adams case happen. The judges turned down our case on principle rather than merit, and point blank refused to look at the issues raised or to address them. The public's attitude was not much better. In the Texas "hang them high" mentality, it was better to occasionally kill an innocent one than to let a guilty one go. Nobody wanted or needed Canadian reporters crying "human rights" and "justice." They wanted to continue doing justice Texas style.

To my amazement, Debbie was not like them. "You know, I am married to a cop," she confided. "And I have to tell you, some of what is going on is not at all right. I know innocent people go to prison in Texas, more than people realize. And nobody here will speak out for it, because the average person on the street does not know. I have seen Errol Morris' film, and it did not surprise me. I think it's wonderful that you foreign journalists are coming here, good on you. I hope after you and Errol there will be many more."

Debbie was so enthusiastic about my undertaking that she wanted to know what she could do to help. She asked the question and came up with her own answer in the same breath: "You know what? I'll charge you only half price for grooming the dogs, and then you can put the rest into financing the case. I know that a capital murder appeal can be costly."

And so it came that Tiny and Mike had their first meeting with Debbie the following Thursday, when I was on route to my weekly visit at death row. Debbie had a way with dogs, and they took to her instantly, especially Tiny. She understood his reluctance to be addressed and treated as a D person, and allowed him his illusion that he was a small human of enormous importance. Tiny was permitted free access to all the grooming cages, where assorted dogs were being blow-dried after Debbie and her assistant had given them a bath. Tiny enjoyed it enormously to walk down the corridor and look into the cages as if he owned them, sniffing each dog, wagging his tail at some and growling at others (usually the biggest ones).

When I came back from Huntsville after my death row visit, I hardly recognized the two rascals. They both wore bow ties, smelled most exquisitely and Tiny had even a purple ribbon behind each ear. Their fur shone healthily and there was not a flea to be found. I couldn't believe it.

"You... wow, that's my dogs?" I asked Debbie. "I can't believe how beautiful they are."

Years of dog show experience had taught Debbie how to turn out a dog, looking its best. "Can I bring them again?" I asked her.

"Sure thing," Debbie replied. From them on, Tiny and Mike spent every Thursday afternoon with Debbie. She became like a generous aunt to them, spoiling them with tidbits, always having their lunch and sometimes even breakfast waiting - all without charging me. Before long, Debbie began to take charge of her new protegees' well being.

"What are you feeding them?" she asked me about three weeks after we had met.

"Lucky dog, why?" I replied. "They seem to like it well enough. Especially Tiny enjoys the fact that there are four different flavors, and he can pick and chose."

"You can't feed them that junk," Debbie said. "That's just like feeding a person hamburger. Tastes good, but nutrient value is almost nil. If you want your dogs to have a long life, you need to start with a good diet."

From then on, Tiny and Mike, upon Debbie's recommendation, and to the joy of our local vet, began eating Iams mini chunks. When Tiny developed a sensitive stomach, his diet was changed to Iams lamb and rice, which he eats to this day.

When Mike, who tends to put on weight easily, became a little large around the girdle, Debbie announced: "I've just discovered a really great, top-class dog food for overweight dogs, recommended by a champion dog breeder I know. I think we should try this for Mike. Actually, I've already started her on it, I hope you don't mind."

From then on, Mike ate Natural Choice Lite. Naturally, the price difference between the "good" and the "junk" dog foods was enormous, but, as Debbie and my vet assured me, they were well worth it.

From then on, I discussed my dogs' diet with Debbie, as well as other little problems as they arose: ear mites, flea infestation, Tiny's flaky skin problems for which Debbie got some special protein conditioner. Debbie and I discussed even what brand of dog biscuits to feed them and switched to Iams lamb and rice, allowing only for the occasional milk bone cookie.

Before too long, Tiny and Mike began looking forward to "Debbie day." There was always so much to do and see at Debbie's, new friends to be made, and Debbie never could give them too many hugs or kind words. They looked forward to her good food, gentle baths, and had great fun under her blow dryer. When I took the exit off the freeway, we had to take a left turn at the Shell gas station on the Woodlands exit, then go back on ourselves, as Debby's place was off the one-way feeder road. The moment we stopped to turn at the gas station, Tiny and Mike grew frisky. Mike started whining, impatient to get out of the car. Any worries I might have had that I was leaving them alone with a stranger for too long were soon dissipated. As soon as we stopped at Debbie's, they jumped out of the car and walked into Debbie's house, with excited tailwags and without bothering to look back.

"Bye guys," I shouted after them, but they were already around the corner, eagerly inspecting the blow-drier cages, to see what dogs were in there for them to play with today. "Oh well," I remarked to Debbie the first time this happened. "I suppose they are beginning to like it here."

From then on, Debbie looked after them when I was on business trips, at the ridiculously low charge of only 5$ a day for both of them, which worked out at 2.50$ a day per dog. In comparison, the average price for an in-house, private pet sitting service runs somewhere between 10 and 15$ per dog.

Thanks to Debbie, I was able to travel for long periods of time, and I was able to travel in peace. There is nothing worse than having the stressful job of being a journalist, somewhere in a strange city, interviewing a succession of strangers and trying to meet deadlines and then worry about your little dogs that you left in the care of a stranger.

With Debbie, I knew that even when my work on one occasion took me from Houston to Germany to Central America, to Germany again, back to Central America and then finally back to Houston, on a trip that lasted a total of 4 months, not only would I be free of worry for my dogs' safety, know they were given the right food, allowed to exercise as often as need be, I also was secure in the knowledge that they were being given so much love that it was a vacation for them to be there. When I returned, I was on no account met by two pathetic, whining creatures. On the contrary, they looked very happy, extremely clean and ran tailwagging through Debbie's house, which adjoined her grooming business, clearly having taken it over as the new owners.

Mike had even conned Debbie into feeding him little bits of pancake on Sunday mornings... They were happy to go home with me, but would have been just as happy to stay a little longer aunt Debbie's...

When the time came for us to leave Houston, after five long years of which the dogs spent a fair amount with Debbie, the good-bye came hard for both sides. Just before we had to leave, they had spent another 3 months with her as I was jetting around the world. When I had to leave, I breezed into Houston for a mere two-night stay, long enough to pick up any clothes and other personal effects and long enough also to pick up the dogs from Debbie one last time.

"That's it, then?" Debbie said when Phil and I dropped by to pick them up. "Yes, I'm afraid so," I replied.

"You guys really leaving town?"

"I was only here for a death penalty appeal, Debbie. I have done all I could, interviewed all the witnesses. The lawyer said it is time for me to go home again, and I want to. I miss the Laurentians, the cool, fresh air, swimming in a clean mountain lake ... and so do Tiny and Mike. We don't belong here, Debbie."

"Okay then," she said, "Let me get them for you." A few seconds later, the two little guys came round the corner, wagging their tails. They had been given one of Debbie's famous summer clips, wore pretty bowties and smelled wonderful. Debbie hugged me, Phil, and then finally, the two little dogs.

"Look after yourselves," she reminded them. "Don't eat too much, Mike. And you, Tiny, stop being so bossy. If you ever get back to Houston, make sure that you stop by and say hello. I'll always have their lunches ready..."

When we got back to Montreal, I sent Debbie a thank you card. I affixed a photo we had taken of Tiny and Mike, shortly after our return, on the steps of the old fortress on Montreal's Isle St Helene. They stood side by side, curiously looking out into the world, ready for new adventures, wherever the following years might take them. In the card, I had written: "Dear Debbie, Thanks so much for looking after us while we were in Houston. We will never forget you. Lots of love and a big lick from Tiny and Mike."

Then I pressed each of their right forepaws into ink I use for my old style fountain pen and pressed their paw-prints under the photo.

A week later, the phone rang. It was Debbie. "I got the card from Tiny and Mike yesterday. It was so cute. I cried when I read it. How are they? I miss them so much...."

Chapter 15

Status Symbols, Quirks And Favorite Places

The longer I had the dogs, the more it became evident that they were distinct personalities with their very own preferences and dislikes.

For Tiny, for instance, it is very important that he be considered a little human with fur on it, not a dog. To prove this to himself, he demands a series of privileges. For instance, he will not walk on a leash. When he goes outside into the garden, he does not like to be told "come in now." Instead, one is to ask, politely, in German baby language: "Tiny, could you please come in now?," and preferably attach to this request an explanation, such as: "because it is time to eat" or "because I have to go to work and make money, so Tiny can go out and buy some nice things."

Tiny usually will look at me, wag his tail and, just to prove that he is independent, walk the other way, and take his sweet time with doing his morning business. I have lost count of the many times I raced through Houston traffic, down the permanently jammed highway 59, to make it to a downtown interview on time. When I got there, I usually found myself apologizing to my interviewee with a flushed face and the words "sorry about that, my Pekingese was late getting out of bed this morning..."

To further support his delusions of being human, Tiny would not stand for exclamations such as "what a cute little dog" by people we met on our outings. Such exclamations and the subsequent attempt to pat Tiny were greeted by a growl and, if the person did not back off, even an attempt to bite. Due to the fact that Tiny had been delighting in wrapping his teeth around his back fur and then pulling forward, he had succeeded by age three to pull out all his lower front teeth, save one, turning himself truly into a dog whose bark was worse than his bite. The few times he did get to the point where he had to snap at someone to keep them from treating him like a dog, they never got hurt in any way.

Occasionally, a sympathetic passer-by would understand, and comment "Oh, you mean I cannot say the D word, right? Okay, I get it." and then address Tiny in an adult tone of voice, preferably with a question, such as "how do you like Texas?"

Addressed like a person, Tiny would frequently reward his new friend with a tail wag and the special privilege of allowing them to pat him.

Then there is the matter of sleeping time. Both dogs would find the suggestion of a dog basket an incredible affront. Phil and I would not even dare to suggest it. Instead, they both sleep on the bed with us. On the bed, status symbols are important, too. A dog's place is at the foot end of the bed, which is where Mike sleeps. Not because we told him to do so, but because Tiny did. In fact, we frequently call Mike to sleep at the middle or upper end of the bed, but Mike will not come. When this happens, Mike gives us a tail wag and curls up at his designated foot-end of the bed, which is where Tiny puts him.

As for Tiny, he worked out that one of the features which separates man from dog is the ability to sleep under the covers at night. We usually begin the night by placing Tiny at the foot-end with Mike. Then the lights go out. No sooner is this done than Tiny makes his way to the top, always on my side. He positions himself on the pillow, parallel to my head, digs his nose down to sniff out where the covers meet my neck and then starts scratching there with his paw, demanding in no uncertain terms that I lift the covers and allow him inside the bed. This is a process we call kriecheln, which means "to crawl inside" in German baby language. He then makes his way under the covers and curls up right into the duvet itself. Having done so, he soon goes to sleep and his rhythmic snoring can be heard for the rest of the night.

The problem with kriecheln is that it results in

considerable less space for me in the bed, which is the reason why I sometimes try to discourage him from doing so. In that case Tiny, in the dark, digs for my nose, gives it a lick, and then continues scratching. I pretend to be asleep. The Pekingese nose comes again, looking for mine. Another lick. Scratching again, this time more furiously, the Pekingese demands his right of sleeping under the covers. The longest I have held out, I think, was about 5 minutes. It has yet to happen that I win...

Both dogs, from watching me work through many a night to meet a deadline and then getting up in the late morning the following day, have somehow come to the mistaken conclusion that it is a status symbol among humans to get up late. They are not morning dogs by all means. I still usually work late at night and rise about 10am. So do the dogs. When I do get up early for an interview, all I get from the dogs is a tired yawn before they roll over on the bed and go back to sleep. Especially Mike is not an early morning dog. With Tiny, it comes down to the toss-up between sleeping in and doing what humans do. When the human gets up to work, Tiny sometimes figures that he has to do the same, to prove to anyone who wants to know that indeed he is flexible, which is another human trait in his calculations. As for Mike, he turns into a vegetable in the early morning hours. Meaning you can sit him up and he just softly falls on his side, still asleep...

When going for walks in the park, Mike always had to be on a leash in our early days in Houston. The reason for this was that Mike, having been used to living on a farm with plenty of space, would simply run off and not come back when let off his leash. I was afraid he would one day get run over when he got too close to the road, and so Mike walked on a leash. Until one day he figured out the reason why he walked on a leash and Tiny did not. From then on, without training, Mike tried to prove to me that he was a good dog. I started letting Mike run free, with the leash dragging behind him, and coming when I called him. If he failed to come, he would be back on the leash the following day. Mike soon figured this out and from then on came on command, being thereafter rewarded by the privilege of running free, just like Tiny, when we went to the park.

Mike soon established his own status symbol by being the "responsible dog." Mike had somehow worked out that in our little hierarchy, Tiny was the human baby and he was the dog. Meaning Tiny had a higher standing, but was less responsible. Mike thus made it his job to be Tiny's bodyguard. When they meet new dogs on their walks, Mike watches over Tiny carefully, and frequently puts himself between Tiny and the other dog when they try to sniff each other, in case there could be trouble. On the one, rare occasion that Tiny did get interested in a female dog, a large Labrador mix we met in a Houston park, Mike jealously chased the dog away, even biting her, a very unusual thing to do for Mike. We have always been trying to get Tiny and Mike to breed, hoping for a Pekingese Shihtzu offspring, but to no avail. Having grown up together, they clearly consider each other non-sexual entities and relate as brother and sister. Mike, thoroughly confused about her gender, will try to hump Tiny when she is in heat... Despite their platonic friendship, Tiny and Mike will not allow the other to elope with an outsider.

Many of Houston's parks have leash laws. We usually did not worry about them, but one little park, in Pasadena on Houston's south side, was jealously guarded by assorted rent-a-cops. The fine for not having your dog on the leash was 200$. The first time we were there, a rent-a-cop stopped us, driving after us in his little cart, to make me aware that I was in violation of the leash law, had I not seen the signs? I replied in French: "sorry, but I do not speak English, I am from Quebec," and indicated the license plate on my car. The rent-a-cop, actually a very nice old man, replied in perfect French "what a co-incidence, I was in the army in World War 2 and stationed in France." It turned out that he was half-Polish and had only been in the States since 1950. Prior to then, he had been living in Europe.

"You still have to put the dogs on the leash, though" he told me, in French.

"Well, it's a bit of a problem," I explained. "See, my little Pekingese here thinks he's human, and he will not walk on a leash..." The old man and I worked out a compromise. I would attach Mike on one end, Tiny on the other of the double leash. Then I would let them walk off together, following a few steps behind. That way, Tiny would still have the feeling of not walking leashed to a human, and yet we would fulfill the leash law.

The two little guys took off together, one on each end of the leash. Mike, being faster than Tiny, had a little learning to do. "Mike, wait for Tiny," I told him, and Mike stopped and turned around to look at Tiny and wait for him to catch up.

Since then, Mike was trying to prove that he was responsible, while Tiny was the one who chose where they went and how long they stayed at a given tree or corner of the field. Mike stood by and waited while Tiny did his business, then walking on when Tiny was ready to do so.

On one occasion, they took off together across the field adjoining the park, on the far side of which was a fire station. They were half way there when I called them back. Tiny, as usual, took no notice and kept walking. "Mike, bring back Tiny" I called, "Mike is a responsible dog and comes back now." Mike turned and came back across the field, dragging a reluctant Tiny behind him.

Mike thus found his own status symbol in being "responsible" and "in charge of looking after the little one." Soon, I found out that mention of the word "responsible" worked like the reward of a dog biscuit. "Responsible" was what set Mike apart from Tiny. "Responsible" was Mike's very own niche in life, and he wanted to fill it. I worked out that I could guilt Mike into almost anything, using this magic word.

The Pasadena Park, for instance, had a pond. My dogs

are both not too fond of water, but it was a hot summer's day, and I wanted to see at least one of them swim. I sat down with both of them on the edge of the pond. I put my arm around Mike and looked out over the pond with him. "Now, I know Mike is a really responsible dog, and Mike is a dog who goes swimming now, because that is what responsible dogs do." I pushed Mike's paws into the water, and, indicating the pond, said: "Mike goes swimming." Mike retreated. I laid a guilt trip on him: "Oh, Mike, I thought my Mike was such a responsible dog," repeated this a few times and finally, reluctantly, Mike waded into the water all by himself, swam a few rounds and then came back to shore...

The other people in the park, especially the children, were delighted at seeing a Shihtzu taking a little Pekingese for a walk. Especially the children loved the little rascals and often would ask me "when are you going to be here tomorrow," so they could time their outings with their parents to coincide with Tiny and Mike's. What the kids loved especially were the occasions when the little dogs wrapped themselves around a tree, one of them going to one side, the other into the opposite direction. It was hilarious seeing them work out who would go where. It was usually Mike who ended up having to walk around the tree again, going into the direction that Tiny wanted.

The greatest event of Pasadena Park was the old rent-a-cop who still spoke broken French from his time in the war. Being a rent-a-cop, he had a little cart to drive around in so he could catch up with people to enforce leash laws, litter laws and whatever other laws there were. Texas is a very law and order country, and there were always plenty of laws to cover a public place: from how you could spit on the side walk without being arrested to where and when your dog was allowed to do his business.

The old man and myself always exchanged a few words

in French when I came to the park with Tiny and Mike, him happy to practice his language skills, me glad to have someone talk another language but English to me. Tiny had since long been eyeing the old man's cart, and one day I took heart and asked him:

"Excuse me, this may be a strange request, but could my Pekingese have a ride in your cart? I know it would mean a lot to him to go on one of your enforcement rounds with you."

The old man laughed, and said "sure thing." He lifted Tiny up, put him in the little basket before him and the two of them took off. Mike and I were left behind, watching as Tiny and the old man drove in the little cart around the park, stopping here and there to reprimand someone for littering. When they came back, Tiny was grinning all over, tongue stuck out happily between his teeth.

"Thanks a lot, that was very nice of you," I said to the old man when he stopped his cart and handed Tiny back to me.

"Anytime," he replied, and we took him by his word. From then on, we timed our visits to the park to coincide with his shift. Each time we came, Tiny was given a ride in his cart as Mike and myself looked on. We were talking major status symbol...

The dogs love the beach, as I found out during their first there while we were still in Texas. Luckily, Texas did have a few beaches within easy reach of Houston, and soon our favorite hang-outs were the beaches of Galveston during the week, and the even nicer beaches of Port Aransas and Corpus Christi, some four hours drive from Houston, but worth every mile of it, on the weekends.

Our typical weekend would consist of a four-hour drive to Port Aransas on Friday afternoon and two nights at a local motel there. All of Saturday was spent on the Mustang State Beach park in Port Aransas, followed by a dinner in nearby Corpus Christi on the waterfront, followed by the dogs sleeping in the next morning while I attended 8 am mass at a little Spanish church on Comanche street in Corpus Christi. This was followed by an outdoor brunch buffet for the dogs and myself at Port Aransas' spaghetti house, named so unjustly because it boasted the best food within 20 miles radius, from the most wonderful breakfast buffet to delicious fresh fish dinners to the most incredible home made soups and deserts.

The spaghetti house served a different soup each night, freshly cooked with lots of love, something you could actually taste... My favorite soup, a Jalapeno corn soup with plenty of cream, was only served on Friday nights, which is why we set off from Houston in time to get there before the restaurant closed.

We soon came to define our favorite restaurants by a combination of their food quality and whether or not they allowed dogs. The best food in the world was of no interest to us if they cited "law and order," said in typical Texas drawl: "Ma'am, sorry, but these are the rules. The board of health states clearly..." Some restaurants were, however, willing to bend these rules to exclude outdoor seating areas. The spaghetti house in Port Aransas always welcomed the dogs and me for Sunday brunch on the patio.

"They are travelling dogs," I explained to the owner. "Eventually, they will write a book about their travels. They are journalists, you see..." She saw perfectly, and always had a treat ready for the little rascals when they turned up on Sunday mornings.

Another favorite restaurant of ours was at the "Harbor Front" in nearby Corpus Christi. Tiny, Mike and I usually dined there on Saturday evenings, sitting on the patio and looking out over the water, watching the seagulls soar as the corpus Christi traffic went over the lighted bridge in the background. On my first visit there, I ordered crawfish with potatoes. When the food came, the guys wanted some, too.

166

I gave a piece of potato to Tiny and Mike. Tiny did not like the potato plain, while Mike swallowed it without chewing or tasting it. For Mike, it was a status symbol to eat anything that came off a human table. Tiny is somewhat the same, though he will draw a line with some foods, such as plain potatoes and raw garlic. Both dogs with delight eat lettuce, cucumbers, tomatoes, fruit of all kinds, and Mike, in addition, also eats garlic.

As for Tiny, he decided that potatoes without anything were not for him. I dipped the potato in a little bit of butter. Tiny ate it eagerly. As the waitress stood by, watching the dogs and conversing about them with me, I told her: "I am going to trick Tiny now, let's see what happens." I gave him another piece of potato with butter. He ate it. Then I gave him a piece without butter. He took it eagerly and then, tasting it and noticing there was something missing, spat it back out, with an expression of disgust on his face. When I gave him the next piece, he made me hold up to his nose first, to sniff whether there was butter on it. From then on, Tiny would not allow me to feed him without passing the sniffing test first.

The waitress laughed. "God, I've never seen a dog like that" she marveled. "He sure knows how to keep people under his thumb, doesn't he?"

We were delighted when she came back a little later with a plate of two juicy hamburger steaks, "on the house for the two little ones." From then on, we became regulars there.

In fact, the people of Corpus Christi and Port Aransas were friendly, warm and laid-back people, always ready to smile. Be that as it may, Port Aransas became a solace in an otherwise strange and hostile state, and the friendliness of her people, coupled with the incredible beauty of its beaches, means that we still thoroughly miss Port Aransas.

At the entrance to Mustang Beach State Park, which has one of the most beautiful beaches I have ever seen, was a pretty, blonde lady by the name of Eve. From our first meeting onwards, Eve always had a dog biscuit ready for Tiny and Mike whenever we passed by her booth on Saturday mornings. The beach is an island of solace from a hectic world, equal to none. There is something very special and serene about the place, from the salty way the air smells, to the fact that you can walk for miles and miles, and after that miles more on a lily white sandy beach, watching the waves break out on the reefs, meeting nobody.

Tiny and Mike, once off the leash, usually walked off by themselves, side by side, and kept going and going and going... If I had not called them back at some stage to return, they would have happily walked the entire length of the beach, which led all the way down Padre Island and into Mexico. They loved it as much as I did. On the few occasions that we took other people there, Mike walked with us, while Tiny went off on his own, careful not to be seen to be part of our group and, worse still, be mistaken for a dog. Instead, he was always trying to give the impression that he was just another independent person, taking a stroll on the beach.

On our very first visit to Mustang Island State Park, we were treated to a rare sight. Walking along, I became aware of some big shapes, which tumbled about in the shallow water, where the surf broke. I looked closer and eventually made out three shark shapes. Their dorsal fins were sticking out, and sometimes even the entire fish, when a wave broke with the sharks caught up in its tumble. Just as the wave went up before it broke, the sharks swam up into it. I could see their entire length and magnitude as they were being lifted and then everything came crashing down in a tumbling mass of shark and foaming white water. There were three of them, and they were playing in the surf, sometimes swimming side by side, then separating, then coming together once more. I had never seen anything quite like it and stopped to watch, fascinated. Unlike a dolphin, a shark has a straight tail fin that can frequently be seen sticking out when it swims close to the surface. This is in addition to its back fin, and is in fact, the best way to distinguish a shark from a dolphin when both swim just below surface. Here, both fins were sticking out. Also, having seen the shark shapes in the waves as they tumbled, there was no doubt what species I was dealing with.

"Wow, guys, look at that. Look at those sharks," I told them, fascinated. Both little dogs came to my side and did their best to look interested as they glanced out on the water, not quite sure what the fuss was about. I had never seen a shark in the wild, nor had I realized that sharks had a playful streak in them. I had always thought of sharks as killer machines with little minds and big meanness, but watching them interact in the surf with absolute self-abandon, I could not help but think of them as utterly beautiful creatures.

"Hey guys, let's play with them," I called to the little dogs and tried to entice them to follow me into the water. The dogs looked at me as if I were nuts and firmly stood their ground, not moving by even one inch. I went into the water, to where it was just over my foot, taking care not to get into areas that were just about deep enough for a shark. Once I was where they could not get to me, I started splashing as fast and wildly as I could, with good effect.

One of the sharks turned and tried to get at me. But the water where I stood was too shallow. Frustrated, the shark had to retreat. Having paid attention to me and not to the surf, it then got caught in a wave and tumbled under. Surfacing, it swam back out again only to be attracted once more by the splashing. I just about killed myself with laughter at the frustrated shark, which so much wanted to take a bite out of me and could not get any closer than within a few feet of where I stood. Especially funny was that each time he tried he got caught in the breaking waves, and tossed about...

On the way back, I thought I might warn some swimmers who were splashing in the surf some 200 yards away from the sharks that were in the unpopulated part of the beach.

"Excuse me," I called out to them, "You might want to know that there are three sharks playing in the surf a little further up, and they are headed this way. I thought you might want to get out of the water..." I had never seen people get out of the water that fast! On the way out, Tiny and Mike and myself then dropped by at the office of the park rangers, to let them now about the sharks.

It was also Port Aransas where Tiny and Mike became involved in their first fish rescue mission. We had decided to go out to the giant stone jetty for a walk. The stone jetty was a landmark of Port Aransas. It allowed you to walk far out to sea and we spent many an afternoon at the far end of that jetty, watching the dolphins play in the waves. It was also a great place to see Pelicans dive for food, or to marvel at the way the seagulls mastered flight to the point of performing the most difficult aerobatics maneuvers when they dove to the water for food or, as it often seemed, pushed themselves to the limit for the sheer joy of flight.

There were also fishermen, with their sharp hooks and bait, some fishing for sport, some, because they were poor, fishing in the hope to catch the evening's meal. The sun set slowly and majestically as I walked out the jetty with the dogs on that particular day. A warm sea breeze blew across Tiny's coat as I carried him because he had problems negotiating the large gaps between the stones. Mike gaily bounced ahead of us. About half way down the jetty, we encountered two Mexican fishermen. They were excitedly talking among themselves, having just that moment landed an enormous redfish. While Mike charmed the two men and distracted them, Tiny and I walked over to the fish. The fish was a beautiful, silvery white. It twitched on the stone of the jetty, gasping for oxygen. "Wow, Look at that poor fish, guys," I said to the little dogs. "It's beautiful, isn't it?"

170

The fish looked at me. I looked back at the fish. A silent communication passed between us. "Help me," the fish pleaded. "Don't worry, I'll take care of it," I told the fish. I turned to the two Mexicans. "Excuse me, sirs," I began, "you are going to have to return this fish to the water."

"We have to do what?," the younger Mexican asked. I explained to them about the fish and what had just happened. "I promised the fish I would save its life," I concluded. "Please throw it back in."

Luckily, like many Mexicans, they were really nice people. They understood what a capitalist would never understand. That sometimes, soul comes before money. We made a deal: a photograph of them holding up the fish, plus a photo of them holding Mike, in exchange for the fish's life. I positioned the Mexicans and the fish, then got the camera ready. "Smile, please." The Mexicans smiled, holding up the fish.

Then we bent down to the water to release the fish. The older Mexican made one final attempt to rescue what would have been a great dinner. "Do we really have to...?" he asked.

"Yes," I said, "Come on, you won't be left with nothing. Just think of the nice photo we'll send you, which you'll be able to enlarge and frame. Think of how happy the fish will be when it returns to its family. I'm sure fish have family, too, don't you think?"

That did it. When in doubt, always appeal to the family sense of true Latin American. Unlike us Westerners, Latin Americans have a very strong sense of family. When you talk family love, you talk in a language they understand. Before I had spoken the last word, he had let go of the fish. With one final, happy splash, it disappeared in the water.

I then took the promised photo of them and Mike, who performed one of his famous dances for them. The Mexicans were charmed. Smiling and waving, they looked after us as we walked on, immune to the fact that we were the same group that had just lost them their evening's meal...

It was also during our stay in Port Aransas that Tiny and Mike participated in their first and last ever dog show. We had driven to nearby Corpus Christi, a charming sea side city of considerable size, to walk along the harbor and buy fresh gulf shrimp off the fishing boats as they came into shore. Corpus Christi shrimp sold at very good prices and had the most tender, delightful ocean taste. I have yet to find shrimp which tastes better, or a location in the U.S. which has charmed me more...

It was one of the times when Phil had driven from Montreal to visit me in Texas. On our way to Corpus Christi from Port Aransas, we stopped for gas. Doing so, I bought a paper and flipped through it as Phil gassed up the car. TODAY: FUN DOG SHOW. EVERYONE IS WELCOME. PRIZES FOR BEST TRICK, BEST HAIRDO AND MANY OTHERS. FREE ADMISSION I read as I turned to the "things to do" pages.

I showed the articles to Phil: "Hey, look what I just found, let's go, shall we." I turned to the little dogs in the back of the car. "Hey, guys, do you want to go to a dog show?" As usual, they were game for anything and enthusiastically wagged their tails at the idea.

We drove to the address indicated in the story and finally found a huge school building with a banner reading DOG SHOW. As if they knew something exciting was about to happen, both dogs impatiently wagged their tails and rushed out of the car, toward the school building. Inside, it was organized chaos. Dogs of various shapes, sizes and breeds, or of no breeds at all, were being walked around the ring by their owners as the judges looked on. Other dogs sat in the sidelines, with or without owners, waiting for their turns.

"Where do you register for this?" I asked a girl with a large brown dog. She indicated a small desk, and Phil and I marched over, dragging our reluctant dogs behind us, who would have rather stayed with the others and made new friends.

"Hi," I told the elderly woman behind the desk. "We are visiting Corpus Christi. We saw you ad in the paper and thought we'd come along. This is our first ever dog show, what do we do?"

She was a grandmotherly type, with glasses, bun, kind eyes included, and she instantly took a liking to the dogs. Mike did his little dance for her, which was followed by the usual exclamation "My God, your dog is so cute." Tiny gracefully wagged his tail in a short hello, and then couldn't care less about the old lady. She handed us the entry forms.

"Just fill in one for each dog, and pick the categories you want to enter. It is a $1 fee for each category." We went through the list and entered the categories that seemed most suited to us. CURLIEST TAIL was one of them. Another one, SMALLEST DOG was where we thought we would have a good chance with Tiny. LONGEST FUR? Maybe ... so we crossed that one, too. BEST TRICK? We knew Tiny would win in that category, if we could find a way to get our car into the show ring.

"Excuse me," I said to the registrar. "My little Pekingese has a great trick, but he needs a car to perform it. Do you think we could take the judges out into the car park to demonstrate it?"

"No," the lady said, "that would be against the rules." If the tools required for the trick could not be brought into the ring, then the tick could not be considered in competition.

"Okay, don't cross that one, then" I sighed and turned to Phil. "I don't think we have any other tricks, do you?"

"Out of interest," the lady asked, "what does the Pekingese do with the car?"

"Well," I began to explain, "I put him on the roof of the car. Then I say "rutscheln" (that's "slide" in German baby language, I added by way of translation) and Tiny walks up to the windscreen, goes into sliding position and slides down."

She laughed. "I would have loved to have seen that," she said. "Come out to the car with us after the show," I offered, "and we'll give you a free demonstration."

Meanwhile, we had to decide on the other categories. There was an obstacle course, and we decided to enter that. A contest for best costume? Yes, that one, too. And one of prettiest dog. Absolutely!

The best costume was about to start. "Quick, let's get their sweaters from the car," I told Phil. We had come unprepared for such a contest and thus had only their regular sweaters to dress them up in. Phil ran to the car and came back with their sweaters. We stuffed the bewildered dogs into a red and white ringed turtleneck sweater and a blue-green striped one respectively and made it into the ring just in time for the contest to start. We had to walk round and round the ring while the judges looked on. All dogs were to be on a leash, including Tiny. Tiny, for once, did not mind. Both of them walked proudly by our side, Tiny occasionally nodding a star greeting to his fans by the side of the ring, especially when someone exclaimed "Oh, look at this cute little dog" indicating our Pekingese with the oversized ego. We did not win. We lost out to a black Labrador with a baseball cap, a red and blue raincoat and sunglasses. Big deal, he had a nose, our dogs didn't! Nonetheless, we got an impressive, yellow ribbon for an HONORABLE MENTION. For Tiny and Mike, it might as well have been first prize. They had proud expressions on their faces when Phil went to pick up their ribbon and hung it around their necks. As for the lab: well, we were jealous, but just a little bit...

The obstacle course was hilarious. The dogs had to go through it one by one with their owners. We watched as a little Chihuahua was being pushed and shoved by his owner onto a bar, that the dog was to walk along, then get off the other side, jump over a little hurdle made of cans, walk through a hole and out the other side ... The dog jumped off the bar, then threw itself on its back and refused to go any further. We laughed our heads off and were going to do better. "You take Mike," I said to Phil, "and I'll take Tiny."

Phil and Mike went in the ring. I watched them walk in front of the judges, toward the course. Mike was tailwagging and dancing by Phil's side. Our embarrassing Shihtzu jumped over the bar to the other side, then jumped back again. Jumping back and forth along the length of the bar, they made it to the hurdle. Mike ran into it and knocked it over, then danced as someone came to build it up again. Phil shoved Mike through the hole, and out the other side. Then Mike was to jump on a hay bale, something that he had done a hundred times before, back home at the stable. "Mike, jump," Phil called, patting the bale. Mike ran around the bale....

Tiny and I did not fare much better. In fact, Tiny refused to even walk up the bar. Instead, he snored wildly and ran the other way. Suffice it to say that in this class, too, we got an HONORABLE MENTION only...

We carried home three firsts, though. One for the longest fur, basically because there were only five dogs in the class, and aside from a chow-chow they all had short hair. LONGEST FUR went to Tiny.

The second time we got a first price was for CURLIEST TAIL. Mike won this, again in a small class, again competing against the chow, and some others, which did not even come close to having a curly tail at all.

Finally, and most amazingly, we made it for SMALLEST DOG, after the draw for first place came down to Tiny and a Chihuahua. The owner of the Chihuahua was most put out when the judges came to measure the dogs' shoulder height and Tiny won by almost an inch.

As could be expected, success went to Tiny's head. Mike was modest as usual, but for Tiny, it was clear that from now on he was a star. He no longer talked to mere mortals and would not allow himself to be patted, unless it was by other celebrities. Eventually, we were forced to buy a sign that read: VIP ON BOARD and stuck it to the windscreen of our car. Often, when I would drive to interviews or film festivals with my car, which now had the press sticker as well as the VIP ON BOARD sticker, people would frequently ask " which VIP are you transporting in your car." They figured since I was a journalist, going to a film festival with a sticker that said VIP ON BOARD, I must obviously be transporting a celebrity.

"Actually," I would tell them, "VIP stands for VERY IMPORTANT PEKINGESE. If you would like to have your photo taken with him, I will see what I can do…"

Chapter 16

Close Calls, And Their Very Own Guardian Angels

Over the five years that we stayed in Houston, both dogs had a few brushes with death. I ascribe the fact that they didn't get killed to the theory that both little dogs, for the delight they have given various suffering human beings wherever we went, have been assigned their very own guardian angels. But, judge for yourself:

Pasadena

When we could not stand it in the built-up area of Houston any longer, we decided to move to the country, on the outskirts of the city. This is how we came to Pasadena, a lower middle class neighborhood, mainly Hispanic, which suited me fine. I had by now begun to prefer by far the Hispanic culture and mentality to that of white Houstonians, and was happiest when shopping in the Spanish supermarket Fiesta, surrounded by friendly people and able to pick up my favorite foods: Fresco from Mexico, Caldo con Res from El Salvador, as well as assorted Tortillas and Pupusas. I also read Spanish newspapers and watched the Spanish news station Univision. My favorite song was No se Tu by Mexican singer Luis Miguel, and I had recently begun to write for the Mexican editions of Cosmopolitan and Harper's Bazaar. I was by all means on the way to becoming a well-adapted Hispanic.

It took me a while to pick up the language fluently, however, and I remember in my early Spanish-culture-acclimatization days I would sit in the very back of the Spanish church, not understanding a word, terrified that someone would talk to me in Spanish, find out that I did not understand Spanish and wonder what I was doing in Spanish mass.

Truth be told, I wanted to become part of their culture, and I was willing to learn whatever I would have to in order

177

to fit in. The best way to learn was on the job, I figured ... hence I began to watch TV, attend mass and tune in to 93.3, the Spanish radio station, on my car radio.

And one day, as if by miracle, through intense culture and language immersion, I began to understand and eventually speak the language. Until then, I submitted my stories in English to the magazines, and they translated them into Spanish. My highest ambition was to become the first non-native reporter for Univision, but they scoffed at the idea because of my pronounced accent.

I was by all appearances a gringo, but inside, I was turning Hispanic. It became a natural conclusion to move to a Hispanic neighborhood. Pasadena was a high crime area, but this did not deter me. I would be terrified to move after dark in downtown Houston's non-Hispanic neighborhoods, but I was under the delusional impression that no Hispanic would ever harm me. I loved them, hence they would love me, too. This is also how Mike, the dog, reasons...

Crime was hence not a consideration when we decided where to move. The fact that the house we proposed to share with a tow truck driver was adjacent to a horse stable was certainly a consideration, and that it stood on some six acres of ground and boasted a well-kept lawn and a large horse paddock with two outdoor stables, but sans horse.

The tow truck driver, it turned out, had not always been a tow truck driver. Nor had he always lived in Pasadena. He came from one of Houston's finest neighborhoods, Memorial, where he had once owned a prosperous business. When his girlfriend, a pretty blonde whose photo was still on the kitchen table, was killed in a car crash some 8 months earlier, things had gone downhill for him. He had taken to drinking, and crippled with grief, had been unable to keep on top of his affairs. The result was inevitable, and it finally landed him in Pasadena. Nonetheless, because of his background, he had chosen the finest house in Pasadena, which was impeccably kept both inside and outside. It had once belonged to the police chief of Pasadena and had a large fence all around the property. It meant, of course, that we ended up living in the only white street in Pasadena, but it was something I could make do with: the Hispanics were just two miles up the road.

Despite the fact that Mike spent his mornings charging the horse next door and barking wildly at him across the fence, and that both little dogs stuck up a questionable friendship with a Labrador vagabond dog that we named Yellow Dog, everything was fine. It was probably Yellow Dog who was responsible for teaching Tiny and Mike some very bad habits. Yellow Dog's home was a derelict house diagonally across the street, where he was not being taken care of, so he roamed the neighborhood.

The mechanic shop next door fed him his breakfast, and dinner was being provided by Shirley, who owned the horse beside us. Although Shirley was by no means prosperous, she somehow managed to provide for the horse, six dogs of her own, and whatever strays there were. Shirley lived across the street from the horse paddock. When I moved in, I was visited by yellow dog on our first evening.

Tiny, Mike and I had just taken a leisurely stroll across the grounds of our new home, marveling at the warm Texas summer night, when we became aware of a yellow dog in the bushes, who was wagging his tail at us. Yellow Dog was a charmer, just like Mike. Unlike Mike, he was a vagrant, a drifter with no sense of responsibility, but so engaging in his manner that you could not help liking him.

Tiny was impressed by Yellow Dog, because he instinctively understood that it was not enough to be liked by Mike and myself. In order to be accepted, he had to gain Tiny's approval. Yellow Dog pressed himself down to the ground, making himself as small as he possibly could. Then, head sliding along the ground, he wormed himself over to Tiny, submissively wagging his tail. He was desperately trying to make himself smaller than Tiny, indicating, I suppose, his willingness to submit to the control of the little Pekingese.

Once he had reached Tiny, he the rolled over on his back, exposing his belly and wagging his tail. Tiny sniffed him all over, with a superior expression on his face, and then approved. Yellow Dog was allowed to hang out with us, and I went inside the house to get him some food.

From then on, Yellow Dog came every morning and evening, and waited for me outside the gate when I came returned interviews in downtown Houston. I briefly toyed with the idea of adopting him and tried to teach him the basics of acceptable canine behavior. But I might as well have tried to teach a deaf man how to sing opera: he refused to walk on a leash, refused to wear a collar, refused to sit, no matter how many treats I promised. When he got bored in the middle of a teaching session, he simply grinned and walked away, only to surface a few hours later to get some food. He had been brought up with minimal human interference, and he had developed into a free spirit, nice, kind, but totally outside the boundaries of normal canine society. He was going to be owned by nothing and nobody, not even the promise of a permanent home and the security that came with it. He did not want security, he wanted freedom.

I don't know how the dog made it across the street unharmed each time, for the house was situated on a rather busy street.

One morning, I let Tiny out into the huge front yard, which was fenced like the rest of the property. The front yard was a good half-acre, with trees and a patio, fenced off from the main road. While Tiny did his morning business, Mike followed me inside and watched as I got dressed. When I came to collect Tiny, he was gone. I looked for him everywhere, and concluded he must have found an invisible hole in the fence and somehow gotten out. Tiny is able to squeeze through the

180

smallest possible openings, though I have never figured out how he does it. He must fold himself up sideways somehow, then squash his body through the hole and unfold on the other side.

"You have to help me find Tiny," I said, sick with worry, to my housemate, who was in the process of having breakfast. "I can't find him anywhere. He must have gotten out of the yard somehow. I hope he won't get stepped on by the stallion."

The horse next door was a bona-fide, jet-black Quarterhorse stallion. I was afraid what he would do if a little Pekingese wandered into his pasture. While J.C. my housemate, ran around one side of the property, I ran around the other. First, I checked the horse: nothing. I checked the back yard: nothing. I went into our own horse paddock, empty and overgrown, and checked under every bush and tree: nothing still. I called Tiny's name, but I already knew that would do no good, since Tiny never came when called. Finally, JC, the tow truck driver, said, "I heard Shirley's dogs barking across the road, let me just go and check there. Looks like they are excited about something."

"That's a waste of time," I told him. "Tiny wouldn't be so stupid as to wander across the road when he has 5 acres of land to play with here. We'll use valuable time which we could better spend looking around here."

"I'm going to check, just in case," J.C. said, "you stay here and keep calling him."

Sure enough, a few minutes later JC came back from Shirley, holding Tiny in his arms.

"He was over there, playing with her dogs," J.C. informed me. I took the little dog from his arms, thanking him with tears in my eyes. The thought of Tiny crossing the busy road in the middle of rush hour, all by himself, gives me goosebumps to this day...

Tiny was not the only one to have had a brush with death in the Pasadena house. Only a few months later, Mike got into serious trouble. Since we had moved to the big country house, Mike became increasingly obsessed with his crazy episodes, where he runs around in a circles, saying "ra,ra,ra," and is totally oblivious to what is going on around him. Mike was permitted to run free on the big property, although neither dog was allowed outside unsupervised anymore, after the incident with Tiny and the road.

One morning, I was about to go to work, and waited for a friend to pick me up because my car was in the repair-shop. Mike suddenly began to run up and down the property in ever wider circles, "ra-ra"ing as he did. I thought nothing off it; the property was large enough to be a safe for a dog whose brain goes out of gear. I called him, but a usual when he gets into his running moods, he did not respond.

Suddenly, Mike ran straight past me, through the open gate, and along the driveway toward the road. I called him. Mike thought it was a game and began making wider circles. The circle went a few meters into the road, along the side of the driveway, right in front of my feet, and back again. Mike kept going round and round and round, crossing into the road for a few seconds with every circle he made. I tried to catch him, but he was way too fast. In horror, I watched as a huge truck turned into our road and approached at high speed.

Mike kept running circles, and his last circles brought him right in front of the approaching truck, with a split second to spare as he ran past. My friend, who happened to turn in behind the truck, emergency braked his own car, so as not to run over Mike as he raced back into the road again.

Finally, I was able to grab hold of Mike as he came by a third time.

"Wow," my friend, Hoss, said when I got the dog. "I thought Mike was history. I thought that truck was going to get him."

"Me, too," I replied, relieved to have the dog back, but at the same time very angry at his behavior. "Mike is an extremely stupid dog," I told Hoss, "he eats for two, but he has no brain at all."

For the first time in his life, Mike was punished for his actions. He deserved every second of it, but the moment I let him go, Mike wagged his tail and kept bouncing around, as if nothing had happened. "It's useless to even punish that dog," I said to Hoss, "he doesn't remember it the moment I let go of him. I'm just going to put him on a leash for the next week."

And so I did. No matter how good Mike was, no matter that he listened to every word I said when we were in the park, no matter how much Hoss pleaded to show mercy and let Mike off the leash. Even when we were on the beach, I stayed firm and Mike finally got the message. Since then, Mike abandons his circles when I call him...

Guardian Angels?

Tiny is a very greedy dog. If his food is not carefully measured out to him he will literally eat until he bursts. "Bursting" in this case means a dangerous and potentially fatal condition called "bloat," which predominantly affects deep-chested dogs. As a result of overeating, the stomach extends, sometimes filled with gas in addition to food, at others just with the food itself. It is necessary to bring the dog to the vet immediately to have his stomach pumped put when this happens. Otherwise, the stomach can twist and only an emergency operation can still save the affected dog's life.

For various reasons, Tiny and bloat became intimate acquaintances. The first incident occurred when I came back from an overseas trip to Europe and drove straight from the airport to pick the dogs up from Debbie. My car had been at the airport for several weeks. I was amazed at the relative ease with which it started when I retrieved it upon return to Houston. Darkness was falling as I pulled into Debbie's place.

I left Debbie a check for the board and any extra grooming charges she had incurred during my absence, and then tried to drive back to Pasadena, which was clear on the other side of Houston.

The Woodlands is some 36 miles from Houston to the North, while Pasadena is about the same mileage to the south, both of them off the I45. I was facing a drive of well over an hour to get home.

Somewhere outside Spring, the next suburb on the way into Houston, jetlag took over. Fresh off the plane, I was so tired that I actually started seeing double and had extreme difficulties concentrating on the road as I was being blinded by oncoming headlights. In what was probably a wise decision, I pulled off the road and find a motel for the dogs and myself where we could spend the night. After I had checked in and gotten by the "no dogs allowed" rules thanks to Mike's charm and Tiny's cute face, I ordered myself a Chinese take-out from the restaurant next door. The dogs hungrily looked on as I ate. Naturally, I assumed that they had not been fed and made them both a bowl of Iams dry dog food, which I soaked in hot water until it became soft and mushy.

Both dogs ate their entire bowl. A few minutes later, Tiny began whining in agony. He doubled over in pain, walked a few steps on the bed and lay down, only to get up again within a second, whine again, and find another place to lay down. I felt his stomach, which was noticeably distended. I had no idea what was wrong, but decided I had better call a vet. Not knowing the area at all, I had to rely on the yellow pages and pick out a veterinary clinic with an after-hours emergency service that was also close to where I was located. I finally found one and called.

"You better bring him in straight away," the receptionist said after I described to her Tiny's symptoms over the phone. "It could be bloat."

I was previously unfamiliar with bloat, but when she

briefly explained to me the seriousness of the condition, I decided to follow her advice, jet lag or not. I asked her for directions, after giving her the approximate location where I was, trying to remember the nearest exit from the 145.

Next, I loaded Tiny in the car, and - piece of paper with the directions in hand - got on the way. I grew very frightened when I realized that her directions led me along long, deserted country roads with no lights and almost no people. Moreover, they were mostly through high crime areas. I was alone, I was overtired, and I was lost, except for the piece of paper in my hand. In Houston, it takes something as simple as your car breaking down at the wrong hour in the wrong neighborhood.

"If my car breaks down now," I realized with horror, "I will probably not survive 'till morning. Nobody would even come looking for me."

Hoss, my friend in Houston, thought of me safely sleeping in my motel bed. My husband was somewhere at a sailing regatta in the South of France.

In my mind, I already began planning escape routes into the near-by bushes, where I could run and hide until daylight, just in case ... There! I thought I heard the car splutter ... Must be my nerves, I concluded, lack of sleep, all this excitement, jet lag, and then all alone - could happen to anyone. The car coughed again. I held on to the wheel in sheer terror and forced myself to look straight ahead and keep driving. More than once, I was convinced I had gotten lost. The roads seemed to stretch endlessly, they had never told me how many miles it was to the next turn-off, and all I could do was to hold on to the hope that I was still right and pray that, on the dark, deserted roads, I would not miss the badly indicated turn-offs.

It was even more terrifying on the few occasions that a lone car appeared behind us, advanced fast and then kept following...

"I am not scared," I kept telling myself over and over.

"I can handle this. I need to get my dog to the vet and I will keep going until I can go no more." I stepped on my brakes, challenging the car behind me to either make his bad intentions known, or to stop scaring me and overtake. The car overtook, thankfully. So did all the other lone cars that followed.

For the I-don't-know-how-many'th-time that night, I cursed the lonely life of a foreign journalist, which usually leaves you thrown into a strange country, without any friends, often working in total isolation, having nobody to rely on but yourself. I longed for family, permanent friends, stability, and for the luxury of someone who would drive me to the vet when my dog got sick at night, someone who would miss me if I did not get there, the stability of having the same vet, in the same city, instead of having to engage in a nightmare journey toward an unknown destination where I was yet to meet another stranger, who may or may not be competent. That was, if I ever got there...

Finally, the nightmare came to an end and I was able to identify the vet's sign, in a deserted, small shopping center. The neighborhood did not look any more inspiring than the roads I had driven through, but the people inside the veterinary clinic were kind and concerned for Tiny. I watched as they took him to X-ray and gave me the good news that his stomach was not twisted. "So, all we have to do now is to pump his stomach," the vet told me, "and he should be all right."

I watched, cringing, as they put a hose down Tiny's throat and began pumping. When they finished, the vet said "that dog had an enormous amount of food in his body. What on earth have you been feeding him?" "Just his regular size meal," I replied, mystified. Finally, we worked out that Debbie must have fed the dogs their evening meal before I picked them up, a suspicion that Debbie confirmed the following day. The vet decided to keep Tiny over night for observation, just in case.

"Fame at last!" World-famous aerobatics pilot Sean Tucker, Mike and their fans at the Smyrna Airshow, 1996.

"Where are the ice-creams, Mum?" The lucky threesome enjoys a day out on the beach, Summer 1996.

"Hey, that's my cat. Hands-off!" Wherever they went with their cat, Tiny and Mike attracted a lot of attention. At Narragansett Beach, Rhode Island, Mike takes his job as the cat's bodyguard very seriously.

"Stop all the fuss, just pass me the carrot" - Tiny and Mike's horse Wildfire scores a carrot from local resident Dick Alexander in elegant Newport, Rhode Island.

"I'm not going up without a parachute." Tiny at the controls, thoroughly enjoying the illusion that he is a pilot.

"Where did you bury that darn bone? - I don't know" Tiny's ears flow in the wind as they take a walk along the beach, pretending there to be no humans present.

"Even a world leader has to take a break, sometime." Tiny rests in his favorite armchair in Newport.

"Yeah, he does look silly, doesn't he?" Mike had to get spayed, and Tiny keeps watch over his companion who feels very sorry for herself.

"You spelled this wrong here!" As a senior dog, here pictured in 1999 when he was nearly 12 years old, Tiny takes responsibility for editing my manuscripts.

"Where is my nightcap?" Tiny loves his carry-bag that doubles as his bed. Here, he is taking a snooze on the waterfront of Lake Geneva in Switzerland, Summer 1997.

For now, I had to get back home. I could not see myself running the gauntlet of the deserted streets again. In my desperation, I asked the veterinary assistant "are you guys going to close soon?"

"The clinic will stay open all night," the young, blonde man replied. "But I am getting off in 15 minutes, why?"

"I am not from here, and I am terrified to drive back alone. I came all the way from the Woodlands. Would you be so nice and follow me back to the motel, in case something happens to my car or there are some bad guys out there?"

He said that he would be delighted to, if I could wait until the end of his shift at 11pm. "Only if you can give me a huge cup of coffee," I replied and explained that I had just come off the plane this evening, and was still jetlagged, not having had a chance to sleep at all.

"Geez," he replied, "what a nightmare to come back to something like that."

"Tell me about it," I replied. "Stuff like that keeps happening to me in Houston. I don't think Houston likes me too much."

"Don't take it personal," the young man replied. "Houston doesn't like anyone. It's one mean mother. I can't wait to go back home."

It turned out that he was from Minnesota, in Houston to finish his university studies.

The young man followed me all the way back to the motel, where Mike awaited me eagerly and we both fell into blissful sleep. The following morning, I checked out and loaded Mike and my belongings into the car, intending to pick up Tiny. I turned over the ignition: nothing happened. I tried again: nothing. I tried a few more times, and finally called Hoss, who was not only a friend, but also happened to own a car repair shop downtown.

"Hoss, you will not believe this," I told him, "But Mike and I are stuck here, at a motel outside the Woodlands, in

Spring. Tiny is at the vet, and the car won't start. Could you please come and pick me up?"

Hoss took time off work at once, got into his car and drove the 36 miles to Spring to pick up Mike and myself. He looked at the car. "It's your carburetor," he said after a thorough examination. "Did you say that you drove this thing last night? I can't imagine how. By all laws of physics, it should have stopped on you within the first mile..."

Guardian angels? Yes, we believe in them. Not only in the form of Hoss, who subsequently drove the 20 miles to the vet clinic, picked up Tiny and watched as I shelled out a check for 250$, then drove the three of us all the way home before returning to work and arranging for a tow truck to pick up my car. We believe also in the invisible ones, like the one who sat on the carburetor that night, keeping it going, making sure that the little dog got to the vet safely, making sure that I got back to the motel...

We had one more "guardian angel" encounter. It was another occasion of "bloat," when Tiny had been able to somehow break into a carton of Iams lamb and rice dog biscuits and eaten them all while I was away at an interview. By the time I got back, Tiny was in pain. I loaded him into Farley, the car, and called the "Doctor Pet Center" in Clear Lake to let them know we were coming. Tiny frequented the clinic for various ailments ever since we had moved to Pasadena, ranging from cataracts to ear infections, both chronic conditions which the long-eared, bulging-eye breed of Pekingese dogs are notoriously prone to.

"Hi guys, it's Tiny again" I told the receptionist, without bothering to give my name. They were so familiar with us at the clinic by now that she recognized my voice. "We are coming in with bloat."

"Okay, Tess," the girl replied. "We're waiting for you."

As seems to always happen during emergencies. The car

was low on gas and would not make it to the clinic in Clear Lake from Pasadena. I stopped at the corner station to fill up Farley's tank. As I went back in the car and turned the key, the engine refused to start. I tried over and over. Nothing. Not a sound. I knew it was an electrical problem, which Audis are known for, and for which Farley had been in the shop for several times already. In the back seat, the Pekingese was yelping in pain. Although Tiny's threshold of pain is extremely low and hence one never knows how much is real pain and how much is show, I also knew that bloat was not a condition to be taken lightly. I had to get Tiny to the vet at once. I did not have time to phone a tow truck, and wait for it to arrive.

In desperation, I walked up to a black man who was pumping gas at the pump next to me. "Excuse me, please," I began. "I wonder if you could do me a favor. I don't know anyone in Houston, and my car just broke down. I have me dog in the back with a medical emergency and I need to get him to the vet fast. I wonder if you could drive me there, so I can drop the dog, and then drop me back here?"

"Yes, certainly," the man said. "I have an appointment to go to, but I suppose I'll be able to get away with being late. The dog's life is more important."

I let the gas attendant know that I would pick up the car on the way back and phone for a tow truck then. That done, I loaded Tiny into the back of the man's car, and the good man drove us 19 miles to the vet clinic, waited for another 15 minutes outside while I checked Tiny in, and then drove me all the way back. On the way back, he told me that his experience with white people had been a nightmare so far.

"There is a lot of racism here in the South," he told me. "Some people say that the blacks exaggerate, and maybe some do, but as a whole, it is true. There were so many times I was pulled over by police and frisked, simply for being black and treated like a criminal when I had done nothing wrong ..."

"I know," I replied, "I have seen it happen in the prisons,

where I go once a week."

Meeting his questioning glance, I explained to him that I was a journalist and what I was doing in Texas. We talked all the way back to Pasadena. As he was about to pull into the gas stations parking lot to let me out, I asked him: "with all the bad experience you had with white people, how come you decided to help me?"

"My mother taught me something long ago, when growing up," he replied slowly, deep in thought. "She said that we can't always chose what will happen in life, and that much of it will probably be grossly unfair. But she said we can chose how we react to it, and whether we allow it to affect us in our core and change who we are. I have decided not to fight racism with racism. Instead, I have decided to fight racism and injustice with kindness. I was raised to believe in God, and I truly believe that we are all brothers, irrespective of our skin color: white people, black people, brown people, it does not matter. If some others don't believe that, well, so be it."

I never caught his name, and never saw him again. He never gave me his address, though I believe I asked him for it to send him a copy of the book when it was printed. It wouldn't surprise me if he did not have an address. It would not surprise me if he did not have a name. It would not surprise me if he had been sent from some ethereal sphere, to save Tiny's life and possibly also to give Tiny's increasingly frustrated owner the very important message not to be tempted to become as callous, selfish and cruel as was the prevailing climate in Houston at the time. In a city where everyone was out for themselves, it was all too easy to take the same attitude as many people did: "Well, nobody has helped me, why should I?"

Luckily, I never forgot his message, and Tiny never forgot the man who saved his life that day. Until someone can prove otherwise, the Pekingese and myself continue to believe he was indeed a guardian angel, though we are not sure whether his name was Clarence...

196

Chapter 17

Art Garfunkel's Wife, Bhuddist Chants And The Four Seasons Hotel In Austin
Or: Mike And Tiny Go To The State Capitol

It became evident that the courts, as often happens in Texas, had decided to turn down the case of Mike the death row inmate, no matter what new evidence we came up with, suggesting miscarriages of justice and disregard for the law.

Jane and myself realized that the courts were bent on executing our client, and that they were unwilling to address the evidence we presented.

Anyone who has been involved in trying to overturn a miscarriage of justice in the state of Texas will testify to this fact. It soon becomes not a matter of right or wrong, but a cruel game of chess between the state's prosecutors and the attorneys for the convict. The rule of the game is "I am stronger than you are, and I am going to show you, so there." The attorney often loses, especially in death row cases.

We were not helped in our quest for a new trial by an angelic Houstonian mother, a real estate agent by the name of Pamela Lychner who, having been attacked when showing a house to a prospective client, had founded a crime victims' rights group. She frequently appeared on television, calling for tougher sentences and to campaign against a new trial whenever a capital murder case came within a reasonable chance of it. Everybody in the new right movement loved Pamela, who incidentally was destined to die several years later on the ill-fated TWA 800 flight, which crashed in 1996 over Long Island on its way to Paris.

She took a popular side, which could easily be used for inflammatory political campaigns. Nobody could argue with what she said about the victims who had their lives shattered in an act of callousness. But everyone could argue with people who claimed that one or the other "criminal" may have been innocently convicted, such as Randall Adams, or may, due to outstanding conduct, deserve to have his sentence commuted to life imprisonment. In the black and white world of the new "tough on crime" stance in Houston, this did simply not exist.

We had already worked out that we could not go public with the case. Pamela would effortlessly bury us, and anyone who helped us. "Those people are trying to help a dangerous convict get off from paying for a heinous crime," we could imagine her telling the shocked TV audience, maybe even adding "and one of them is even a foreigner, a journalist. Since when do foreigners have anything to say about our laws? I say: the man did the crime, he was found guilty by a jury! He had his chance in court. Now, let him pay for what he did." And so it could go...

As a final resort, we decided to go meet Texas Attorney General Dan Morales in Austin. Dan and I had become friends during his 1991 election bid for state attorney general. Dan had a warm sense of humor. He was compassionate. He was kind. He was very, very intelligent. He hugged. He smiled. Dan was the kind of Texan you had to love. Even Mike the dog, who met Dan on several occasions,

was impressed when Dan shared his sandwich with him. Dan could not help being nice: to dogs, to people and, I suspect, even to houseplants.

I called Dan in his new office at the State Capitol.

"Dan, I have to see you," I told him, and he immediately scheduled an appointment for me two days later, not even asking what I wanted to see him about. To his credit, Dan was putting himself into a considerable bind by doing so. I had heard rumors that he had been reprimanded for his friendship with me, which was inappropriate now that he was Attorney General. I was, after all, working on a death penalty case that Dan was prosecuting. However, Dan had familiarized himself with the facts of the case while still running for office and had agreed that something seemed to have gone wrong. He had promised to look into the case if he were to be elected. I was about to call him to his promise...

The next evening, Tiny, Mike and I set off for Austin in Farley. We had kindly been given complimentary accommodations at the Four Seasons Hotel on Austin's Riverbanks. Upon arrival, we were given the royal treatment, a fact that delighted Tiny greatly.

"And if you leave us a schedule of your meetings tomorrow, we will walk the dogs for you while you are out," the helpful receptionist offered. I promised I would make up the schedule as soon as I had settled in and drop it at reception later that evening.

We walked to the elevator, Tiny with his head thrown back proudly. Mike was nice as always, greeting people to the right and left. We took the elevator up to our designated room, with a beautiful view of the Austin riverside. The river was surrounded by several acres of carefully kept lawns and woods. It was so pretty that I decided to unpack later and take Tiny and Mike for a walk.

Rarely had I seen a city hotel in such a serene, picturesque setting. Right in the heart of Austin, it provided a calm hideaway. We walked the grounds for more than an hour, and met the state girl rowing team as they came in from their late afternoon practice. Mike delighted the girls by doing a little dance for them, as they put away their boats, and basked in the pats and adoration they showered on him. Tiny walked on by himself, as if not belonging with us.

"What's with him?" one of the girls asked, puzzled. "He's your dog, too, isn't he?"

"Yes," I replied, "but he thinks he is human. It is very important for Tiny to be considered to be just another guy out on his own, for a stroll..."

"Ah, I see," the girl replied, and then they asked where

199

I was from and what I was doing here. I told them, and they were immediately intrigued and delighted with the idea of the travelling dogs from Canada. They couldn't wait to find out more. Even more intrigued were they with the fact that Mike had been to a real-life death row inmate, in a successful attempt to teach him responsibility.

"What an amazing story" one of the girls exclaimed.

"You should see the oil painting of Mike that his owner's cell neighbor did of him," I told her.

"Really?" the girl said. "You mean the guys on death row actually paint Mike?"

"Yes," I replied, "and I send them photos, too." They all said they would keep their fingers crossed for the meeting with the attorney general tomorrow and hoped that we would at the very least be considered for commutation to a life sentence.

"If he does get out, are you really going to give him Mike?" a freckled young rower asked.

"Honestly?" I replied, grinning. "No way, no chance..."

Mike and I walked on to catch up with Tiny. We found a secluded part of the lake, in a wooden area, where I sat down, with the dogs on either side, and practiced Buddhist chants, which I had learned from Art Garfunkel's wife Kim after a recent interview.

Following the interview, Kim had invited me to chant with her, wishing to share the experience of Buddhism with someone. "The meaning of the chant," Kim had explained in the lavish Sheraton suite she shared with her husband during her stay in Houston, "is that of a Lotus flower which breaks through the concrete from underneath, blooming after having overcome the impossible obstacle."

If ever I could relate to the image of the Lotus flower breaking through the concrete, it was now. Getting Dan to stick his political neck out for the sake of one man's inconsequential life would be as equally hard a task as the Lotus flower's quest to bloom. As the astonished dogs looked on, clearly trying to decide whether I had gone completely insane, I began to chant as Kim had taught me. As a catholic, chanting felt strange to me, even embarrassing, but I kept going. Finally, as Kim had promised, I arrived at a peace of mind equal to a flattening of waves on a previously stormy sea. Thankfully, nobody saw us. I am not sure how well it would have gone down for a still fairly respectable journalist to be caught sitting in the woods outside the Four Seasons hotel, flanked by a Pekingese and Shihtzu, chanting a Buddhist chant that Kin had written down for me...

In the evening, we dined on Mo-shu Shrimp, delivered by an excellent down town restaurant, since the Four seasons could not provide Asian food for room service. They could, however, provide room service for the dogs and brought up two bowls of Iams lamb and rice, as per prior reservation. The three of us dined from impeccable white porcelain plates, drank imported water from exclusive crystal glasses and wondered what the following day would bring.

Early the next morning, I picked up Jane from Austin's city airport.

"Hey Jane," I greeted her. "We still have plenty of time before we have to go and meet Dan. I hope you don't mind if we go by the hotel first and walk the dogs."

"You brought your dogs?" Jane asked, incredulously.

"Sure," I grinned, "I decided to turn this into a family vacation."

"My, you live in style," Jane remarked when we pulled into the elegant Four Seasons valet parking area.

"Not for my sake," I told her, only half kidding. "Tiny enjoys the luxurious life," and then I added, by way of explanation: "He's my Pekingese."

Jane had not actually met the dogs before, and was delighted when they greeted her at the door to my room. Because it was still early, Mike had his usual, sleepy look on his face. I gathered that both dogs had been sound asleep until they heard us at the door.

"They are not exactly early morning dogs," I explained to Jane and then addressed the dogs, "come on, you couch potatoes, let's go for a walk."

Jane, the tough death penalty appeals attorney, cradled a half-asleep Mike in her arms as we walked to the elevator and went down. Once downstairs, Mike, Tiny, Jane and myself went for an idyllic early morning walk along the riverside, Jane, I might add, being completely enchanted with the little dogs.

"They are so cute," she remarked. "They are almost human, aren't they?"

She laughed as Tiny started walking back and forth, sniffing here and there, then walking away from us, turning around and walking back again.

"What is he doing?" she wanted to know.

"Preparing to do number two," I replied, shrugging. "It takes him a long time to find just the right spot. As a male Pekingese, and one who owns the world at that, it is very important to strategically place it in just the right spot, you see," I said, winking. "Not to mention that Tiny always likes to do it with a view: looking out over the ocean, or in our case he'll look for somewhere with a river view ... watch."

Sure enough, a few seconds later, Tiny positioned himself so he could look out over the beautiful river as he did his business. "You would not believe how many business meetings I have been late for because of Tiny," I explained to Jane.

"I cannot imagine why," she grinned. "Mike is such a good dog. He did his business straight away, and is all ready to go back in."

"Yes" I replied, "Mike takes responsibility very seriously. By the way, Mike is a girl..."

"What the...?" Jane asked.

"Never mind, I'll explain later. Come on, we gotta get them back up to the room and head for Dan's office, or we'll be late."

On the way out, I dropped my meeting schedule with the front desk, so they could co-ordinate walking the little dogs. After meeting with Dan, Jane and I had planned to have lunch. Then I would drop her back to the airport for an early afternoon flight back to Houston, while I would go back to Austin for another meeting. I did not expect to be back before 7 p.m.

There was considerable commotion in Dan's office when his secretary, and assorted assistants that he now had, realized that I had brought someone else with me without having told them in advance. They were even more shocked when they realized the person with me was the official attorney of record on a notorious death penalty case.

I heard muffled, excited voices from behind Dan's closed office door. "She brought someone with her," I heard a female voice hiss. "Without telling us. It's that attorney."

"That's all right," Dan said, "show them both in."

It was good to see Dan again, though he now wore a suit and tie, sat behind an imposing looking desk and no longer put his feet up on the table like he used to. He had become a politician.

"I hope you don't mind that I brought Jane," I began. "I didn't want to tell the secretary, so I decided to bring her on the spur of the moment. So much for not telling," I grinned, "seems the whole office knows. Sorry!"

"That's all right," Dan said, surprisingly casual. "It won't be a problem. What can I do for you?"

We explained the case to Dan once more. "You've already seen all the documentation, Dan, you know the facts. The courts don't even give us a break. If they give us a hearing, we can prove at the very least the need for a new trial. That guy really might be innocent, Dan, we have to do something. If you are going to have the death penalty, at least have it for

203

people who are guilty."

"I quite agree," Dan said, and listened to Jane's arguments in detail. "Just ask your bloodhounds to hold off with filing long enough to give the judge a chance to consider our issues," she pleaded. " Right now, they are turning us down in summary denial, without even looking at the stuff we file. We found all this new evidence..."

Dan, Jane and myself talked for several hours. In the end, Dan promised to do what he could, agreeing with us that there was the danger of a possible miscarriage of justice. He also saw, however, the danger of this case being highly unpopular, whether the man was innocent or not, due to the fact that our man had in the past been involved with a prison gang and had a bad prison disciplinary record prior to 1989.

"What does that have to do with the facts of the alleged crime?" I asked.

"Nothing," Dan replied. "But it makes it more difficult to make people sympathetic to care what is happening to him in the first place."

"But he is no longer with the gang, and he has cleaned up his disciplinary record and become a model prisoner."

"Never mind," Dan said. "It is still on his record. Now, if he were black, you would have a better chance. At least there would be the black advocacy groups. But with a white guy, and then that kind of record ... anyway, I'll see what I can do."

Jane and I were in high spirits when we left Dan's office, notwithstanding the dirty looks his associates and various helpers gave us. "He is a really nice guy," Jane remarked. "I would have never thought that. I am sure he'll help us."

"Me, too," I replied.

We had lunch in a small but excellent Thai restaurant in downtown Austin, by way of celebration. Then I took her to the airport. "Have a great evening with your dogs, and give Mike a hug from me," she said as she boarded the plane, "and I just wanted to say: well done. We're a good team. We're going to win this case yet."

When I got back to the hotel, it was not yet 7pm. Instead of going up to the room, I decided to go straight to the hot spa, rewarding myself for a long and tough day with a well-earned and relaxing soak... The gym and hot spa of the Austin Four Seasons overlook, through giant windows, the garden and river. It was the most beautiful hot spa I have ever been in, because you can enjoy the bubbly hot water while watching a true Texas splendid sun set over the lazily flowing Austin river, right outside the hotel's gardens, through a giant window on the far side of the tub...

As I did so, suddenly the little dogs came into view. I had forgotten that 6:30pm had been scheduled as their final walking time of the day. There they were, right on schedule, leashed as I had instructed, dragging a hapless hotel employee, uniform, prissy little shoes and all, behind them. I watched with intense interest as Tiny tried to go off to the right, and Mike pulled to the left.

"Oh my God, they are so funny" a lady in a pink bathing suit, who had eased herself into the spa next to me, remarked. "I know" I grinned back. "They are my dogs."

I told her the story of how they came to be walked outside the spa window, and once again remarked on the excellent service at the Four Seasons.

As we watched, the young man tried to get the dogs back inside, apparently having decided they had had enough time to do their business. Tiny planted all four paws firmly into the ground and refused. The man tried to drag him. Tiny threw himself on the floor. The young man bent down and made an effort to pick the little Pekingese up and turn him on his four paws again. I watched, through the giant glass windows while deliciously soaking up the hot water, as Tiny first turned his face into a grimace and then snapped at the man. Mike danced in tune, as the hapless man jumped back, petrified.

After that, Tiny walked where he wanted. The young

man and Mike followed, the former no longer daring to tell Tiny what to do, the latter having since long gotten used to the fact that subjugation was the only way of dealing with the Pekingese who did indeed own the world...

Meanwhile, the pink lady and I were doubled over with laughter in the tub, soon to be joined by several more gym guests, all of them now watching, because it was far better entertainment than the televisions in our rooms could ever provide. We saw Tiny and Mike wrestle with the poor hotel employee as the sun set picturesquely behind them, over the river...

I met the three of them as they were on the way in, just as I came out of the gym to cross the corridor into the changing rooms.

"Hi," I told the dog walker, greeting Tiny and Mike at the same time. "They are mine. Giving you hell, are they?"

"Never again," the poor man sighed. "Your little grey dog is a terror, I tell you. Here, now that you are back, would you mind taking them back up to the room yourself?" With that, he threw the leashes at me and left before I could say a word. I stood, still in my bathing suit, between gym and change room, with Tiny and Mike and a throng of their admirers in the background, waiting for us to come up to the gym door so they could pat the dogs who had entertained them so well while we were all in the tub...

Unfortunately, our Austin visit had been in vain. A few days later, a petition was filed from the Attorney General's office, regarding the case of our inmate. It said, in almost the same wording, that the courts should not listen to us under any circumstances, that we should not be allowed any further hearings and that it was high time to execute the inmate.

The petition, though not written by Dan, was signed with his name and bore the stamp of his office. We knew it had passed his desk and been read by him. Dan went on to become the Attorney General who sought and succeeded in executing the most inmates ever in his term of office, thus securing himself the re-election the following term through support of the "Hang them high" mob, making him the only Democrat to be re-elected in the State cabinet.

The State of Texas, headed by Dan, thereafter went after our inmate with a vengeance and finally succeeded in having him executed in December 1995, rehabilitated and innocent as he might have been, without having given him the chance to present new evidence or to have his petitions properly considered...

Chapter 18

Tiny In Hospital

At the beginning of 1991 I noticed a couple of pronounced lumps under Tiny's skin, to either side of his shoulder blades. I observed them for a few months and when they refused to go away and, on the contrary, proceeded to increase in size, I called the hospital in Clear Lake and was told to bring him in for a check-up.

The Clear Lake Pet-vet center was a large animal clinic that had several different, experienced veterinarians on staff. We were this time waited on by Dr Koenig, who had such a kind, warm way with the animals that even Tiny found it hard to resist him and refrained from his usual growling and other veterinary intimidation techniques. Instead, he sat on the examination table, meekly wagging, as Dr Koenig felt for the lumps I pointed out to him.

"Oh yes, I can feel them," he said, following my directions. "They are certainly quite big. I think we are going to have to do a biopsy."

While Koenig prepared Tiny for the biopsy, I tried to find out more. "What do you think it could be?" I asked nervously. "Don't know," he replied, "But I have to warn you that it could be cancer..."

"You mean Tiny could die?" I asked him, shocked.

"Not necessarily. With cancer, it depends at what stage you catch it and whether it is possible to control the spread of the disease in time by operating on the animal."

Koenig performed the biopsy on the still tailwagging Tiny as he kept talking to me, explaining what he was doing as he was doing it. Thankfully, he did not send me home to sit by the phone, nailbiting, for the results. Instead, he immediately took the time to investigate the tissue samples he had taken while Tiny and I were left in the examination room to wait.

No thinking what would happen if I were to lose the Pekingese ... and poor Mike! Tiny had become such an integrated part of our family that it was impossible to even imagine the thought that he could have a life- threatening illness and might not be with us one day soon.

As usual in situations like this, I tried bargaining with God. "Please God, don't let it be cancer. If you don't let it be cancer, then I promise that Tiny, Mike and myself will go out and do some good deeds. See, that is why we can't have Tiny dying. So that he can out into the world and do your works..."

While I tried to convince God of the importance of the Pekingese in doing good works for the poor, Koenig was at work in the lab. No sooner was I finished than he came back.

"So?" I asked anxiously.

"Well, to be frank, I do not know. They seem to be benign lumps of tissue, but there are some cancer cells in them. Not enough in numbers to justify a diagnosis of cancer, but I think we should cut all the lumps out immediately, just to make sure."

"So it is not life-threatening then?" I asked, trying to fully understand what he had been saying.

"It does not appear to be." Koenig patiently explained. "But it could become so in future, which is the reason why I want to cut all the lumps out immediately, and then, if no new ones appear, we should be fine."

He scheduled Tiny for surgery that very afternoon and promised to call me as soon as it was over, re-assuring me that the risk for an operation complication with a healthy dog of Tiny's young years was very slim.

"But there is a risk?" I asked, always the journalist.

"Yes, there is always a risk, as with any operation, but, as I said, it is not a very high risk at this time..."

"Well, how much of a risk is it, then," I kept insisting, "and what exactly could happen?"

Any other vet may have well dismissed me with an

impatient wave of his hand and a characteristic, superior, know-it-all attitude, not so Dr. Koenig. He understood the attachment between animal and man all too well, having a few of his own at home. He spent another 20 minutes with Tiny and me, touchingly explaining every detail. Finally, I was satisfied.

Okay, I'll leave him with you then," I conceded. "But only if you are going to be the one to operate."

"Yes, I will operate," he promised.

"And you will call me as soon as it is over to let me know how it went?"

He promised to do so. Finally, he was nice enough to let me take Tiny into the back, to put him into a holding cage. "Oh, I better leave him something of mine," I remarked, "so he has something to sleep on with my smell on it. Could you turn around for a minute, please?"

"What the...?" Koenig asked.

"I am going to leave him my T-shirt," I explained. "I am wearing it under the sweater, so if you could please..."

Koenig did, and when he turned around, Tiny and T-shirt were both deposited in the cage. I left a list of what to feed him with a nice veterinary assistant who walked up to Tiny's cage with the usual exclamation "oh, what a cute dog..." only to be rewarded with a sneer and a growl.

"He's always like this with new people," I offered by way of explanation. "After a few days, he'll love you."

"Uh-huh," she replied, not quite believing me. "He's certainly cute, though..."

I left Tiny, the T-shirt, and a reassuring Dr Koenig at the clinic and headed for home. There, I sat by the phone for 4 hours, biting my nails, unable to concentrate on my work. Mike came and sat by the phone with me, thoroughly tense, not quite knowing what was going on, but sensing that my nailbiting was somehow connected with Tiny's absence and this little apparatus which made a ringing noise from time to time and that people talked into.

Finally, the phone rang. I picked it up first time.

"Dr Koenig?" I gasped into the phone. "How is he?"

"Excuse me?" a strong male voice on the other end of the phone asked, puzzled.

"You're not Dr Koenig?" I asked, equally puzzled.

"What's going on, who is this?" the voice on the other end of the phone was growing impatient. "Is this a joke or something? I am looking for Tess, the journalist. I obviously have the wrong number."

He was about to hang up. I pulled myself together, in a last-minute rescue of my career and reputation. Swallowing hard, then real fast, to catch him before the receiver left his ear, I blurted out: "No, this is me. You have the right number. I am sorry, I'm a little pre-occupied today, my little dog is in hospital for an operation this afternoon and I am waiting for the vet to call me back to let me know how it went."

He luckily understood, being a dog owner himself. He turned out to be the manager of David Copperfield, the magician, who had called to informing me that David had read and approved the magazine for which I was seeking an interview with him and that the interview would go ahead. I muttered something like "great" into the phone and absentmindedly jotted down date and time of the interview on a piece of paper.

The call after Copperfield's manager, thankfully, was Dr. Koenig.

"The operation went fine," he reassured me. "He is in the recovery room, sleeping off the anesthesia. I want to keep him here another day or two, but if you like, you can come and visit later this evening."

By the time I got to the animal hospital in the evening, Tiny had the situation under full control. He sat in a big cage reserved for large dogs, with a series of stitches on his shaved fur from the back to the sides, and - as the only dog among some dozen or so which ranged from German shepherds to Rottweilers to Pittbulls - proudly displayed a sign "CAREFUL, BITES" on the outside of the cage. Tiny totally ignored the stitches or the fact that he had just had an operation. He was as bossy and full of himself as ever.

I could not help laughing and asked the veterinary nurse, "so what did he do to you people to deserve that sign?"

She informed me that Tiny had put the entire clinic in its place with a carefully dished out mixture of wags, growls and "wa wa wa"s, asserting his right as the alpha dog. "Once we submitted," the girl laughed, "everything was okay. This sign is really for the nightshift, who may not know about his emperor complex."

That was a way of putting it. As for Dr Koenig, Tiny greeted him with a tail wagging grin. "How did you do that?" I asked him, surprised. "Tiny isn't usually like that with strangers?"

"Ah, he is just a cream puff, once you get to know him," Koenig replied and ruffled Tiny's fur at the tip of his tail. As I spent more and more time in the back entertaining Tiny in his cage, I should soon learn that Koenig had a way with animals surpassed by none. No matter how frightened, mean or superior a dog acted with others, when he was around Koenig, he became as mellow as can be. Maybe this is the difference between a good and a bad vet, I mused, as I watched Koenig calm down a growling Rottweiler with his voice alone. I had never seen animals abused or even roughly muzzled in this clinic, and I had gotten to take a good look behind the scenes in the time I came to spend there.

For now, Koenig asked if I wanted to get Tiny a little toy or other cheer-up tool. "He can have a cookie or a chew toy" Koenig explained, "but just one."

"Great," I replied, "I'll be right back."

I got into my car and went to the neighboring mall, where I entered a big pet store, incidentally of the "Doctor Pet

Store" chain, the same where Mike had come from. "Hi, my dog is in hospital across the road," I told the sales clerk, "and I need something to cheer him up. What can you recommend?"

The clerk laughed and said, "Boy has he got a good mother. What kind of a dog is it?"

When I had explained Tiny's size, breed and personality to the girl, we both settled on a small chewing toy and a rawhide stick which Tiny referred to as Stoeckchen in his vocabulary of German baby language.

The stick was greeted with a joyous lick on the donor's nose, whereas the expensive rubber chewing-toy was discarded without a second glance. "Oh well," the veterinary nurse shrugged and grinned. "At least you tried."

I left Tiny to chewing his stick and drove back home, after having been assured by Koenig that he would call me in the morning and let me know whether I could take Tiny home.

He called and said that I could. "Tiny is recovering so well from the operation that I have no problems sending him home with you this evening," Koenig informed me. "He will need a week of rest to let the stitches heal, and then everything should be fine.

Mike and I got into the car to drive to pick up Tiny. We took with us our old pet carrier, which I was to transport Tiny home in, so as to avoid him jumping around in the car and opening his stitches. Mike had to wait in the car while I went in to fetch Tiny. The veterinary nurse brought him out. The little Pekingese was wagging his tail, and looked out into the world with proprietorial rights from her arm. "He's come to like it here," she explained. "This morning, he even let me play with him."

She put Tiny down and let him run over to greet me. While I waited for her to prepare the (presumably large) bill for services rendered, Tiny and I took a stroll into the back part of the clinic, where a variety of dog foods, leashes, flea collars and other dog utensils were on display. Tiny loved to go shopping for his own items, a habit he had picked up when I first took him to a giant pet supermarket in Houston which allows dogs to shop with their owners. The joy he had felt when sniffing for various flavors of dog food before making up his mind which one to "buy" had never left the little Pekingese. Having survived his operation to stoically, he obviously decided that he should be rewarded with a shopping trip. He walked among the shelves with me in tow, climbed on a bag of dog food here, sniffed a leash and collar there, but nothing was really to his liking. Until Tiny came to a row of dog carriers in the lower shelf at the far end.

He instantly fell in love with a pink, medium sized dog carrier and jumped up to its door, wagging his tail wildly. "Ah come on Tiny, we have one of those, let's go," I said trying to get him to walk on by. But Tiny ran straight back to the dog carrier scratching at its door again. "Very well then," I sighed and took the dog carrier from the shelf, placed it on the floor and allowed Tiny to have a closer look.

He walked all around it, inspecting it in detail. I placed a brown one next to it. "How about this one?" I asked. Tiny was not interested. It had to be the pink one, or none at all.

"Want to try it out for comfort?" I asked and opened the door to the carrier. Tiny crawled inside and refused to get out again, wagging his tail. I placed the grey carrier back on the shelf, picked up the pink one with Tiny inside and carried it to the front desk. "You better hold it before making up the final bill." I told the girl. "Tiny here has decided that he wants this pet carrier for his house. I am going to get it for him, because he just got through an operation."

The girl nodded with an understanding grin and added the 25$ for the pet carrier to her bill. When she handed me the bill, it came to some 850 odd Dollars, with operation, overnight stays and special night nurse included. I swallowed a few times and coughed. "Er, that's a lot of money," I remarked.

"Yes," she said, "they sure cost a bundle, don't they?"

"Do you believe there is any way I could get a discount?" I asked. "Because Tiny is so cute, and because today is Wednesday?" I added in desperation as an afterthought.

"I don't know about that," the girl mused, "we are already the cheapest on the market, as far as the big clinics go. If you can't pay ... we are supposed to hold the dog until the bill is settled."

"No no," I hastened to say, "I have my credit card with me. But still, do you think you could ask?"

"Wait a minute if you would," the girl said and disappeared into the back. She came back with a woman veterinarian who I learned was Dr Kriegler, the other staff veterinarian. Dr Koenig was not on duty today. Just my luck!

"What can I help you with?" Kriegler said with a pleasant smile.

"Well, I know you don't know me or my dog," I began, "But he's been here for an operation the past two days, and now I have this big bill to pay, and I was just wondering whether we could get a discount of some sorts?"

"Is that Tiny you are talking about?" Kriegler asked.

I nodded.

"I know Tiny, I met him this morning when I did my rounds. Lovely little dog," she remarked. "Let me have a look at that bill."

She took the bill and went through it with a red pen. "There, we can discount the overnight stay, because he is so little. That'll be half price... and the anesthesia, same thing, didn't use as much as we would have done on a big dog... As for..."

By the time Kriegler was through and handed the bill back to the girl to be added up again, it only came to $500.

I smiled a grateful smile at Kriegler, handed the girl the credit card and watched as she processed it. $500 was still a stiff bill to pay, but it could have been much worse.

Tiny and Mike performed a stormy greeting ceremony in the car, through the bars of Tiny's pet carrier, and then we made our way home. I kept in mind the advice of the doctors Kriegler and Koenig: "don't let him jump around, keep him quiet or the stitches could open again."

I couldn't very well keep Tiny confined to the small pet carrier all night, and so I opened the door to let him out. So much for keeping him quiet. The result: Tiny and Mike wrestling, ignoring my orders to stop doing so. Tiny jumping up the bed, down the bed. Tiny dragging Mike by the ear, running around him in a circle....

The next morning, Tiny was as happy and chipper as ever. On his right and left side were big, soft balls. Despite Tiny's happy appearance, something was obviously wrong. I called the hospital. Dr Kriegler was still on duty.

"Dr. Kriegler, there is something wrong with Tiny. I couldn't keep him still last night, and now he's got these big bumps where they operated him. He doesn't seem to be in any pain, but they seem very odd."

"You better bring him in straight away," Kriegler suggested. "I am about to go off shift, but if you can get here right away, I'll wait for you."

I packed Tiny into his new pet carrier, which had now become his Haeuschen or house, and which he defended against Mike, and drove him back to Clear Lake.

Kriegler exclaimed "oh my" at the sight of Tiny's large lumps and then performed some tests which showed that the lumps were filled with blood.

"I am going to have to keep him here and drain the blood out," she explained. "It will be a few days before you can take him home again, maybe by Monday."

Kriegler and I decided to leave Tiny at the clinic longer than that: until he was completely healed, after I had explained to Kriegler: "Look, my life is so hectic. He won't get the rest he needs at home. He's better off here, at the clinic."

Thus it came to pass that Tiny spent some two weeks at the clinic. The first few days, I drove there on my own in the afternoons to visit him, only to be presented with Tiny in a white blanket, with tubes sticking out of his skin through which blood was oozing at continuous, though slow, speed. Tiny smelled coppery from the blood which kept dripping from him, but he was oblivious to the sight he made as I carried him around the hospital grounds and then outside to go window-shopping.

Several people asked what was wrong with Tiny, and having been given an explanation, tried a comforting pat on the head, only to be snarled at by Tiny and, if they didn't back off, put in their place in no uncertain terms.

"You can't treat him like a dog," I explained to the astonished Samaritan in question, "he takes exception to that."

When we got back through the clinic doors, the girls laughed at the expression on Tiny's face. He had his tongue stuck out in a superior grin. "Just look at him," one girl remarked. "It looks like he is saying: my mommy is here now and I am on top of the world."

Having informed Mike, the death row inmate, of Tiny's admission to the hospital, get-well cards began to arrive from the inmates on wing J21. One of them, Mike's cell neighbor, sent a beautiful oil painting of Mike, the dog, suggesting that I leave this with Tiny at the clinic, so he would not miss his significant other too much. I had to write regular reports to the men on death row, via Mike, to inform them of what was happening to Tiny. Hardened criminals as they were, they had all discovered a common soft spot for a certain, prissy little Pekingese, and they worried alongside with me for his well-being.

Luckily, things went well. As Tiny got better, he was allowed to roam around the clinic freely, and soon came to see himself to be the owner of the animal hospital. He entertained courteous relations with all "his" staff, who had taken to bringing him little tidbits when they came to work in the morning.

"Dr Tiny" made his rounds every afternoon, looking into the cages of freshly operated animals, or those who were still waiting to be tended to. He got such intense pleasure out of being the one who ran free while the others were in cages that even the regular afternoon visits from myself and later from Mike were treated more as a distraction, even if a pleasant one, rather than as his main event of the day.

Mike and I tried to win Tiny back by going on extensive shopping trips in the pet store across the road in the mall, but our gifts were treated with polite and passing interest, as were we. Tiny clearly had more important things to do with his life now, such as running a big veterinary clinic and making sure that "his" staff performed up to standard.

Through Tiny's taking over of the clinic, Mike and me got to meet sick cats, dogs who wouldn't eat, got to watch veterinary assistants prepare medicine and food for their charges and in general learned a lot about how to run a clinic. When it was time to go, we paid a - heavily discounted - bill of $1500, and then Mike and I stood in the sidelines and watched as the staff lined up to bid Tiny farewell. Tiny dispensed licks and tailwags, not unlike a respected superior who was leaving to go to another facility.

We took Tiny home with us, overjoyed to have him back. He was fully restored and showed no adverse signs from the ordeal he had been through. Except that adjusting to our humble life style came somewhat difficult to Tiny. For months afterward, he would fake various ailments, whether it was screaming and whimpering with "stomach pain" or waking up in the morning and walking on three paws, holding the forth one high up in the air as if it was broken, at an odd angle. Each time, I rushed Tiny to the clinic immediately, only to be baffled to find that the symptoms disappeared the moment we walked through the door. After expensive tests and X-rays, I was told each time that there was nothing wrong with him - finally, we figured out that Tiny was missing his old friends, and that he was making up excuses to go back to the clinic. From then on, we made it a point to go there once a week to visit until Tiny had been dutifully weaned from his "doctor complex..."

Chapter 19

We Make Good On A Promise
Or: Humans Don't Bite

Tiny left hospital completely cancer-free. As soon as he was well again, the three of us were looking for a way we could make good on our promise to make the world a better place.

Tiny, Mike and I got into our new car (Farley had long since died of old age and broken CV joints. We were now driving around Houston in a blue Ford with Quebec license plates), in search of somewhere we could put ourselves to good use. Finally, we found it in the form of a derelict, little park. It was located in the middle of a high crime district off the C/59 exit.

Our first stop at this particular park came because Tiny had, as usual, taken his time in the morning. Now, we were on our way to the usual weekend break at Corpus Christi, he began yapping. In true Pekingese fashion, he demanded to go to the restroom at once to complete his urgent business, complaining because I had not given him time enough to do so in the morning.

Just before we entered the freeway, I pulled into a park I saw on my right. As I mentioned in an earlier chapter, Houston is a racially divided city. We were in a black neighborhood and it came as no surprise that I found myself to be the only white person in the park. Everyone else was black, except for a handful of Hispanics.

They looked at the dogs and me, clearly surprised, when they saw us pull up and get out of the car. Was the surprise because we were the wrong race, the wrong color? Was it because the dogs here were mongrels and they had never seen someone like Tiny and Mike before? From conversations with the men on death row, who for the greatest part originated from neighborhoods like this, I had to my amazement learned that

Pekingeses and Shihtzus were generally not known to children in the lower class neighborhoods of the United States.

Ignoring the piercing stares in our backs, we walked around the park, as Tiny sniffed a tree here and a shrub there. Mike, his usual bouncy self, became aware of three little children playing by themselves under one of the picnic tables. The Shihtzu took it upon himself to introduce our little group to the children. Wagging his tail, he ran straight to them. To excited Spanish-language exclamations of: "what a cute little dog," Mike performed his regular dance for their benefit: tongue hanging out to one side, grinning into one child's face after the other. A little girl began to pat Mike. Joyfully, he jumped into her lap. Now the other children did the same. Mike jumped from one lap to the other, freely dispensing enormous doses of doggie love.

As usual, I had to wait for Tiny to complete his business. When we finally caught up with the little group, Tiny was immediately greeted with shrieks of joy such as: "oh, and look at this one, isn't he adorable."

Tiny rewarded their attention with his best "stay-off" grimace and a deep growl. "What's with him?" a little boy asked, surprised. "Never mind Tiny," I explained, "he likes to think of himself as human. You just treated him like a dog. He takes exception to this."

"So what do I have to do?" the little boy, who had introduced himself as Miguel, asked me. He was determined to become friends with Tiny.

"Well, for one, you always have to ask Tiny. Never command. Treat him politely, like you would a person. Ask him: "how are you." Or compliment him by saying: "you have a very pretty coat," instead of exclaiming "how cute." Get it?" The little boy shook his head in wonder. He had never met a dog that wanted to be human before, but he was child enough not to question my explanation and do as he was told. He kept doing what I told him, and Tiny finally wagged his tail at him.

Miguel and his sisters, Carmen and Maria, had a wonderful time playing with the little dogs. Soon, other children joined us. When I asked them where they lived, all of them pointed to a run-down, government-subsidized apartment building on the far end of the park as their home. All of them reported home lives of extreme poverty, and some spoke of physical abuse at the hands of one of both their parents. Most of them had always dreamt of owning a dog, but there was no money to get one. These children, judging by how they described their lives, were living in hell.

They were serious children with old eyes. The hopelessness of their existence had wiped the smiles off their faces long before they ever reached adulthood. With Tiny and Mike, they found them again for a little while. Tiny occasionally graciously invited one little girl, with a tail wag, to come closer and permitted her - to the admiration of the other children - to pat him.

Mike, true to his good nature, allowed himself to be picked up, carried around, lowered to the ground once more, being watched while he did his business, called from here to there and back again. The eyes of the children shone with excitement as the little Shihtzu danced for them. Together, they ran with him across the length of the park. When it was time for us to go, a throng of children followed us to the car. They were begging me to return the next day with the dogs.

I realized with sadness that these children had nothing in their lives to give them joy. Nothing. Except the few hours they had spent with the dogs. I realized that many of them were probably beaten at home, maybe even sexually abused. Most did not have much of a future. What would it be for me to come back here once a day and give them their smiles back? Even if it was just for a little while?

"We will be back," I promised, "but not tomorrow. We are on our way to Corpus Christi. We will be there until Sunday. How about we meet next Monday?"

Eager faces nodded with pleasure. Little mouths opened and joyfully exclaimed: "Yes. Yes! They are coming back." After working out a time which would be mutually convenient, fitting it in between together interviews in my case and school times in theirs, we parted. Behind us, the children waved until we disappeared, smiling with the joy they had just experienced as well as with the excitement of already looking forward to the next time.

The following Monday, they were there. All of them, not one little face was missing. Before I even opened the car door to let them out, shouts greeted me: "Did you bring the dogs?"

"Ah, there's Mike. Hey Mike!"

"Oh, look Tiny!"

When the dogs were finally lifted out of the car and on the ground, Mike being supported by many little helping hands, the children at once laughed and danced around the small canines.

"You don't have any dogs?" I asked the obvious question of little Miguel. "No my mum and dad are too poor to feed a dog," he replied, swiping a black curl from his forehead. "But when I grow up, I am going to make a lot of money. And then my mum will be able to have a dog, and I will have many dogs."

His little sister Carmen bounced up and down next to us, filled with youthful eagerness. Enthusiastically, she commented "si, si."

"I am going to be a doctor when I grow up," Miguel added. "I want to study medicine at university."

"Do you get good grades at school?" I asked Miguel, before the background noise of the little dogs, who were putting on their show for the benefit of the little children. "Because you'll need good grades if you want to go on to university, you know..."

"Yes, I am good," the little boy replied. "I get almost all A's. But is hard at our school right now. There's a lot of drugs."

"You don't take them, do you?" I wanted to know, shocked. Having grown up in Western Europe in a sheltered, all-girls private boarding school, the concept of drugs and violence in high schools was still alien to me.

"No, I don't," he replied. "But there's a lot of pressure on us to take drugs, you know."

"Pressure by whom, Miguel?" I asked.

"There's some older kids who sell them," he explained. "And they sometimes beat you up when you don't buy from them. Same with the gangs. They have been wanting me to join a gang. So far I have said no, but it is becoming very difficult to hold out."

"And the teachers?" I asked. "Can't you go to the teachers for help?"

"They are scared, too," Miguel explained.

Not knowing what else to say, I replied lamely: "Well, you just keep in mind that drugs are for losers. Smart people don't need drugs. And gangs are for people who don't have any self-confidence. You have no need of either one or the other. Remember that."

"Yes, I know," Miguel replied gravely. In that instant, he had aged beyond his years. The little boy's eyes betrayed a deep weariness, which had no place in one so young.

The following instant, he became a little boy again, joining happily into the group of children and dogs who wrestled on the ground, laughing and shrieking. I could not help wondering how much of a chance Miguel stood to reach his goals. Would he be able to hold out against the gangs, and the drug pushers? Would his hopeful young life one day end in prison or, worse still, somewhere in an alley from a drug overdose? The time with Tiny and Mike might be the only childhood this young boy and his friends would ever get...

For several months, we drove to the little park almost every afternoon. Tiny and Mike delighted the children of the Barrio. It was lovely for them, but I knew that the situation could not last. I had never felt quite safe at the park, and I knew that no women went there alone. In addition, I realized that most other adults in the park seemed to be either gang members or drug pushers. Then came a segment on Houston's evening news, highlighting "our" park as one of the most dangerous gang territories of the city. The story ran complete with interviews of notorious gang members, whose faces I all recognized.

Clearly, it was time to re-think our park. There were serious considerations of personal safety, versus the joy I saw in the children's eyes when they played with Tiny and Mike. The children could move without problems in the gangs' turf, having grown up there. I wondered how long the little dogs and I would be able to continue doing so.

The question answered itself before long. As usual, we had spent a nice afternoon with the children. When the children had gone home, I took Tiny and Mike for a walk around the park, so they could complete their personal business in a more relaxed fashion. It was getting dark fast. The dreary Texas winter had arrived, without much warning, a few days earlier. A group of young men played soccer on a big field in the middle of the park, their women watching from the sidelines. I felt fairly safe, considering that it was not yet dark.

We passed a group of men who were stood under a tree, talking among themselves. One of them came up to us and, squatting down to pet Mike, he remarked: "That's a very nice dog you have there."

"Thank you," I replied my standard response, used to such compliments. The other young men drew near. As one of them tried to pat Tiny, Tiny snarled. I explained. The man backed off.

"Can I have your dog?" the fat young man who had first come over to us asked.

"No, of course not," I replied.

"Why not?"

"Because he is my dog."

"I want him."

"Well, sorry you can't have him. You are going to have to get your own dog."

"But I want this one."

"Sorry." I shrugged genuine regret. "We have to get going now."

"What if I just take your dog?" the young man insisted with a dangerous undertone in his voice.

"That would not be very nice."

"I am not very nice," he replied. "They call me mad dog."

The others looked at him admiringly as he kept trying to corner me and I kept trying to get on my way.

While I kept explaining why he could not have Mike, I somehow managed to keep walking backwards, toward the car. Still talking, I inserted the key into the door to unlock it behind my back, while giving the impression that I was casually leaning against the car.

"Frankly, lady, I am beginning to run out of patience," the fat boy said.

"What a coincidence, me too," I grinned at him. "I think we better get going."

Before they knew what was happening, I had opened the car door, shoved Tiny and Mike inside and driven off.

The incident left me quite shaken. For the first time, I realized how vulnerable we were in the park. There was nothing to stop this young man, or anyone else, to grab Mike and walk off with him. How was I going to defend myself against a 200 plus pound guy and his six buddies? I resolved to put my safety and that of the dogs first.

Change number 1 to come out of this incident was that I resolved to take up something Chuck Norris had suggested to me earlier in the year, when we had spent a few weeks together on the movie set of Sidekicks: I would take up karate. I dug out a phone number Norris had left me with of a Houston based instructor-friend of his and made appointments for private lessons.

Change number 2: I would be more careful and not take the dogs for a walk in the park after the children had gone home.

All went well for a week or so. If only it could have become a permanent condition, but this was not to be. I pulled up one overcast afternoon to find the children, parked in my usual spot. As always, my car stuck out like a sore thumb, with its Quebec license plate and white female driver. A man in an imposing red Ram Charger noticed us. As I drove into my usual parking space, he pulled in behind me, parallel-parking his car along the curb immediately after mine.

The children were nowhere to be seen. I got out of my car. He did the same. The soccer players were on the field again, with their women. I sighed with relief. The man sat down on the hood of his truck, legs dangling, arms folded before him. He was looking at me, not kindly, but in a very menacing fashion.

I took the dogs and walked away, accompanied by the man's cold stare. His eyes followed me as I walked around the park. He would not move. Just sat and stared. Besides the soccer players, nobody was around. My heart began to thump. I became very scared.

There had been a series of serious incidents in Houston recently, and it was making its way up the top ten chart of America's most dangerous cities. Women had been followed in their cars in broad daylight, thumped off the road, raped, murdered, and their dead bodies dumped in a ditch. In fact, one body had been found not too far from where I was living. A few days earlier, a woman sheriff, who had been carrying her gun, had been abducted from Greenspoint mall (where Mike came from) as she was loading groceries into her car. Her body had been found the night before, badly battered and bearing traces of brutal sexual assault. This had happened in the "good" neighborhoods.

I was wondering whether the menacing young man who sat on the hood of his car and kept staring at me was indicative of the fact that I was in the process of living my final hours and whether Tiny, Mike and myself were about to become part of the ever-rising crime statistics of Houston. Perhaps we were soon to be taken up by Pamela what's-her-name in one of her causes:

"...and now they murdered that poor, Canadian journalist, and her innocent dogs (blend in for a close-up photograph of Tiny and Mike, both grinning into the camera). I say: no parole for Hispanics! I say: bring back the chain gangs. I say: let's take away their televisions and make them bust rocks!"

To the cheer of a right wing crowd, waving large photographs of Tiny, Mike and myself on sticks, Pamela would endorse yet another hang-them-high politician, who would yet again make the prison system a little tougher, ensuring that rehabilitation became a concept of the past, ensuring an even higher rise in the very crime she claimed to fight against.

The image of Pamela and the politician, using the cute faces of the dogs in their campaign did it: my survival instinct took over. They would not have the little dogs as their campaign mascots, nor would they get themselves the tragic story of young Canadian journalist murdered by Latino thugs to further increase racism against Hispanics.

I walked up to a very large black woman who sat by the soccer field, watching the game. "Excuse me, I wonder if you can help me," I began. She looked at me in surprise. From Houston's racial wars, she was used to white people being scared of black people whenever they were on black people's turf. To me, lucky enough not to have grown up there, people were still people: green, yellow, white or black.

"Yes what can I help you with?" she asked.

"Listen, there is this guy over there...," I began and explained the whole story, leaving out the part about Pamela, but ending with the words "I don't want to become a Houston crime statistic. Will you help me?"

She grinned. "You are not very street smart, are you?" she asked. "Those guys sense the fear. They home in on it. Let me walk with you, we'll walk right by him, and I'll tell you whether he's really dangerous or not."

She walked with me and the dogs, whom I dutifully introduced to her and whom she instantly became smitten with. As we turned the corner, I pointed him out to her.

"Girl, you got yourself a problem," she remarked, deliciously drawing out the "girl" and "problem" part. "He's got his eyes on you. He's gonna get you."

"Do you know him?" I asked, heart thumping even faster.

"Not personally, but I know of him," she replied. "He is bad news, that one is."

"Is there anything I can do?" I asked, now truly frightened.

"Not really, considering that he sitting on his hood there, behind your car. If you leave, he'll follow you and run you off the road. If you stay, he'd be waiting until we all gone, then he gonna come and get you."

"You have to help me," I implored.

"Not much I can do," the girl said. "He be wanting you. He gonna be gettin' you. But if you be lucky, he be lettin' you live. Sometimes he lettin 'em live."

My brain was working overtime, desperately trying to find a solution. To my utter horror, the soccer game had just finished. I watched as the players went to the side of the field, grabbing their towels, chatting.

"Well, I'll be seeing you," the girl said. "The game is over, I have to go with my husband, good luck."

She began to walk to the middle of the field. Life had

become very cheap in Houston. If you got killed, you got killed. So what? Those who were not in danger shrugged and walked on by. Not this time they wouldn't.

I ran after her, finally having worked out what to do.

"Listen, can I borrow your husband for a minute?" I asked her.

She looked at me as if I had lost all reason. When I explained that I wanted to drive off with her husband and then let him out on the other side of the park, she laughed and said, "You are a smart girl." She agreed. We went to her husband. The husband was a large, black man who looked like a bodybuilder, with the weary look of a street-smart gang member on his face. He was very kind and allowed me to "borrow" him.

A few seconds later, I hugged the girl good-bye, planting a grateful kiss on her cheek. The husband and I walked to the car together, talking. The look on my potential rapist/killer's face read "what the...?" as he watched the man get into my car, behind the wheel. He watched with folded arms, his menace now giving way to a mixture of respect (I could only assume that they were rival gang members) and surprise as the little dogs and I got into the passenger side and the four of us drove off. He did not dare follow. He just sat and stared, with his jaw wide open.

On the other side of the park, I pulled over.

"He can't see us from here. Drive out of here fast, because once he sees me going back to the park, he'll realize he's been tricked. If you want my advice, don't be comin' back here. He's got you marked, if he finds you again, he'll be goin' after you, next time he may be shootin'. This is no place for a white woman to be anyway. What have you been doin' here in the first place, anyway?"

I explained about Tiny, Mike and the children. He was appreciative of what we had been trying to do, but added "sometimes you have to think of your own safety first."

I thanked him, shook his hand and watched him walk away. Just another one of our many guardian angels sent to rescue us in Texas! They must be working overtime, I mused, to get Tiny, Mike and myself out of the situations we kept getting into. I drove off, shaken but glad to be alive, and never went back to the park.

From time to time, the three of us still wonder what became of Miguel, Carmen and the other little children. We wonder how long they waited for us before they gave up, and whether they would understand.

To this day, I carry an image of little Miguel buried deep inside my heart. The image: Miguel and his sisters walking over to pat Tiny. Tiny growling. Miguel asking: "what's with the dog?" Me explaining: "he wants to be human" and listing the many ways in which he is: he makes his own choices about color of dog biscuits, he understands every word, he sleeps under the covers, he watches television, he goes to the movies, he walks off by himself trying to give the impression that he is just another human taking an afternoon stroll...

I recall that list getting ever larger, as Miguel listens with interest. I recall him sitting down on the ground to address Tiny like a person: "would it be all right if I pat you?" Tiny rewarding him with a tail wag and grin, but snarling and putting him into his place when the little boy pets him without having been given permission by the royal dog.

Miguel, to me: "You have to tell Tiny (being aware that Tiny requires a translator, speaking only German) that his human impersonation act works quite well, except for one thing that shows him up to be a dog. One thing he still has to work at."

"What's that?"

"Humans don't bite when they get angry."

Chapter 20

Willie Nelson, His Drummer's Dog, Mike, Tiny, The POW And Operation Desert Storm

I had been in Texas for a little over two years when I was sent to interview country and western star Willie Nelson. I had arranged the interview through the manager of a big country and western venue where Nelson was to perform. "10 minutes is all I can get you," the man informed me, "and you can be glad you are getting that."

Before the show, Nelson and I met in the manager's office, with a photographer by my side. "What a shame we will only get to talk for 10 minutes," I began. "I would have liked to have done a really nice in-depth interview with you."

"Who says you couldn't?" Nelson wanted to know.

"Well, your manager said I could only have 10 minutes," I replied.

"I am still the one who calls the shots," Nelson said. "How long do you need?"

"An hour?"

"Done. Come to my hotel tomorrow morning at 10, and we can have an hour or however long you might need."

We used the ten minutes we had been allocated before the show to allow my photographer to take some pictures of both of us. I then watched Nelson perform and got to know his ground crew.

The next day, Nelson and I conducted part of the interview, but did not quite finish. He invited me to Austin some two weeks later, where he was involved in a country and western benefit concert, featuring himself and several big country stars.

"If you come there, we can complete the interview and I can introduce you to some of the other singers you will need for your series on country singers," Nelson offered.

A few weeks later, I sat in Nelson's RV van in Austin, finishing the interview while being interrupted by knocks of fans on the doors, all of which Nelson patiently accommodated by signing autographs between answering the questions I asked him.

When the interview was finished, Nelson, ever so proud of his home state, asked me how I liked Texas.

"Frankly, I hate it," I replied truthfully.

The singer, shocked, wanted to know why. "Well, for one because I am working on a death penalty case and nobody is interested that the guy might be innocent. They are going to kill him anyway, no matter the evidence. Secondly, because I have just done a story on police brutality, and you wouldn't believe the kind of stuff I found out. Thirdly, because there is a lot of racism here. I just can't relate to these people. I can't wait until I leave again."

Nelson responded by asking me to send him a summary of the case of James Briddle, a copy of my story on police brutality and by saying "if you would like to meet some nice people, why don't you come up to our place on weekends and holidays? We have plenty of space, and you'd be very welcome to stay overnight. I am determined to prove to you that Texans are not all bad."

"I have dogs" I mentioned, knowing from experience that this usually terminated any such invitation. One lawyer I had to interview in San Antonio even made the dogs sleep outside in my car while I stayed at his house overnight, having talked with him well past 11pm.

To my surprise, Nelson did not mind at all.

"That's just fine," he replied. "We love dogs, we have some ourselves, just bring them along."

This was how Tiny and Mike, the following weekend, made their way up to Willie Nelson's ranch, along with me. It is located just a little outside Austin, the state capitol of Texas. Nelson owns a wonderfully secluded acreage, on which he built a few dozen houses, for himself and his then-girlfriend Annie, whom he has meanwhile married, and for his friends and band members. They all lived together on the same ranch, each in their own house.

I was delighted to discover that Willie's drummer also owned a Shihtzu, a beautiful sable male who took an instant liking to Mike. "Wouldn't it be wonderful if we could mate them?" I thought aloud as the drummer, Willie's business manager and several other people stood in Willie's kitchen and watched the two dogs romp over the grass outside.

Tiny, as usual, was being his "charming" self. He would grimace and growl when someone approached him and was nowhere near as big a hit as Mike, who immediately guilted Nelson, with his usual cute dance and a big dog grin, into picking up his guitar and singing for us.

We soon became regulars at Nelson's ranch, something like weekend lodgers. Tiny and Mike became known by name and sight by all of Nelson's entourage, as well as by the assorted rock stars who visited on occasion. We watched as Nelson screened his latest movie, fresh off the studio executive's table, the dogs with more or less of a passing interest. At Nelson's place, there was such a multifaceted assortment of characters that someone always felt like setting out in search of some hidden, comic truth.

A white-haired, kind man from Hawaii, for instance, who had become something like Nelson's spiritual advisor, explained to me that God lives inside of you and if you look closely enough, deep into your heart, you can see him there.

Interesting!

Despite being able to explain ever other mystery of the universe, he did not have an explanation as to the consistent refusal of the drummer's Shihtzu to mate with Mike. "Maybe she isn't in heat," he offered, but this theory defeated itself through the mere fact that we had been trying for more than 6 months, almost every weekend, and Mike came into heat once every six months.

It was one of Nelson's friends who finally came up with the most feasible answer: "Mike is obviously in love with Tiny. A platonic lover perhaps, but it does not leave room for anyone else."

Considering how the two of them stuck together, we all conceded that this was the most likely explanation and abandoned forever the since long cherished hope little Shihtzu puppies romping about the ranch and accompanying their daddy to autograph sessions with Willie.

Having given up on the Shihtzu mating scheme, Willie Nelson and I instead turned our efforts to a more important matter at hand. In the midst of the idyllic and peaceful time we spent discussing the wonders of the world and little dogs, the Gulf War, Operation Desert Storm, arrived.

I was reporting on it for a variety of overseas newspapers and magazines, keeping an eye on events as they unfolded. There were anti-war and pro-war demonstrations, yellow ribbons to be worn by those who supported the war, white ribbons by those who wanted peace. A questionable local literary agent arrived and ordered a book to be written about the war, vaguely and unrealistically promising huge sums of money if such a book were to be delivered on his desk within 10 working days. Still naive enough, at barely 24 years of age, I believed him and went to work.

Interviews followed with Jewish, Palestine, Moslem advocates, with White House politicians, with people representing Veterans for Peace. There was even a phone call to Camp David, where the President had gone on vacation, and a quick talk with the very nice FBI agent in charge of his protection, whom I had met at an earlier George Bush dinner and introduced to eating with chopsticks and the wonderfully exotic cuisine of authentic Vietnamese food. This time we talked not food but war, and he assured me that there was nothing to worry about and everything would be over swiftly and smoothly.

But this was not to be. There came the matter of various allied POWs who had been shot down by Iraq. They appeared on television, badly bruised and beaten, along with the threat of Iraq to use them as human shields. It got nasty. Living up to my reputation as the Mother T of journalism, it did not take long for me to become involved in their plight.

Enter one unfortunate British POW by the name of Jon Peters, who had a young wife named Helen and two very cute children. Poor Helen was only a few years older than I was. I tried to imagine her as a widow, and the smiling faces of her smeared with tears when told that their father's would never come home again.

For some reason, everyone seemed to think that Peters was the least likely of the captured POWs to survive, mostly due to the fact that he had been beaten worse than the others. Nobody could put their fingers on the exact reason why they thought he would never return home again, but almost every politician I spoke to agreed that he would not make it.

This I wanted to avoid. I called everyone involved with negotiating the release of the hostages and informed them that Peters was a personal friend of myself and of several other high-profile journalists, including those from CNN. This, I hoped, would ensure that he would not be overlooked if and when the release of the first batch of POWs was negotiated. I became known to a fair number of people at the State Department, who after a few weeks would greet me with the statement "No more news on Jon Peters today, Tess."

Things did not look too good. Rumors began to fly among the negotiators that Peters had been killed and his body had been dumped at a busy road in downtown Baghdad. I thought of Helen, the poor unknown young mother on the other side of the world, and I decided to fight to bring her husband home to her.

The following weekend, when Tiny, Mike and myself

were at Willie Nelson's place once more, we carefully worked out a strategy. While Mike sat on Willie's lap with a proprietorial look on his face, Tiny snored in a corner and I told Willie Nelson the story of Helen and the two children in England.

"We have to do something," I urged him. "We can't just let the poor man die. I already have a promise from the State Department's Secretary, to I don't know whom, that they will put him on the list first when the names of people to be released are negotiated, but how can we make sure he stays alive until then?"

I honestly do not remember who came up with the bizarre idea, whether it was Willie, myself or either of the two dogs, but the latter is probably most likely. We reasoned that Willie was known all over the world, hence also in Iraq. There had to be Willie Nelson fans in the Iraqi army. Hence, if we made out that Peters was a personal friend of Willie, and if we sent him a letter handwritten by Willie, if this letter got through to him, and was read by those who guarded him and if maybe the ones who did happened to be Willie Nelson fans, this might ensure good treatment for the poor man.

Thought out, discussed, done. Willie Nelson and I sent a letter to Jon Peters care of Royal Air Force in London. As an afterthought, we added a photograph of Tiny and Mike in their Christmas tree dresses, in case the Iraqis needed a laugh, but mainly because we thought it might cheer the hapless young pilot up to see a photo of two little dogs in Christmas garb as bombs were dropping to the right and left of him.

A week or so later, I met a self-important senator who knew everything, and his aide, who knew everything, too. We were at some press luncheon. The aide said to me, regarding Peters: "Hey, we got this bulletin in that one of the POWs has been killed. They did not name names, but we are certain it is Peters. Just to let you know."

Having complete faith in the scheme that Willie Nelson and I had come up with, and "knowing" that whoever had been ordered to shoot Peters would have found the letter, happened to know English and also happened to not only know of Willie Nelson but be a big fan of his, I announced to the senator's aide: "Well you just tell the senator and everyone in Washington that they are wrong. Peters is alive, and he will be released soon."

"Oh yeah?" she asked in her broad Texas drawl. "I assume it takes a Canadian to come down here and tell us about our politics. Maybe you know something we don't then?"

"I certainly do," I boasted, but when she pressed me for details, I did not wish to elaborate on the fact that my faith was based precisely on two things: Willie Nelson's fame in Iraq, and a photo of a Pekingese and a Shihtzu with ridiculous bow-ties on their heads.

Jon Peters was indeed released some days later, with the first batch of the POW exchange. I watched the happy event gloatingly in the wee hours of the morning on some national TV show, and then I called Nelson to share the good news with him. Hanging up the phone, I hugged the dogs, gave them an extra cookie and called a Democratic State representative who had been a Peters-believer all along to take him for breakfast.

Having returned after a sinful breakfast at Houston's French Bakery extraordinaire, I realized that the next task at hand was a rather difficult one. There was the matter of a somewhat embarrassing letter that had to be written as soon as possible:

"Dear Jon Peters, you are probably wondering why you are at this time in possession of a letter by Willie Nelson and several international journalists, all of them claiming to be your personal friends. You will perhaps wonder even more about the photograph of two charming little dogs dressed up in most absurd Christmas dress. Perhaps I ought to explain. You see, the little dogs are mine..."

PART 4

BACK TO CANADA

Chapter 21

We Turn Our Backs On Texas

Enough was enough. After four years of withstanding oppressive heat in summer and terrible floods in winter, of having fun made of Tiny's nose or lack thereof, of being verbally abused as a "bleeding heart liberal shit-ass Canadian do-good journalist," of being harassed by prison officials on Texas death row and putting our lives in jeopardy on the unsafe streets of Houston, we decided to abandon the idea of saving the life of our death row inmate. It was very obvious that the Texas courts were going to break the law anyway, and there was nobody who could stop them. Even the lawyer, who had been initially enthusiastic due to the new evidence we had found, increasingly lost hope in a system that elects its judges and is heavily dictated by political interest.

The decision was taken during a reporting trip to Latin America. Seated in a sauna-like press center down there, and trying to whip out an article for the San Antonio Express Newspaper at short notice, I made two significant decisions. One, I was going to give up journalism until further notice. This was easy enough. I sent a fax to my editor at the newspaper and explained that I had given the story to someone else, and subsequently recruited a wire service journalist to do the work for me.

Two, I was not going back to that hellhole of Houston. From Latin America, I called Phil in Canada and asked him to meet me at the airport in Houston. "I've had enough, I'm getting out of there," I informed my happy husband.

Two weeks later, the flight from Latin America touched down in Houston for what would be my very last arrival there. I was so happy to get out of there that I hugged the immigration official upon arrival, for once not being sad to get to Houston because I knew it would be a last time.

"You had a rough time down in Latin America, haven't you?" she asked, grinning, not used to such emotional a hello from the passengers.

"Sure did," I told her. "It feels good to be in a civilized country again."

It felt even better to tell her that I was only going to stay for three days, "on my way home to Canada."

But with every good-bye also come some regrets. There is always someone you grow attached to, no matter how distasteful the place might have been. We had met some kind people in Houston, and had become regular faces at certain restaurants about town.

There was, for instance, the little Italian Cafe on Kirby Street, just behind Myako's Japanese Restaurant, which always served ice-cream to Tiny and Mike in a little dish and informed all its waiters to serve the little dogs a bowl of water the moment we sat down, so Tiny and Mike could have a drink while they decided on the day's ice-cream flavor to pick.

There was our nice mechanic friend Hoss, who had for several years loyally looked after whatever car we transported ourselves in, had offered to baby-sit Tiny and Mike when I was away during long working days and had let us stay at his apartment during a story on fire-fighters because he lived close to the station I was riding from. This spared the dogs and myself the long drive home after our shift ended well after Midnight. Hoss was usually also the person who drove me to the airport when I had to fly to interviews in various parts of the world and delivered Tiny and Mike to Debbie's house after that.

"You should see the look on their faces when you are gone," he once remarked to me. "It's as if someone has died. They are so depressed. I say, "Guys, cheer up," but they won't have any of it. Once I get them to Debbie, they are okay again."

There was the supervisor of the fire fighters, a certain

244

Melville Wallace. He had boasted, when I first starting riding with him: "I don't stop for a dog in the road when I am racing at 100 miles an hour to an emergency. I can't, it would put me in danger, and it's not worth the risk for a stupid dog," and had looked at me with amazement when I explained to him "But you have to. Dogs are little people with fur on them." With great interest, he had listened as I told him about Tiny and Mike. Bonding happens quickly when you are on the road 12 hours a day, cruising the streets, waiting for an emergency. He took me by his old high school and told me recollections of his past as a Paramedic Supervisor on the emergency team.

Then came the inevitable time of all new friendships, when family photos were whipped out of wallets. His family: a lovely wife, two beautiful children. He smiled proudly as I commented what a nice family he had. Then I showed him my family: Phil, Tiny and Mike. The tough guy Paramedic smiled. Only days before he had scraped a zoo-keepers remains out of the lion cage without batting an eye and I was to observe him wiping someone's brains from his shoes with a piece of kitchen roll as he remarked wryly "that's life."

A few hours after we had exchanged our family photographs, it was night and slippery, we were on the way to the shoot-out which was to result in the brains on his shoes. Wallace pleasantly surprised me with his reaction to the following scene:

We: in the car. Very fast. 11pm. No other car on the road. A curve. Bushes on the side of the road. A little dog. Darting out in front of us.

Me: covering my eyes. The tough guy had warned me that afternoon: if you ride with me, don't be sissy. I don't stop for them.

Me: opening my eyes as the car did a sidewards slide at lightening speed because the tough guy had slammed on his breaks and grabbed the wheel firmly with both hands, carefully maneuvering to avoid hitting the dog.

Me: beaming. "You saved the dog. My hero!"

He: embarrassed the next night because I told everyone in the station.

He: losing his tough guy image forever.

He: instructing everyone else in his team to brake for dogs whenever possible. Reformed by the photo of Tiny and Mike? Who knows, but what a great guy...

There was, last but not least, our death row inmate, on whose case I had worked for so long. For one last time, I drove up to the hated prison in Huntsville and subjected myself to their harassment. Good-byes were due to some nice prison guards who I had gotten to know over the years: the man at the gate who, when he was at shift, would always go out of his way to minimize inconveniences to visitors. The young man who worked inside death row but was a Christian and worked in this job only because he had no other means of supporting himself. He always tried to give an extra ten minutes of visiting time and would constantly seek ways to show kindness to the dejected men on death row. He also took a keen interest in Tiny and Mike and often went to our inmate's cell to admire each new batch of photos I sent to him.

Our inmate, who had long since resigned himself to the fact that he was going to die, had only one concern: "You are going to keep sending us photos of the two little dogs, aren't you?"

"Yes," I nodded. "I promise that I will."

On the way back from Huntsville we stopped by Debbie's house, where Tiny and Mike had been given a final, complimentary bath and grooming session.

"Are you going to come back and visit?" she asked.

"Don't think so," I replied. "You will have to come and visit us."

"I will miss those two so much," she said. "After five years with them, I almost feel like they are my dogs." She hugged them both for the last time, and wiped a tear from her eyes as she went into her pantry and gave me a box of dog cookies for them.

All good-byes said and done, we loaded up the car and set out for the long drive home. Because it was the height of Texas summer, we drove nights and slept days to avoid the heat. As usual, we relied on Mike to charm assorted motel attendants into letting us stay, even when the sign at reception said Pets not allowed. Mike did not fail us...

Finally home in Canada, we took three months off, recovering from our turbulent adventures in Texas. We went for long walks around Park Mont Royal and Ile Ste Helene. I briefly considered a career change, into a world without corrupt judges or violent policemen.

I explored the option of studying biology with the head of department at Concordia University. He prophesied a 10 year study program, "Full-time, and you won't be able to do any other work, because you'll have your hands full with studying."

I tried to visualize Tiny, Mike and myself starving, all of us living on Phil's salary as I studied day and night and finally hit the job market at age 40 to become a field biologist, competing against much younger graduates. No!

Phil and I drove to Connecticut to visit the world's most famous field biologist, George Schaller. "I want to quit journalism.

"Can I work with you?" I asked him.

"What exactly would you do?" he, ever the practical German, asked. "You are not qualified."

"Cook coffee?" I offered hopefully.

"I can take a graduate student for doing that," he replied, but then offered "If you want to do a book on an expedition, come with me as a journalist, that's a different matter."

While I was contemplating what to do next, Christmas had come up. As always, we had a Christmas tree and presents underneath it to be unwrapped. As always, the dogs thoroughly enjoyed the ceremony, and both participated actively in the unwrapping of presents, sticking their noses enthusiastically into the wrapping paper as I unwrapped the presents that bore my name. Mike chewed a corner into a package that had his name on it and contained dog biscuits. He skillfully extracted a biscuit before we had assisted him with the unwrapping of it.

The next day, as always, we had a German Christmas goose and dumplings and red cabbage to go with it. Because Phil and I have no family in Canada and all our friends have their own families, we always celebrate Christmas alone with the animals. Hence, the goose usually lasts until the New Year.

On the 31st, we were still eating goose, and - to finish it off, I offered Tiny and Mike a piece each. What a silly idea. Within 10 minutes, Tiny began to show signs of bloat. At 10:30pm, we were sitting comfortably by the log fire, drinking a cup of hot chocolate before us. Outside raged a wicked snowstorm. This was, after all, Canada.

"We are going to have to drive Tiny to the vet," I announced to Phil. "Sorry about that, but I fed him a piece of goose and it looks like he is bloated again."

Sighing, Phil put on his coat. We wrapped Tiny into several blankets and made our way into the biting cold outside. The temperature change almost knocked us over. It was -20 degrees Celsius, with a wind chill factor of -40, and the wind was blowing hard.

The vet was 35 minutes drive away, and the car took at least 10 of these 35 to warm up. It was the worst possible situation in which to take a whimpering dog to an emergency veterinary clinic. We spent New Year's eve in the waiting room, watching several other dogs be treated for emergencies ranging from being hit by a car to having fallen out of a window. It was our turn shortly after midnight. We watched Tiny be taken away to X-ray, and were relieved to be told 10 minutes later that once again, we had been lucky: his stomach had not twisted, but they wanted to keep him overnight for observation and an IV drip.

We got back home at 1:30 am in the morning, realizing as we walked through the door that the New Year had arrived and that it was now the first of January 1996. "Happy New Year" I said wryly to Phil. "Yes, you too," he replied, frozen to the bone and so tired that he dropped into bed and fell asleep within 5 minutes.

January 2nd we were allowed to pick up Tiny from the clinic. We were presented with a bill for: emergency attention, extra charge for it being New Year's eve, two nights supervised stay at the clinic, X-rays, IV drip, emergency consultation. It came to 565 dollars. Not a bad start to the New Year...

If this wasn't an indication that 1996 was going to be another adventurous year for the little dogs, a call that I received some ten days later from Germany certainly was. A literary agent in Munich had split from his well-known agency and was opening his own firm. Already, he had several book-projects lined up with the big publishers. He had heard that I was looking for a break from journalism. Would I be interested to come on board as US representative, in charge of translation rights and as a staff writer for the US and Canada?

This was how Tiny, Mike and myself came to meet Ian Stephens and walked into the heart-breaking world of Aids....

Chapter 22

Ian And Nini
Or: The Aids Guy, His Pekingese,
My Pekingese And The Good Shihtzu

Ian Stephens was a prominent Montreal writer who had contracted the HIV virus. Having written a best-selling book about his fight against the virus, the former journalist had become and instant celebrity. His photo and profile featured on the cover pages of the Montreal's largest newspaper, as well as on a number of weeklies. He became known as the "Aids guy," after the title of one of his poems.

When his HIV processed to full-blown Aids and he was facing his last summer, he wanted to document his death. He needed a journalist to work with him, and the literary agent thought I ought to apply for the job.

Our preliminary phone conversations were strained. Stephens was a reserved man and not very good at small talk. I wondered how I would ever get him to open up enough to write a book, in case that we would come to work together.

But I need not to have worried. Very soon, it turned out that this was not a pure writing matter, it was primarily a Pekingese matter.

Prior to our first meeting, I had bought a copy of his book and had read it several times. I also studied the dedications in the front of the book. Aside from writers and editors, his family and his boyfriend, it contained a special thank you to someone named Nini. Who might that be? His sister? His girlfriend? A close friend? Another writer? Having identified everyone but Nini in the dedication section, she remained a mystery to me.

A few days later, I drove to his house for an introductory meeting and lunch. When I rang the doorbell, I was still rehearsing what I would say to this talented but difficult writer, and how I might break the ice. Slowly, the door was opened and in the doorframe appeared ... a Pekingese! The Pekingese walked past me, out into the front yard, stood there, and smiled a typical, wide Pekingese smile.

"Well, hello there," I greeted the Pekingese and bend down to pat it just as Stephens, its owner, appeared in the doorway.

"I have one of those, too," I introduced myself, grinning.

"You have a Pekingese?" he asked, incredulously. I could understand his surprise. These days, Pekingese owners are a rare breed, and this has become usual way how one Pekingese owner reacts to another upon first meeting them, the "what-you-too?" syndrome...

"This is Nini," he explained, pointing to the Pekingese. Ah, the mysterious Nini!

"Nini from your book?" I asked.

"Yes," he replied, and added, "I see you read the dedications. Not many people do..."

One point for me! I had identified the Pekingese...

Waving any formal introductions, he asked "and what is the name of yours?"

"Excuse me, my what?" I asked.

"Your Pekingese."

"Tiny," I replied, glad to see that Stephens was a typical, besotted Pekingese owner. This would be easier than I had thought, much easier...

He asked me in immediately, already deeply involved in a conversation about Pekingeses ... He wanted to know everything about Tiny: how long I had had him, where he was from, how old he was. In turn, he filled me in about Nini.

Nini, I learned, was a lady of 11 years. Like Tiny, she was a travelling dog and had been all over Canada with Ian and his boyfriend Alex. We sat down on his sofa and ... just like two proud parents ... began to brag about our Pekingeses.

His Pekingese could stand on two legs. Yes, but mine could slide down windscreens of cars. His understood every word. Well, so did mine! Did he know that mine spoke German...?

Next came the scrap books, and I was treated to snapshots of Nini and Alex, Nini and Ian, Nini without Alex or Ian ... He, in turn, got to see the five photos of Tiny and Mike which I keep in my appointment diary, usually to show them to my interview partners when they whip out snapshots of their kids: Tiny and Mike on the beach in Texas. Tiny and Mike in Montreal's Ile St Helene. Tiny and Mike facial close-up...

"Who is that hairy thing in the picture with Tiny?" he wanted to know.

I told him the story of Mike. He laughed. He said he had never met a Shihtzu before, and could I bring him over when I came by next time, together with Tiny. I promised to do so. I bent down and tried to pat Nini. Nini looked at me with an expression that said..." And who are you? Urgh, get away from me," and then she ran to hide behind Ian's feet. Nini and I were not a success story....

" She'll get used to you in time," Ian said, trying to make me feel better. He was very wrong...

Ian and I went to lunch at a little Thai restaurant around the corner from his house. Between bites of lemon grass chicken and satay beef, I tried to talk about literary subjects.

"So, where did you study"? I began.

"I got my Masters in Creative Writing from Concordia," he said and, in the same breath "You know, I always thought that Pekingeses were more special than other dogs. Have you grown up with them? I have, my family always had Pekingeses..."

We exchanged stories of Pekingeses long past and gone. Business could wait...

"We had this little black Pekingese when growing up," he said. "We have a country house and a road runs through it.

Once a day, a school bus comes down that road. The rest of the time, nobody uses it. The dog liked to go to the lake to swim, so he would cross the road. And one day, he did so just as the school bus came by and..."

"Got run over?" I asked.

"Yes," Ian replied. "Real sad."

"Absolutely, a Pekingese death is like a death in the family. Let me tell you about the ones we had..."

It was clear that Ian Stephens and myself spoke the same language. Unlike others, he listened not with the patience of a martyr, but with real interest as I told him about Snoopy, Ganti, Drecki and Herbert ... all our Pekingeses of days gone by. He eagerly listened as I told him how they lived and died.

The waitress came and politely reminded us that we had been here for 3 hours and they were closing the restaurant. I got up. He got up. Still talking about Pekingeses, we walked to the register and paid. We left the restaurant, still talking. He walked me to my car, 10 blocks away. All the way there, we were talking. About Pekingeses. And books. Books about Pekingeses.

"I always wanted to write a book of short stories about Pekingeses," he said. "I think I may start to do it this summer."

"Great," I told him. "Can Tiny be in it?"

"Sure," he promised. "Listen, I have a great Pekingese book, if you want to borrow it. Gives you the history of the breed, and has photos of the world's most famous Pekingeses."

"I would love to, thank you. Next time when I come by, if that is okay?"

We had now reached my car.

"Sure, when can you come back?"

" Next week?" I asked. He said that would be fine.

Just as I was about to drive off, I remembered something.

"Ian?" I shouted after him, as he had already started to

walk away. He turned.

"Hey, about that writing business?"

"Oh yes," he laughed and came back. "I had totally forgotten."

"Me too," I grinned. "Do you realize that we met at noon. It is now 3:45. We spent almost 4 hours talking about Pekingeses."

"Simple: you can do the book. I'm sure you'll be a good writer."

"Are you sure?" I asked, amazed how easy this was.

"Of course, us Pekingese owners have to stick together," he grinned. "Not too many of us about these days..."

Chapter 23

Ian's Last Summer With The Dogs

It was not long before Ian and Alex became good friends with Mike and myself. Unfortunately, the same could not be said for Tiny and Nini, or Tiny and Ian.

Nini kept giving me the cold treatment, and Tiny growled at Ian whenever he came near him. Unless, of course, Ian had a cookie. As Ian kept a good supply of dog biscuits in his kitchen, he succeeded several times to bribe Tiny into giving him one of his prized mmm-nas, or: dog kisses on the nose. Mike would dispense his kisses freely, with or without biscuits. Ian and Mike bonded quickly, as did Alex and Mike. Nini wanted nothing to do with either Tiny, or Mike, or me.

Unless, of course, I had a cookie. In which case Nini would come up to me, wag her tail, and then sit up prettily, pretending that she loved me deeply. Usually, she would also smile. I, proud to have my presence acknowledged by Nini at last, would happily give her the cookie. Nini would thereafter take off into Ian's bedroom, with the cookie, and proceed to ignore me. Her expression would return to a superior one, reading something like: a fool and his cookie are soon parted...

Tiny and Mike soon became part of Ian's regular cheer-up routine. Because his boyfriend worked during the day, Ian often spent his afternoons alone. Tiny, Mike and myself decided on an impromptu program of "pet therapy." We went to visit the terminally ill writer almost every afternoon, to take him to the park or to sit and have a quiet cup of coffee with him in his back yard.

The more Tiny acted in an aloof manner, the harder Mike tried to prove to Ian that he, at least, was a good dog. Mike was always friendly, attentive and kind to Ian, and became known as the good Shihtzu.

We, that is Tiny, Mike and myself, would drive the 30 odd miles to Ian's house four to five times a week, have a cup of tea with him and Nini and take them to the park. Typically, Tiny and Mike put on their famous wrestling show for Ian's benefit, helping him to forget the problems that came with his disease for a few precious hours.

One sunny afternoon, we decided to have lunch at Montreal's Mont Royal Park. We loaded Nini, Tiny and Mike into my car and drove to a sandwich store to pick up lunch for ourselves. Unfortunately for us, we ignored Mike's urgent pleas to buy lunch for the dogs, too. We should not have done that, but little did we know what would happen...

Park Mont Royal is set on the beautiful Mont Royal Plateau, overlooking the city of Montreal. Lush hills, wonderful hiking paths and giant oak trees make it a perfect place of peace and repose.

As the city provides picnic tables and chairs and in summer, many people come there to have lunch in the shade of the oak trees.

Ian and I parked the car, got the dogs untangled and proceeded to one of the picnic tables. We were followed by Mike and Nini. Tiny, as he often does, stopped, wagged his tail in a demanding fashion and stuck his tongue out in a typical Pekingese smile. It meant" "carry me, please."

I had no choice but to leave our food, Ian and the other two dogs at the picnic table and go back to fetch Tiny. When walking past an oak tree not far from out table, on the way to getting Tiny, I noticed a group of Indians sitting in its shade, on the grass. In their midst was a pizza, of which they were cutting off slices with a pocket knife to share out amongst their group.

I picked up Tiny. As I walked back, I heard Ian's screaming "Mike, noooo..." and witnessed Mike as he ran over to the group of Indians, wagging his tail. The Indians were nice about Mike, and one of them reached to pat him.

Mike acknowledged the Indian briefly. Then, to my utter horror, he jumped straight into the circle, grabbed the pizza and ran off.

I ran to the table, put Tiny down and then - profusely apologizing to the Indians - ran after Mike, trying to retrieve the pizza. Mike kept running away from me, gulping down the pizza as he ran, so he would not have to give it back.

By the time he allowed me to catch up to him, the pizza was gone. Ian Stephens, though an aggressive performer, was a shy man in his private life. I could just about see from the expression of his face that he wished the earth would open up to swallow him. He was not happy at all with this kind of attention being lavished on our small group, thanks to Mike.

I walked over to the Indians. "Listen, I am real sorry about my dog," I began. "He has two stomachs and no brain."

They laughed and assured me that it was no problem at all. By that time, Mike had finished the pizza and had found out that he could not score additional food from Ian, as the writer had finished his sandwich. Mike came running over to the Indians and me.

"He really is a nice dog..." I assured the Indians and bent down to Mike to introduce him more formally. I could not believe it when Mike ran straight past me and jumped into the circle again to retrieve the last piece of pizza...

Thankfully, Mike can be very charming when need be and the Indians forgave, probably last but not least due to the fact that Mike put on his starving Ethiopian look, which I am sure he has been practicing for a long time secretly at night, while I am sound asleep. The Ethiopian look is good enough to convince anyone that this sweet, innocent dog is on the verge of starvation and in urgent need of food...

Through the summer, Ian and Alex saw a lot of Tiny and

Mike. While I was working at the Formula 1 Grand Prix, they babysat Tiny and Mike for me. I would drop the dogs off on the way to the track and then pick them up after work.

The first day I went to the race track, I was unsure whether I would get a VIP parking pass to park my car on the track itself. I was sure that parking would be impossible at the general car parks. Thus I decided to leave my car at Ian's house after dropping the dogs there, and took the underground to the racetrack.

When I finished with my interviews at the Ferrari race team, one of the executives offered to give me a ride back to Ian's house.

"That's very nice of you," I said to him. "I have to go and pick up the kids."

"How many you got?" he wanted to know.

"Oh, they aren't really kids. They are two little dogs. That's them..." I said and handed over the famous photo from my business diary.

"Very nice dogs," he replied, "why don't you bring them to the track tomorrow."

But this was something I did not want to do after all. As glad as I was that Tiny and Mike had received an invitation to be VIPs at the Ferrari lounge at the racetrack, I was worried they would not like the noise of the cars roaring by.

Soon, I found out that Ian and Alex told everyone about their new canine friends. One day, I was to meet Ian at his family's country home in St Agathe, in the Laurentian mountains. When I arrived, a group of his friends were there, expecting me.

"Where are Tiny and Mike?" everyone asked with disappointed faces. "We heard so much about them, we wanted to meet them." Never mind about me... It was my dogs who were becoming the talk of the town.

Chapter 24

Nini, Tiny And The Aids Floor At Montreal General Hospital

When Ian's T-cells dropped to 4 at some stage in late autumn, we both knew that he might not survive the winter.

Nonetheless, I was a little surprised to return from a brief trip to the United States in November and find out that Ian had been admitted to hospital in my absence, suffering from severe Aids complications.

I had bought a Pekingese calendar and a Pekingese mug, which I had found after some long searching in the States in a specialty pet store. I had brought them back for myself, but now decided to give them to Ian instead. I put the calendar, the mug and some fruit into a bag and wrote a get-well card with it, which I signed with Tiny's name and to which I attached a photo of Tiny. Because my car was in the repair shop at the time, I asked a friend to drop the bag at the hospital for me and to tell Ian that I would come and visit within the next few days.

When I got my car back a few days later and was able to drive to the hospital, Ian was happy to see me. His private room was decorated with pictures from the Pekingese calendar. Right over his bed hung a photo of Nini, grinning on top of a mountain somewhere in Vancouver, a photo of Alex and Nini on the same mountain, and the photograph that I had sent him of Tiny.

"I will tell Tiny you have his photo on the wall," I said to Ian. "I am sure the Pekingese will be pleased."

"Can you bring him?" he asked. "I miss having a Pekingese around. You of all people will understand. I miss Nini. But Tiny would do for now..."

It was a typical case of Pekingese withdrawal syndrome!

"Okay, I'll see what I can do," I promised. "How does

tomorrow 3pm sound to you?"

"Fine" he said, and assured me that it would make a big difference to his speedy recovery. "After all, there is such a thing as pet therapy, right?" he grinned.

The following day, I did my best to explain to Mike why he had to stay at home and Tiny would accompany me. I am not sure how well it worked, because Mike sported a very hurt, poor done-by expression on his face when Tiny and I left the house together. But Mike is a boisterous, conspicuous dog and there was no way I could hope to smuggle him into anywhere without being caught.

I loaded Tiny, a big travelling bag and my long overcoat in the car and set off for the hospital. Just before we pulled into the hospital parking lot, I stopped the car and explained to Tiny, using his pet name "cake": "The cake is going to have to be very quiet now, because they do not allow cakes in the hospital and we are going to have to smuggle the cake in..."

Tiny listened attentively to every word, stuck out his tongue in a broad grin and wagged his tail.

"Is the dog a chocolate cake with Marzipan glazing, or a Marzipan cake with chocolate glazing?"

Tiny always got a kick out of choosing what kind of cake he wanted to be, and this time he wagged his tail at the latter.

"Okay, then, all chocolate cakes have to go inside this green bag now," I explained to Tiny, who understood perfectly as I stuffed him in the shoulder bag.

"Don't move now," I told the dog as I drove by the parking lot attendant, one hand on the bag with Tiny in it, my coat hung loosely over it.

I parked the car, waited until the parking lot attendant looked the other way, and scooped up the bag with Tiny in it. I had done the zipper up only partially, so Tiny could get some air. Just as we were about to walk past the parking lot attendant, Tiny's nose pushed through the hole, in an attempt to stick his head out. I squeezed Tiny's head back down into the bag, while smiling at the attendant, trying to distract him and struggling to keep the coat over the moving bag.

Tiny and I made it to the hospital front door, and we walked right in, me with my green shoulder bag, smiling guiltily at passers-by as I tried to keep the bag from moving. We passed hospital security. I held the bag in both hands, hoping they would not see it move. The elevator came. We went inside. The bag was over my shoulder. It moved. A guy looked at me, then at the bag. I grinned at him:

"Nice day today, isn't it?"

He grinned back. Tiny made a push for it and stuck his nose through the zipper to see what was happening, just as the elevator doors opened and a doctor walked in.

"Oops," I said and threw my coat over the black nose that came out of the zipper. I grinned at the doctor. "Hi"

"Hi" he said. He looked at my bag.

"Steiff?" he asked.

"Excuse me?" I replied, my hand on the bag working overtime under the coat, trying to push the little black Pekingese nose back inside.

"Couldn't help seeing that toy you have in your bag there." he explained. "Looks so life-like. Thought it must be Steiff, you know, that German firm. They make the best ones. I collect them myself..."

"What?" My brain had momentarily gone out of gear. I had been wondering what they would do when they discovered Tiny. Ban us from the hospital forever? Fine me? Suddenly I understood that this doctor either really didn't know, or he was giving me a way out...

"Ah yes, Steiff," I smiled at him. "I'm going to visit my daughter."

Thankfully, the doctor got out on the next floor, sparing me any embarrassing questions about my "daughter," or further conversation about Steiff animals. Not to mention what could have happened if he had asked to see my "toy animal."

That elevator ride turned into the longest of my life. Naturally, the AIDS floor would have to be at the very top. Tiny kept moving in the bag. People came in and out of the elevator, staring at the bag. I did my best to pretend that there was nothing wrong with the picture I presented: a young woman standing in a corner, with a moving green bag casually slung over her shoulder. Ian was on the 18th floor, and it seemed to take forever.

Finally, the doors opened on the 18th floor. Now it was just a matter of making it down the corridor to Ian's room. Tiny stuck his nose through the zipper once more just as we passed the nurse's desk. I quickened my steps and hastened past.

By the time I pushed open the door to Ian's room, I felt like I had run the gauntlet. Alex and Ian's mother were both there, visiting. I closed the door, walked up to the bed and deposited the bag next to Ian, beside the IV hose and the Oxygen machine.

"Here you go, someone's come to visit you," I said and let Tiny out of the bag.

"Oh my God, what a wonderful Pekingese he is," Ian's mother, a hobby Pekingese expert from England, exclaimed at the sight of my little grey terror. Tiny, who was clearly pleased to be the center of attention, held court with Ian and Alex. I answered the questions that Ian's mother bombarded me with: which breeder was he from? He looked like he had a champion pedigree, did he? Etc etc.

By the time I had finished giving Tiny's history, from the time he was a baby to the present day, Tiny had succeeded in taking over Ian's bed. Like he does at home, he had managed to spread across more than half the bed. Ian tried to move him to the side a little. Tiny growled "get away, this is my bed now."

I said: "Tiny, you're not supposed to growl at the patients you're coming to visit."

Tiny clearly had to learn some hospital bedside manners,

before he had a hope of becoming a proper pet therapy dog...

Just as I was prepared to pick him up and move him to the side, the nurse came in, without knocking. On reflex, Alex quickly threw my coat over Tiny.

The nurse stood in the doorway, talking about medical procedures. The coat moved. The nurse looked at the coat. Ian, Alex and I looked at each other. Ian looked back at the nurse and kept her talking. The coat kept moving. The nurse kept looking, from Ian to the coat and back again. Ian would not let her get one word in, outside the medical procedure she was discussing with him.

"I am very tired now, I think I am going to get some sleep," he told the nurse. The nurse looked at the coat once more, which I was trying to control with my hands. She then looked at Ian. "All right, then, I better leave you alone," she said and left, giving us all a look that clearly indicated she thought we were very weird.

As soon as she was gone, we all burst out laughing.

"That was a close call," Ian grinned. He fed Tiny a piece of cookie from his bedside table, for having been so "good," or probably for encouraging him to be better next time....

"I better get going, guys," I told them. "This nurse thinks we are mad. She is bound to send the doctor in here to check up on you," I said, addressing Ian.

When we said our good-byes, Ian told me: "I would like to see Nini. Could you coach Alex on how you got Tiny in here?"

Then, addressing Alex, he asked: "Do you think you could bring Nini tomorrow then?"

I left with Tiny stuffed into the bag once again, but only after Alex and I had made a date for a "smuggle-the-pekingese-into-hospital" coaching session....

When I next went to the hospital, I pushed the door to Ian's room open to be greeted by Nini who rushed straight past me, out into the corridor. Luckily, it was 11pm, and not many people were about. Flying by me, after Nini, came Alex. "Give me a hand" Alex said as he threw himself on the floor and on top of Nini. Together, Alex and me shoved Nini back into Ian's room, grinning and waving at a young doctor who walked past.

As Ian became sicker, all of us spent an increasing amount of time at the hospital, enough that the doctors and nurses at the Aids ward got to know us quite well. They had become used to weird occurrences surrounding Ian and his visitors, such as moving blankets, people crawling onto the corridor and waving, as well as an occasional growl coming out from behind Ian's closed door. They didn't know what we were up to, and I am sure they decided it might be better not to find out.

Ian was somewhat of a celebrity in Montreal, and known as a brilliant though eccentric artist. My guess is the staff at the hospital decided such odd occurrences were just about what could be expected from the city's most famous alternative writer. So what if, between giving private readings from his latest best-selling book for the duty nurse at 3 am and signing autographs for the doctors who had read about him, Ian had the occasional bark coming out of his room - he was an artist. When artists died, they did it differently, and their friends were...well...somewhat different too. So what if they enjoyed jumping out of the patient's door on the spur of the moment and crawling along the hospital floor, grinning and waving...

As Ian's disease progressed, towards death, I began to spend the nights at the hospital to document his final weeks. We often sat up all night, between shots of morphine, talking. Ian was only allowed a certain number of morphine shots through the night to keep from interfering with the other medications he needed to keep Aids related infectious diseases in check. When one morphine shot wore off and the next one was yet another 20 minutes away, Ian would often become argumentative with whoever was around. Usually, this was me.

One night, he had woken up as the morphine wore off, at 2:30 am. His next shot was due at 3:15. He couldn't go back to sleep.

"Can we go and sit out in the corridor, by the elevator?" he asked me.

"Sure," I replied. "No problem."

His room was at the very end of the corridor. To get to the elevator, beside which was a row of benches, we had to walk along the entire length of the hospital corridor. I helped him get up and steadied him as he walked along the wall, holding on to it with one hand, and to me with the other. The hospital corridor was spooky, and completely deserted this time of night. From behind one of the open doors came a moaning scream, a man's.

"I wonder what's wrong with him?" I remarked to Ian.

"He's lonely. He does not have any visitors," he explained. "He is dying and he is afraid. He often screams all night..."

We walked on, by other doors, all of them open. From the inside of them, I could hear the eerie beeping of the heart monitors, ventilating machines...

We passed the nurse's desk. The nurse briefly nodded at us as she talked into the phone. "Your sister has taken a turn for the worse," I overheard her say. "You'd better come tonight. We don't expect her to survive until morning."

If there was a hell on earth, I knew this was it, I contemplated as I walked further along the dark corridor between dangerously quiet rooms in which death seemed to reign, beside this writer whose body was being eaten by Aids and whose sole connection with me was that we both owned a Pekingese...

We finally reached the benches and sat down.

"Did you ever think," Ian began, "how badly brought up

your Pekingese is?"

"Excuse me?" I asked.

"Really, I mean, Tiny is such a brat. You know, if he were my dog, I would teach him manners. Your dog actually snaps at people..."

"Hey, come on, my dog spent 10 minutes in a hot, stuffy bag the other day, just to visit you."

"Yes, and then he took over my bed and growled when I tried to shift him," Ian reminded me. "You are such a bad mother, it is incredible..."

"Yes, and I suppose your dog is better?" I snapped. "May I remind you that your dog treats me like dirt."

"Well, she's shy," Ian defended his Nini.

"Bull," I spoke up. "Your dog is arrogant and socially disturbed, if you ask me..."

We spent the time until his next morphine shot, arguing about which Pekingese was worse mannered, mine or his. On the way back, we passed the lady whom the nurse had called, coming out of the room of her sister. She was crying. She had come too late....

Ian and I walked on by, still arguing about our "children."

The next day, I called him.

"Ian," I began, "do you ever realize how ridiculous we are? Do you know we spent almost 2 hours last night, arguing which Pekingese was better, mine or yours?"

Ian passed away on a sunny afternoon in March, three months after I had moved from Montreal. As soon as I heard, I went back to Montreal to visit Alex. The funeral had been only a few days earlier, and Alex was still visibly shaken. They had been together for 10 years.

"How did he die?" I asked.

"Peacefully," Alex told me. "We all gathered around, his closest family were are there. I had been to see him at the

268

hospital every day for the last month of his life, and Nini was always with me. Nini and I spent the nights with him at the hospital. In fact, Nini was there when he passed away. He smiled at her one last time, and then he was gone...."

Figures...

Chapter 25

... And Cat Makes Three

Tiny and Mike had both grown up with cats. At the horse farm, there were always at least three cats around the stables. Later, in Texas, there was the KittyKat.

After that, due to the unsettled life we lived there, the absence of a cat was not much noticed: we moved from place to place, often at short intervals of only a month or two. They were too busy with new smells and places to miss a cat.

But once we were in Montreal and no longer traveled as much, everything changed. The little dogs wandered around the house, somewhat lost. They were clearly looking for something. A cat lived across the street from us, and Mike kept gazing at it longingly. Mike had always been a big cat fan. Both dogs seemed somewhat depressed. Finally it dawned on me:

"Do you guys want a kittykat?" I asked. This was greeted by enthusiastic tail wagging from Mike. Tiny did not understand. "Will der Hund ein Kaetzchen?" At last, there was tail wagging from Tiny. Both of them started to wrestle with each other, thoroughly excited. They ran round the house, panting. Then they came back and looked up at me expectantly.

"I am afraid that we will have to get a cat," I announced to Phil that evening. "Mike and Tiny really want one."

"A cat?" he moaned. "Do we have to?"

"Not for my sake," I replied. "But the guys really miss having a cat. Especially Mike. He is so much happier when there is a cat around. Come on, let's get them a cat."

Finally, Phil relented. He does, after all, love the dogs as much as anyone, and we have an unwritten rule in the house, the little dogs come first.

We made elaborate plans about a well-pedigreed Persian cat, from one of the best breeders in North America. The cat

271

was going to be cream-colored with dark brown ears and tail: a Himalayan. Of course, as always, everything came different than planned. Circumstances conspired against, so we ended up with the cat from hell, rescued from the local SPCA.

We had made contact with the ill-fated SPCA of Montreal long ago, when I first returned from Texas. This was due to the fact that I was now working as correspondent for a German animal magazine. The SPCA was under-funded, badly administered and in very poor shape. From week to week, they did not know whether they would be able to keep going. When we went for our first visit there, we found a chaotic, badly run institution. A handful of idealistic staff and volunteers with haggard faces, all of them Type A personalities on a roll which caused you stress just by watching them, tried to keep everything going: walk the dogs, feed everyone, organize veterinary services, look for money donations, and try to find homes for the animals to keep them from being destroyed.

The SPCA also turned out to be a treasure chest for interesting personalities, pathetic fates and weird stories. For instance, there was Rose from Germany. She had survived two heart attacks, was "mother" to several adopted native Indian children and married to an unemployed German. She lived in a large, strange house, with assorted animals and children. Rose was also a "psychic." In addition, Rose had cancer and refused to submit to chemotherapy treatment. She believed in the healing of the mind, and mistrusted modern medicine. Rose was always involved in a more or less armed conflict with her neighbors, over the six dogs she kept at home along with assorted cats, parrots, mice and ferrets. She also battled the SPCA over the way everything was being administered and the Canadian government over its treatment of native Indians. Despite her combative nature, Rose was basically a kind soul, who spoke and complained a lot but whose heart was in the right place.

There was also Sandra, who was crazy about animals.

She had closed down her successful boutique in the heart of Montreal and used the money to keep the SPCA going. One year later, the pretty young woman was broke. Single-handedly, she had provided food for the animals during "dry periods," when funding at the SPCA was low. She took surplus animals home to find them new owners when their "grace period" had run out and they were facing destruction. At Sandra's house, there were always assorted stray cats looking for a home. Sandra never had time for anything. She was always bathing a cat, rescuing a cat from an abandoned building in the midst of a snow blizzard, or nursing cat bites in iodine and hot water...

We liked her dedication to the welfare of the animals. Sandra and we had exchanged phone numbers after our first meeting at the SPCA. She was an interesting girl: a writer who stemmed from a well-known Mafia family, very pretty, ex-girlfriend of famous men from all over the world. Casually, surrounded by cat food bowls, Sandra would show photographs of herself in the "humble home" of some friends: Sandra in the palace of a Royal family somewhere in Saudi Arabia, Sandra as guest of honor at the Royal wedding in Morocco, Sandra and a famous Formula 1 race driver at his home in Monte Carlo. The contrast between the world she had left behind and the world she had entered to help these animals could not have been greater. She was a woman who had had the world as her oyster. Yet, she had turned her back on fame, fortune and success to channel her energies into helping a bunch of stray cats. Sandra cared more about animals than about anything else in the world.

When Phil and I had to fly to Cannes in Southern France in the summer of 1994, Sandra arranged for a friend of hers to look after our dogs. The friend was named Crystal. Sandra knew her from the SPCA. Sandra regretted that she could not do it herself, but she had her house full of stray cats.

We went to visit the Crystal one dreary afternoon, two days before we were scheduled to leave for Cannes. It was not the fact that she lived in one of those horrible, high-rise buildings, or that her apartment was not very tidy. It was that Crystal was weird. Like Rose, Crystal was a "psychic." Unlike Rose, she had "strange" written all over her. Crystal supplemented her welfare check with "readings" for the local psychic hotline. It was not until I met Crystal that I became aware of these networks and the scams that they were. Instantly, journalistic curiosity took over and I made a mental note to infiltrate and check them out later. For now, I had the dogs to deal with. The situation was not ideal. But Crystal, who was being paid handsomely for the job, promised to look after the dogs. " They will get their own bedroom and mattress to sleep on. I am always here. I work from home. They will always have company. I will take them out at least four times a day. I know this place is small, but they will be so much happier here than at a kennel. I have looked after other people's dogs before. I am very good with dogs."

Finally, she convinced us. We left our "kids" with Crystal. After all, Crystal volunteered at the SPCA. Crystal was a friend of Sandra. If anything happened, surely Sandra would be able to help out. We paid her in advance, delivered the dogs two days later and got on our plane to France.

Three weeks later, we had an emergency phone call from Sandra: I sat in a beautiful hotel in Cannes, looking out over the picturesque ocean walkway, watching the waves break to shore on the picturesque Cote d'Azur and listened to a horror story from the other end of the world. Crystal had broken her leg. She had been admitted to hospital. Living alone, she had not been able to find anyone to look after the dogs. She had left them at her apartment, unattended. Sandra found out two days later and had gone to pick them up. Unable to put them anywhere else, she had dropped them with a vet. There, the dogs were now lodging in a cage at the rate of 20$ per day. Tiny, especially, took badly to being in a cage: he refused to eat and was suffering from bad diarrhea. Could I please come home at once and pick them up?

We were not thrilled, but what is a good dog owner to do? There did not seem to be much choice: sighing, we packed our suitcases and checked out of the hotel. We took one final trip to Monte Carlo in the afternoon, walked the cobble stone streets, fondly stopping at a well-known market stall her or there. We climbed up to the royal palace and looked out over the majestic ocean. We watched the seagulls soar proudly in the wind as we reflected on the days which were to come, or which had been planned to come. Sadly, we waved those days good-bye. Then we cut short our vacation and hurried home. The dogs awaited us, deeply depressed, in a cage at the vet clinic. Sandra was there to hand them over to us. She swore up and down that she could not understand how Crystal could have flipped. Trying to make up to us, she swore glumly: "I will never speak a word with her again."

We learned from this not to have any further dealings with the SPCA or anyone associated with it. It was not a good place. It was not run by good people. In addition to people like Crystal, there were stories about it in the paper every week: constant change of directorship, corruption charges, mass destruction of animals. The whole place was pathetic.

Why then, did we choose to go back there, one year after our distasteful experience with Crystal? Sandra! She was such a lovely girl that we stayed in touch. One night, when my business in Montreal took longer than anticipated, she allowed me to sleep over at her apartment. Phil and I lived at the foothills of the Laurentians, over 30 minutes drive from the city. It would have been a long and exhausting drive home in the dark.

The next morning, the dear girl had gone out especially to buy some lobster mousse and fresh croissant. Over breakfast, she pointed to one of the "new" cats in her apartment. The tail of the tabby was missing. So was one ear.

"I rescued that cat in a snow blizzard," she explained.

"We got a phone call that someone had abandoned two cats on the roof of an old house. Nobody else wanted to go, so I went to get them. It was dark and it was dangerous, but I didn't mind. All I could think of was to get the cats. When I arrived at the address they had given us, I immediately climbed up on the roof. One of the cats was no longer alive. In temperatures of -40 Celsius, he had simply frozen to death. The other cat was this one. His tail had frozen to the roof. I picked the cat up and the tail just came off. Later, the same happened to his left ear. The cat had been out there for too long. He was about to freeze to death, like his companion."

When she saw the shocked expression on my face, she went on, "That's not even half of what people will do to animals..." Sandra went on to speak of other cats who were awaiting homes at the SPCA.

"I try to re-home as many as possible," she exclaimed. "But I can't keep looking after the entire reject cat community of Montreal. It is getting too much. They will start putting some animals down soon."

I felt guilty at once. Phil and I had spoken of getting a Persian cat! The thought of forking out 400$ for a feline while at the SPCA so many cats were in danger of losing their lives because they were not wanted suddenly seemed wrong. Things like that always seemed wrong when in Sandra's house.

"Well, I suppose we could consider adopting a cat," I began. "Phil and I have been thinking of getting a cat. But we really wanted a Persian cat..."

"No problem," Sandra exclaimed joyfully. "There are plenty of Persian cats at the SPCA. Let me just call Rose and tell her you are coming over. She'll show you around. It won't be a problem to find a cat for you. I am sure of that."

With the rest of her croissant in one hand, Sandra jumped up from the table and before I was able to utter another word she was on the phone. She came back to us a few minutes later and said: "All set. Rose is waiting for you."

We had not meant to get a cat so soon. But what could we do? I called Phil to let him know that I was not driving home. Instead, I was going straight to the SPCA.

"To the SPCA?" he asked. "But why?"

"To get a cat."

"But I thought you wanted a Persian cat."

"I do. They also have Persian cats there," I informed him. "Anyway, I just had breakfast with Sandra. She convinced me that it is absurd to buy another animal when there are all these cats waiting for homes. Can you meet me there?"

Half an hour later, my long-suffering husband met me outside the SPCA. We walked through the doors, hand in hand. Immediately, we were greeted by Rose.

"Sandra told me that you were going to come by ," she beamed. "I am so glad you are going to get a cat. Please, have a look around. Take any cat you want. Take two, three even! You don't have to pay the adoption fee either. Just take one and go."

She was clearly desperate to match us with a cat. As we walked into the cat area, we could see why. There were cats in every cage, three rooms full of cats, all of them looking for a new owner. Some of them had been abandoned, beaten, starved. Others had been given away by owners who no longer wanted them or were able to look after them.

We made acquaintance with an incredibly fat Russian Blue, a seven-colored house cat and a litter of kittens that were temptingly cute. We forced ourselves to go on, past the cages in the first room, and into the "long-haired cats" section. This was not easy, as Phil and the Russian blue spent a too much time together and almost got married. He began to argue his point, why a Russian blue would be better than a Persian, and why this particular Russian blue would be perfect for our house. Finally, I was able to tear him away and guide him into the next section.

Here, at last, were the Persians, even one Himalayan,

just like the cat we had envisioned. Unfortunately, it had been abused badly by its owners. It had been found by the SPCA, wandering along the side of the 640 motorway. The cat was extremely hostile to humans and hissed or scratched when anyone came near it. Whatever had happened to this cat in the past, it had become psychotic as a result. We had visions of the cat scratching our dogs to pieces, who were both considerably smaller. As beautiful as it was to look at, we decided against taking the cat home and trying to "reform" it. It was clearly the feline equivalent of a dangerous criminal, though it had been turned dangerous through abuse.

Besides the psychopath, there was a choice of a white Persian with badly infected eyes, a beautiful cream which had no faults except that it slept in its litter box all day and shed hair where it went, and a black with strange eyes which was 12 years old. We were about to leave a very disappointed Rose and the SPCA with empty hands. At the last moment, Phil spotted "our" cat: a ginger and white Persian, hardly recognizable as such for its knotted fur.

The cat had just come in that morning and had not yet been inspected by the SPCA vet. Hence, it was not with the other cats but in a cage on its own in a separate corridor behind doors marked "Staff only." Phil, having been granted unlimited access by Rose, had ventured behind these doors and found it.

"This may be nothing," Phil mentioned casually as we were about to leave, "but there is a ginger and white cat in the back there. It's kind of scruffy looking, but it appears to be a Persian."

We went together to see the cat. The cat had a beautiful, flat Persian face. At once, I recognized that he had to be of champion pedigree. He came to the bars and purred. He was very kind and nice. I used a bit of artistic imagery and saw the cat before my mind's eye, combed and washed. Gorgeous!

"We'll take him," I announced to Phil and Rose.

"Don't you want to think about it?" Phil asked.

"No, he's perfect for us," I answered confidently.

So it came to pass that a cat joined our household. From his papers, we learned that his name was "Tommy."

"That won't do," we decided in unison at the SPCA counter. "We'll have to re-name him."

On the spot, we dropped Tommy's name. For lack of a better one, he was from then on referred to as "the cat." We assumed that the correct name would manifest itself with time. It didn't. The poor cat went through a variety of names, or rather pseudo-names, which ranged from: Miau-person, Miau-queen, Beauty-queen, Sweetheart person to an entire arrangement of other such sillies. At the time of writing, some three years later, the cat still does not have a name.

For the past three months, he has been answering to "Mau-mau." This is the longest he has ever had any one name. We hope for everyone's sake that this name will stick.

But now back to the SPCA: Tommy, we learned, had indeed once been a high-priced, champion-pedigreed Persian cat. He had been a Christmas present for a wealthy Westmount girl two years earlier. Recently, the girl had left home and gone to college. She was unable to take her cat. Her mother did not have time or patience to look after an animal that required such intense attention. Hence, the knots and neglected appearance. However, "Tommy" had been well attended before, he had undergone a costly gall stone operation, and he had been neutered. Due to the gallstone problem, he was on a special, expensive diet. He would need this diet for the rest of his life. His fact-sheet bore the remark, underlined in red, "Do not destroy." At least his owners cared for him more than most that drop their animals at the pound.

Now Tommy was about to become "the cat," and prepared to go to his new home. While we negotiated with Rose to have him vaccinated (which she agreed to) and combed (which she did not agree to) and to pick up our new cat the next day, another SPCA drama unfolded before our eyes. A little dog, a cute, black and tan puppy, was brought in inside a pet carrier. The man who brought it explained that it had been run over by a truck. The little dog appeared to be fine. We watched as a girl from the SPCA staff opened the door of the carrier and called the puppy. It walked over to her, wagging its tail. It held its head to one side and could not stop panting. It appeared a little dazed. Besides that, it was as attentive to humans as any other young dog.

"What's going to happen to the puppy?" I asked Rose, while filling out the appropriate forms to take the "cat-person" home with us.

"Don't know, we'll have to check with the vet. Call me later this afternoon and I'll let you know."

I watched as the puppy, still wagging its tail, was guided back into the carrier and taken downstairs to the vet chambers. I hoped that it would recover soon.

Before we left, Rose gave us a tour of the dog premises. In a cage, we saw a little Pekingese who - true to Pekingese nature - growled at us self-importantly when we approached. A Pekingese will usually defend his territory against anyone, even if the "anyone" happens to be three times its size. But the growling is all show. Inside, the little dogs have a heart of gold. Once a Pekingese trusts you, it becomes a loyal friend for life.

"I've had enough of pushing this snowball." Mike takes a break from building a snowman. This picture is taken outside our house in Rhode Island.

"I don't care, I am not smiling for yet another photograph!"
Tiny and Mike love the beach, especially at sunset. This photo
is taken at Second Beach in Newport, Rhode Island.

Tiny and Mike with Auschwitz Concentration Camp survivor
Judith, who doted on them.

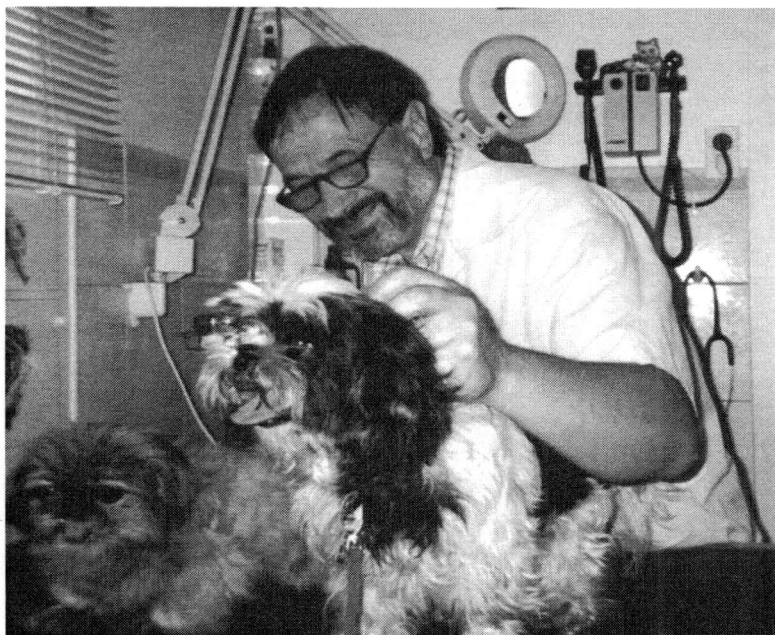

"Him first, not me." Tiny and Mike always went to the vet together. Here, they are at their vet in St Eustache, Quebec, preparing for their move to Rhode Island.

"I love my Mum." Tiny and me in Geneva, Switzerland.

"All say cheese for the family photograph." Tiny and Mike in Munich, Germany, with my grandparents.

"Where's my breakfast, I shan't wait any longer." Tiny, who thinks he is human, sits down to eat.

"I've got the wrong end, haven't I?" Tiny rides "his" horse, Wildfire.

"Got my seat, where's my table?" Tiny, Phil and a sailing colleague at breakfast in a five star hotel in Geneva, Switzerland, at the International 8 Metre European Sailing Championships, 1997.

"Ha! Got through the customs..." Tiny and I prepare to fly to Europe. Lufthansa airlines allowed Tiny to come into the cabin in his little blue carry-on bag. He ate yogurt and beef fillet, and thoroughly enjoyed being the only canine passenger on the plane.

"Pekingeses should not be in cages." I told Rose. "When did he come in?"

"Only yesterday," she informed me as we stood in front of the angry little creature.

"Is he up for adoption?" I asked. "Because if you can't find anyone to take him, we always have place for an extra Pekingese. Call me anytime."

"No, that's all right. I am taking this one myself. I can't keep him at home because of the council restrictions on the number of dogs I can have. But I will keep him here at my office. I am just waiting until he goes through the veterinary checks. Then I'll pull him out of here."

Unfortunately, both dog stories of that day ended in tragedy. Rose informed me later that afternoon that the puppy had to be put down. As for the Pekingese: she kept him for two months and then - when her cancer flared up and she had to go to hospital - in an idiotic move which I do not understand to this day, she elected to have a perfectly healthy Pekingese put to sleep. She made the decision despite the fact that it had a welcoming home waiting for it. Rose never told anyone of her intention. She just did it.

When she informed me of her action some six weeks after the event, I wanted to rip her head off. Remembering that she was very ill, I decided against it. It must have been one of the absurd stress reactions that come with having a fatal illness.

Our dogs were overjoyed to have a cat in the house. Once cleaned up, and rid of all his knots, the cat had transformed into one of the most beautiful Persians we had ever seen.

Beauty appeared to be his best feature, however. The cat had a few odd habits, we soon discovered. For instance, we found that he had a fascination with asphalt streets. When left alone to roam outside, he would run to the middle of the road and sit there with a happy expression on his face. Cars seem to be of no worry to this particular cat. When they come, he purrs and looks straight into the headlights, assuming them to be benign creatures. We tried the cat-car thing only once, before deciding not to allow the cat out on his own again.

We also found that snowflakes delighted him. When winter arrived, we built a snowman in front of the house. Supervised, the cat was allowed outside with us. Predictably, he ran into the middle of his beloved street. Snow was falling in immense amounts, true to Montreal winter reputation. The cat raced up and down the street with great enthusiasm, trying to catch snowflakes. The roads had been closed down because of the heavy snowfall, so we let him play to his heart's content. Laughing, Phil and I watched our usually aloof Persian cat fool around with the snow.

There is not much else I can report about the cat. We found that he makes himself absent for most of the time, even from his closest "friends." Around the house, the cat ate and slept. That constituted the full extent of his life. If he did not engage in these two favorite activities of his, he would sit on our leather sofa, eyes in two slits, and stare straight ahead. We discovered that the cat purrs only when he feels that he is unobserved. There is an immense blasé attitude about him, which causes him to take great care so as not to appear to like or appreciate anyone or anything.

At the SPCA, when trying to secure a new home, he was the nicest he would ever be. In fact, we never saw our cat being that nice since. At home, when picked up to be cuddled, he sighs and rolls his eyes to heaven. This is the distasteful part of the day, which the cat considers as doing his duty as a cat. Only when you listen very closely can you actually hear him purr, deep inside. He purrs only if he cannot help it. In that case, he tries to hide the purr somewhere in his belly, trying his utmost to keep it from escaping to his throat, where it could be discovered. That would be awful, because it could show he actually likes being held. That is something the cat would never admit.

The dogs were treated from the start with disdain. Tiny soon gave up trying to make friends with the cat. Not so Mike. To the indifferent stares of the cat, Mike bounced up and down in front of it. Mike is an extremely nice dog and will never cease trying to make friends with anyone. It took a lot of patience from Mike's side until he made some headway. Today, they are as close as the cat will ever be to anyone.

With three animals, a strict rank order has been established in our house by the dogs. To them, it is very important to define who stands where. First comes Tiny. Then Philip and me (for some reason, we are on equal standing). Then comes Mike. After Mike comes the cat. The rank order is, for instance, very obvious at bedtime. The cat is not allowed on the bed. That is by rule of Mike and Tiny. Philip and I have nothing to do with this. In fact, we frequently take the cat on the bed with us. If we do, Mike gets up and jumps in front of the cat, staring him down until he leaves, or he turns his head from where he lies on the foot of the bed and glares at him in no uncertain terms.

"Mike, stop glaring at the cat!" is one of the most frequent exclamations to be heard in our bedroom. Mike will usually stop glaring for a minute or two, but in an unattended moment, he will resume his intimidation tactics with the cat. So long as the rank order is respected and the cat does not try to sleep on the bed, Mike dotes on him. When they are outside together, Mike will defend the cat, just as he does with Tiny, against any other dogs. They are often walking outside together. After we had learned that the cat could not be trusted to be left on his own, we trained him to walk on a leash. At first, this experience was not too dissimilar to the Garfield cartoons. Bemused neighbors giggled behind closed windows as they observed a certain ginger and white Persian cat dragging his owner behind him on a leash, wrapping both of us around trees, throwing himself on the ground to be dragged on his back … until I picked up the cat one day and carried him to the beachfront. On the beach, I let him go. Intrigued, he walked to the water and tried to catch the waves with his paw. He spent hours watching the ocean. His paw shot forward to catch the wave, withdrew in disgust as he got wet, came out again. And so it went…

Once the cat understood that the reward for walking on a leash was the beach, there were no further problems. Except when there were people about. In the early days, I was still misguided enough to want to show off. "Look how great. My cat can walk on a leash," I would call out to the neighbors as we passed their front yards. I did not take into account my feline partner. The moment he noticed that I had an audience, the cat sat down and refused to walk one step further. "You mean how well he can sit on a leash," people laughed. Or: "That poor cat. Cats aren't made to walk on a leash. You should let him go."

To this, a grinning Persian cat purred in the background. Sometimes, I did not like my new cat…

When he had run out of things to do to humiliate me, the cat behaved quite decently. Finally, I bought a double leash for Mike and the cat. In unison, they walked down the road: cat on one end of the leash, Mike on the other. Side by side. Waiting for each other as one of them sniffed at a tree. Or caught a snowflake. On the beach, they ran together. Tiny followed, as usual by himself, a little aloof. Soon, the cat had came to consider himself to be a dog.

He started by sniffing Mike on the nose, the way he had observed Mike and Tiny do it. This expanded to walking on the leash. Being with a dog, it was natural for him to do what the dog did when they encounter other dogs. Both would sniff the other creature. The cat's sniffing them hello was being greeted by smaller dogs with a warm welcome. Big dogs were often confused as to the cat's species. They could not make out whether he was a dog, since he behaved like one, or a cat, since he smelled like one. Some of them got nasty when they found the ginger, furry thing to be a cat. This is where Mike stepped in. As a self-appointed bodyguard, he jumped between the cat and the offending dog, growling to keep him off. This is a habit Mike keeps to this day. He takes his position of defending his "family" very seriously, felines included.

In the end, I must admit that the man who wrote Garfield could have easily modeled it on our cat: he eats, he sleeps. He treats our home like a hotel. He scratches us when he is through playing. He stands in the bedroom door at 6am, miauing loudly for food. He sits outside the bathroom door while Phil is having a shower, miauing. He complains loudly when his food is not in his bowl by 6:15am. Even on Sundays. On Sundays, we usually wake up with the cat staring into our faces, purring loudly. Or miauing. Or swiping Phil on the nose with his paw. He also drinks out of the toilet bowl. He sleeps on my keyboard while I try to write a book or article. He crawls into cartons, brown paper bags and bookshelves. This happens also when the brown bags still have groceries inside. In that case, the groceries frequently crash to the floor, bag and cat included. The cat casually shrugs and wanders off. On the floor, there remains a puddle: orange juice perhaps, sometimes ketchup, Mayonnaise, vinegar, even olive oil. The dogs are delighted with this habit of the cat. When the groceries he sends crashing to the floor contain bags of edible material, these bags are expertly ripped open by Mike, and the contents shared out between the two little rascals before we discover them.

As for us: the cat allows us in his life only in the capacity of litter-box changers, food providers and occasional back scratchers. Tiny and Mike are accepted by the cat on a slightly higher level than we are. Mike because he is a friend. Tiny because he, as always, runs the world. I really don't know why we own a cat.

Chapter 26

Next, We Get A Horse - And We Are Ready To Move Again!

We had not intended to buy a horse. This time, it was even hard to blame the additional family member on the little dogs. Except, perhaps, for the fact that Tiny had always wanted a horse. Well! That may be a little far fetched. Tiny had always enjoyed "owning" the stable when we still had one. So it was a reasonable conclusion that he wanted a horse to make up for the fact that Mike now had a cat. Let me revise the start of this chapter, then, to say: it was Tiny's fault that we got a horse to go with the cat...

It happened somewhat by accident. We were in the process of moving to Newport, Rhode Island. Philip had managed to secure a good position there as vice president of the American branch for a British based company. I needed to go to New York for my work anyway. A move to the United States, away from the cold and snow of Montreal, into economically more prosperous territory, would do us good. The only problem was that Phil had to move by the end of September if he wanted to get the position with the British company. I was caught up in work for the literary agency. I was also still working with Ian Stephens on his book/documentary of the final months of his life. There was no way I could move before the middle of December. Hence, we decided that Phil would move at the beginning of September, leaving me behind.

We tried to find reasonable living quarters for me, but nobody was willing to rent a house or decent apartment for only three months. Thus began our time in purgatory: the little dogs, cat and I moved into the only place we could find that was being rented at such short notice. It was a small basement apartment, which consisted of one tiny bedroom, a small lounge/kitchen area and an even smaller bathroom. There were two tiny windows at the very top of the ceiling. The place was so dark that you had to keep the electric light on at all times. When I looked straight ahead of me, I saw walls. When I looked up, I saw walls. I had to lift my head way up to see the one small window, and could only look outside it if I stepped on a chair to elevate myself.

In contrast, the house to which the apartment belonged was beautiful. The owner of the house ran a taxi business from home. He had decided to pay his mortgage by converting his basement into three apartments which he rented at 435$ per month. The dogs or myself have never before or afterward lived in circumstances quite like it. Naturally, I was the only professional there. When I moved in, the apartment opposite me was occupied by a drug addict and his drug addict wife or girlfriend. On the far left lived a neglected young man who was being visited by equally neglected young men. Together with them, he smoked tons of marihuana and stank up the corridor that was shared between the three apartments.

I would not have stayed there had it not been a choice of doing either that or leaving the rest of my work unfinished. The problem with the kind of life Phil and myself had been leading it is that, exciting as it may be, you have to be very careful to start new projects in case that you don't get to finish them before you are transferred again. I had been brought up to always finish what I started. Therefore, although the cost would be considerable to Tiny, Mike, the cat and myself, we decided to stay and complete the project of documenting the final stages of Ian Stephens' life.

Everything started under a bad star. Phil, who suffers from Diabetes, had been moving furniture from our old house into the small apartment. His sailing colleague Barney, from England, helped. When the move was finally completed, our exhausted threesome decided to get something to eat at a local St Eustache restaurant. St Eustache is a picturesque, historic town some 30 miles outside Montreal, on the foothills of the Laurentians. It has many nice, outdoor restaurants where one can dine on wonderful, French food. But that evening, we were too tired to eat much. The men just had a big salad, and I listlessly ate some profiteroles, followed by a soup. Tired as I was, I decided to have Desert first, then the soup, then perhaps the main course. After the soup, I was so tired that I decided to forget about the main course and we all called it a night.

Phil and I headed back to the new apartment, where we were to spend our first and only night together. The following day, he was off to Rhode Island. Exhausted, we both dropped off to sleep immediately. An hour later, I came to because Phil was behaving strangely. He was suffering from a low sugar reaction, a potentially fatal condition that afflicts Diabetics when they inject too much insulin for the amount of food they subsequently eat, or if they have exercised too much. With diabetics, the body does not produce enough or, in some cases, no insulin at all. In healthy people, the body releases the right amount of insulin to process the sugar content of the food we eat. If diabetics inject too much insulin for the amount of food they eat, their blood sugar plummets because the insulin has no food to work with. A low sugar reaction is easily treated in its early stages by giving orange juice, dextrose or a dextrose-based paste designed especially for diabetics.

The problem was that we had finished moving at 9pm that evening, and we had not been shopping afterwards. There was nothing in the kitchen, no orange juice, no sugar, nothing. I did not know the phone number for the local ambulance service. St Eustache was so far out in the countryside that it was not on the 911 system. There was no phone book. Even if I had a phone book, I did not know the address of our new place. Phil had rented the apartment and driven us here.

I knocked on the door of our drug-addicted neighbors at 2:30 am. Predictably, they were still up. They listened to strange music and were smoking an even stranger-smelling

297

substance. They gave me their phone book. They did not have the number of the ambulance, but suggested it should be "in there." When I told them I had just moved in and that my husband was sick and could potentially die, they shrugged said "nothing we can do about it." They did, at least, give me the address of our new apartment.

The dogs looked on with great interest as I finally found the number and dialed for the ambulance. Then I had to wait outside, in the parking lot of the elegant house that hid such dreadful a row of basement apartments for the ambulance to arrive. When the paramedics came, they immediately rushed down to Phil and fed him dextrose paste.

"Close call," one of the guys said. When I told him this was our first night here and that we had been working all day, he remarked something to the effect of "welcome to your new home. Let's hope this is not going to be an indication of things to come."

Phil had recovered instantly after administration of the sugar paste. Now he laughed and said "No, let's hope not."

The paramedics were in fact very nice. They informed us that we lodged in a most expensive house situated in the most exclusive street of St Eustache "Pity just about the basement part," they grinned while patting Tiny and Mike. Excited at this unexpected late night visit, the two little dogs were putting on a wrestling match for the benefit of these strangers whom they assumed were coming to stay at our new quarters. The paramedic warned us against moving anywhere without at least orange juice in the house. "Even when you move into a place in the middle of the night, stop somewhere at on the way and pick up a carton of juice," he advised us. "With diabetes, you always have to be careful. Better safe than sorry, right?"

This was followed by a conversation about our "cute" dogs. They were at their funniest: after the wrestling match, Mike danced for the tired paramedics. They were so enthralled, they even would have stayed for coffee - if we had had any to offer them. I told them that I was a former journalist and in the process of writing a book about Tiny and Mike.

"You guys will probably be in it," I grinned with a note of warning.

"How did you end up in a place like this?" the paramedic wanted to know. "If you don't mind me saying so, it's not usual for journalists to live like this."

We told him the story. He nodded. "You must be very dedicated to your job." he remarked.

Finally, they left and we were able to go back to sleep. Mike curled up at the bottom of the bed, as is his habit. Tiny, also true to habit, waited until the lights had been switched off and then wandered from the foot-end of the bed to the top, scratched at the end of the blanket to be granted admission under the covers. As is his custom, Phil growled a little when Tiny was admitted under the blanket. As is my custom, I said, "he only wants to stay there for a little while. It is a status symbol for Tiny to sleep under the covers." I explained to Phil, as always, that I did not quite understand it myself, but that it apparently had something to do with being the alpha dog. Then, as is our habit, we all went to sleep, Tiny loudly snoring under the covers. Mike modestly rolled up at the foot-end of the bed with Phil and myself sharing half of the bed between us, while Tiny lay clear across the other half.

This was the start of a rather difficult period in the lives of the little dogs, the cat and myself. Phil was lucky enough to leave the following day. In Newport, a lovely, four-bedroom home awaited him, in one of the most exclusive streets. It had a view of the water, a private vineyard and a secluded beach. Meanwhile, Tiny, Mike and myself stared up at the walls in an apartment that had the total size of the Newport house's dining room. I made my phone calls from these tiny living quarters, wondering what my editors colleagues would say if they knew what kind of a hole I was working from. I was very careful not to let them notice. When I drove to meetings, I drove impeccably dressed and coifed. When I came home, I stared at the walls.

After two weeks of living like this, depression set in. It was not psychological, it was physical. I had problems getting out of bed in the morning because there were only these dreadful walls to look at. Breakfast was taken by neon light, staring up at nothing but walls. The dogs grew listless and hardly touched their food. The cat jumped up to the sill of the tiny window and miaued mournfully. I began to understand what prison must feel like, perhaps a little worse because there would be more noise, no animals, and no freedom to make your own day. I began to understand that I would never be able to live in prison.

Prison, incidentally, was one of our problems at the time. The death row inmate's attorney had called to advise me that an execution date had been set for December 12.

"This one will probably be a go-ahead," she warned me. "I think it is your job to call his parents and tell them. You need to tell them that we have no further legal recourse. They turned every issue down we raised."

Thus, I had the difficult task of informing an aged, catholic couple of the fact that their son, who had never been given a fair trial and who was most likely not guilty, was going to be executed by the State of Texas.

"I am sorry," I said, "but is nothing we can do if the judges refuse to uphold the law. Legally, we have won the case. We have presented all the evidence. If the judges refuse to look at it, there is nothing we can do about it."

Not that this made it any easier for the poor parents, but at least it was the truth.

After this, the dogs and myself took refuge in the Laurentian mountains. We drove there every afternoon after work, and our spirits improved a great deal. The Laurentians are one of the most beautiful spots on earth, as far as I am concerned. Lush green hills extend to the shores of crystal clear mountain lakes. The air is so fresh that you can almost drink it. There is an atmosphere of utter peace as you drive through the small, windy roads, surrounded by green to the right, left, and even from above as the trees close over your head. In autumn, spectacular colors can be seen from the top of the mountains of St Saveur, Mont Tremblant or Ste Adele, gorgeous Swiss-style villages with the best in food, wine and people.

Every afternoon, we drove up Autoroute 15, heading north. Listening to the music of Montreal's Cirque du Soleil on the tape deck, Tiny and Mike hung their heads happily out into the wind as we passed St Jerome and headed toward "our" mountains. We usually returned by 10pm, our batteries recharged after long walks in the woods and good food at the Thai restaurant in St Saveur. On weekends, we drove all the way to Brebeuf, where Mike and myself went swimming in the warm waters of the red river as Tiny, who does not like getting his little paws wet, sat on the beach and looked on.

Afterwards, we went to one of our favorite little restaurants that had an outdoor terrace overlooking the forest. The man there served Tiny and Mike a bowl of water and myself a wonderful sandwich. We drank local spring water so pure that it tasted like liquid silk, and a cup of hot chocolate to finish up with. The terrace had been built directly over the hills, and I sat surrounded by lush green, or bright red (depending on the season) foliage as assorted guests took photographs of the dogs and me.

We had a wonderful time, and the dreary nights at the apartment did not seem so bad anymore. But winter came soon enough, and with winter came disasters of various shapes and forms. The arrival of the snow meant for instance, having to scrape a built-up of ice from the car, in the biting cold with an average temperature of - 25 Celsius. In addition, there was the need of shoveling several feet of snow from the roof of the car. Winter in Quebec also meant having to freeze for the first minutes of driving, until the car grew warm thanks to the efforts of the heater.

Our death row inmate's execution date grew closer. Ian Stephens went to hospital with severe Aids complications and I began to spend the nights there. Life became difficult, to say the least. My typical day looked like this: at 10am, I drove back from the hospital in Montreal to my apartment in St Eustache.

Often, there were dreadful snowstorms when I left the city. I arrived home to let the dogs out, then fell into bed, exhausted. Often I did not have time to eat before sleep overcame me. When I did have time, there was nothing in the fridge. There was rarely enough time to go shopping.

I usually awoke by 5pm, by which time it was dark once more. I took the dogs out again, then drove to the store to buy a roasted chicken and have a hasty meal while I made phone calls to publishers who were all very understanding and had given me their home numbers. By 7pm, I went outside into the bitter cold again. I scraped the snow off my car and drove through the darkness, listening to Susan Aglukark on the tape recorder, all the way back to the hospital. I had a few close calls when the car slipped on dark, icy roads. I realized that if anything happened to me, it would be until morning before anyone noticed. Thus, I always put out a pot filled with water for the dogs before I left: that way, if something happened, they would survive until people found them.

For the dogs, it was worse: they spent all their time in the dark, small apartment. During the day, they watched over my sleep. At night, they anxiously waited for my return just as the sun came up again. To add insult to injury, it became necessary for me to have a root canal. The doctor I went to, a country local, botched the job up so badly that my mouth infected. He put me on antibiotics, which I took religiously but which had the side effects of such bad stomach cramps that I could hardly eat at all thereafter.

Surviving on very little food while spending night after night in Montreal's General Hospital with a dying stranger began to take its toll, as did the cold drives along icy roads to get there and sleeping during the day and often seeing the sunshine only as it set over the horizon. We all grew horribly depressed: the dogs because they got to spend their time locked into the horrible apartment, and me because the life I was living was simply not feasible.

Something had to change. But what? In the past, no matter how bad things got, riding a horse had always cheered me up. One Sunday afternoon, I decided to go pack the dogs in the car and find a place where to go riding. My idea was to find a horse, rent it for an hour or two, ride out into the spectacular Canadian mountains and return, refreshed in body and soul. It was not that easy: people did not rent out horses the way I envisioned it. At most stables, you had to ride with a stranger, a "trail-guide." With him would be a group of other strangers, your fellow riders. That was the last thing I wanted. I had owned horses all my life and did not want to be told when I could walk, trot or canter. Not to mention that I was absolutely not interested in making conversation with strangers at that point in my life.

The dogs were clearly perked up by our visits, albeit unsuccessful, to various stables in my attempt to rent a horse. Tiny went immediately into "stable owner" mode: head thrown back, chin high, he walked through the corridors of the stables we visited, "inspecting" various horses. Eventually, we drove back to St Eustache. None of the stables would allow me to take out a horse on my own.

"Guys, it looks like we will have to buy a horse," I announced to the excited little dogs. Mike recognized the word "horse" and began dancing around the small apartment. Tiny did not understand, until I translated into German: "wollen wir ein Pferdchen kaufen?"

He thought it was a great idea, indicating so with an enthusiastic lick on my nose. With both dogs approving, I now had to get the idea past Phil. I realized this would not be easy. A few years earlier, we had owned 18 horses and it turned into a lot of work. To Phil, the word "horse" was a red flag since then, but as it happened, Phil was in England on company business. What better time to go looking for a horse...?

Our new next door neighbor, after the drug addicts had been evicted, was a very nice Eskimo girl. I decided to see if she knew anyone around the area who sold horses, and went across the hall to knock on her door.

"Hi, the dogs and I want to buy a horse. Do you have any idea where we could go?"

"You want to do what?" she asked, laughing. "Buy a horse?"

I nodded.

"Now?"

I looked at my watch. It was 7pm, and time to leave for the hospital again.

"Well, maybe not right now," I told her. "But tomorrow afternoon. I was wondering whether you know of someone who might have good horses for sale?"

Horses in Quebec were hard to come by. Except for the run-down sales barns that sold equally run-down horses, everything happened through private contacts.

"Not really," she replied. " I know a few horse places around here, but their horses are no good. There is one guy, though..."

"Yes?"

"...but I don't think he sells his horses. He is a Hollywood stuntman. He does a lot of the horse scenes in the movies. He's got about 40 horses; some of them are very nice. As I said, I don't think they are for sale, but you could drive by his house and ask him."

Take it that we would not buy an ordinary horse. We

bought a movie star. When Tiny, Mike and I turned up at the door of Frank, the stuntman, he was not against our request. He was indifferent to it.

"If you want a horse," he said, "just go out into the paddock and pick one. We can negotiate the price later. I don't usually sell my horses, but since you are already here you might as well have a look."

"What do you live on, Frank?" I asked. "Do they pay you that much at the movies that you don't have to worry about an extra few thousand here or there?" I was really curious. It was 11 am when we got to Frank's house, and it looked like he just got out of bed. He did not seem to be working at all.

"You know, it's a funny thing," he grinned. "Until a few years ago, I was struggling like everyone else. Then I won the rodeo world championship and Hollywood came knocking on my door. Since then I provide the horses and stunt rides for them. I work six to eight weeks a year, that's it. The rest of the time I have to myself."

"That's great," I replied, not without envy. "You really have it made, Frank."

"It's not a bad life," he smirked. Frank was a good-looking guy in his early thirties. I was sure that before too long, some Hollywood starlet would snap him up, with his fancy car, horse-stable, movie connections and all.

As for his horses: there were rows of them in his stable and another group on the paddock. When we entered the stable, we were greeted by two dogs, a German Shepherd and an Australian sheepdog mix. "That's Randy and Gringo" a young stable-lad informed us. Tiny and Randy eyed each other with great suspicion. I picked up Tiny, not wanting to take the risk of an "armed" confrontation between the German shepherd and my miniscule Pekingese. Tiny was in fact just preparing to bite Gringo, indicating this by his typical pre-bite snarl. I did not want to find out what would happen if Gringo refused to allow the little Pekingese to put him in his place.

On the paddock, we saw the most amazing black horse. "You can't have him," Frank said, when I asked him about the horse a little later. "That's Wildfire. I just drove all across Quebec to find a beautiful, black horse like that. I need him for a Dracula movie. A film crew is coming here next week from Hollywood to start shooting."

"Sell him to me when the movie is finished," I pleaded.

"I need my two black horses," Frank explained. "When there are horror movies, they often require black horses for the carriages. A pretty black is hard to find these days..."

Finally, "we" talked him into it. The deal was definitely aided by a few tail-wags and cute, puppy-dog faces. We waited six weeks and, after shooting was completed, we took Wildfire with us. It turned out that our new equine had an affinity with dogs. He had been best friends with Gringo, the Australian sheepdog mix and so he immediately took a liking to Tiny and Mike. When the little dogs first made intimate acquaintance with the horse, Wildfire bent his neck down to give Mike a friendly sniff. Mike thanked him with a bite on the nose. Hurt and aghast, the horse withdrew and has been weary of Mike ever since. The little dog probably could not help it. Since having been stepped on by a horse in his youth, Mike has the irresistible urge to bite or at least bark threateningly at any horse that crosses his path. Poor Wildfire...

A few weeks after we got Wildfire, Phil and myself loaded Tiny, Mike and the cat into one of our two Mercury sables and drove across the boarder into the US. We were about to spend one year in historical Newport, the most famous city of the state of Rhode Island, on the way to new adventures...

At the time, we had no idea what to do with Wildfire. Newport, I had already found out, did not have many riding stables. Initially, we left Wildfire behind in Canada. When we first arrived, Tiny, Mike and I drove around the area of our new home in search of a place for the horse.

We found Stone Gate farm, a Morgan horse-breeding farm. At $400 monthly boarding fee, it offered only a tiny riding arena, and nowhere to ride outside. There was Glen Farm, a beautiful historical building that was under the directorship of a famous show-jumper. Glen Farm was famous for its international Polo matches and was the playground of Newport's wealthy. Unfortunately, it was also overcrowded and up to sixteen people rode in their large indoor arena at any one time. The daughter of the former governor of Massachusetts ran Sandy Point Farm, our next stop. It had a riding arena inside the stable area; it was overcrowded and also very expensive.

At last, there was the ill-fated "Newport Equestrian Center." They were constantly in financial trouble and most of their horses were starving. They offered trail-rides to the public, and one girl had been killed when she fell off her horse as the jittery equine had bolted on the road. The owner had filed for bankruptcy to avoid the legal damages, and had re-opened the riding school under a new name. Never mind that they had an indoor arena and accepted borders. This place would never see even one hoof of Wildfire...

Finally, as often, "accident" helped. Tiny, Mike and I got lost on our second day in Newport. We could not find our way home to the beautiful house we had rented on the prestigious Indian Avenue. On third beach road, we pulled into a driveway at random and knocked on the door of the house. Not only did the woman turn out to be the long lost widow of Phil's oldest journalist friend from England, but she also happened to "know this private stable just up the road from me. I am pretty sure they take in boarder horses..."

Within two weeks, Wildfire followed us to Rhode Island, delivered by Frank, the stuntman.

PART 5

TINY, MIKE AND FAMILY IN NEWPORT

Chapter 27

The Lesser Adventures Of Wildfire
Or: Shake-A-Leg, Kindergarten, Round-The-World Sailors And A Horse

Before too long, the six of us had settled into our new home. Newport turned out to be a charming little town, with cobblestone streets, enticing shops and three lovely beaches. The town's famous Ocean Drive wound itself along picturesque cliffs and rocks that overlooked a beautiful ocean.

"I think we are going to like it here," I remarked, unnecessarily, to my husband. Our house was gorgeous. Situated on some four acres of land, with its private beach and an ocean view. Our neighbors lived in mansions, one of which even housed the city's newspaper publisher.

Thanks to the lady I met when I had gotten lost, Wildfire ended up in a stable just around the corner from where we lived. From there, Phil, the dogs, the horse and I ventured out for walks along the beautiful Newport roads.

We had only been doing so for the second day when we met some children by the roadside. A little girl was walking with her two younger brothers. All three of them stopped when they saw Wildfire.

"What a lovely horse," the girl remarked longingly.

"Would you like to have a ride?" I asked her. I could see in her eyes how much she wanted to. I knew from asking around that prices in Newport for riding were very high: the going rate was $50 for half an hour of a guided trail-ride. No way that a young girl would be able to afford it, unless she had well-off parents to pay for it. This girl did not look like her parents had money enough to pay for riding lessons. We put the smiling girl on the Wildfire's back. Phil led the horse by the reins as we walked toward the beautiful nurseries, the little boys skipping behind us in the sunshine. We learned that the girl's name was Kathryn. She came from a family that was living off Welfare, and she had four brothers, of which e had just met the younger two. Her mother, Sue, had been abandoned by her military husband several years ago, leaving her to fend for herself and her five children. The family lived in the once impressive home of Kathryn's grandmother. Now, it was slowly falling apart, because there was no money to fix it.

Sue, Kathryn's mother, had been forced to abandon her studies for a psychology degree in order to work. Kathryn's grandmother, now an arthritis-ridden woman of eighty, had a Masters in Mathematics from the University of North Carolina at Chapel Hill. She had led a life worthy of a book in itself: educator for the Navajo Indians in El Paso, fluent Spanish speaker with regular travels to Mexico, university lecturer at some of the best schools in the nation. Now, she was languishing in the neglected house, trying her best to help her daughter who struggled to make ends meet.

There was no money for horse riding lessons. As many young girls do, Kathryn loved horses and riding was one of her fondest dreams.

"If you would like, you can come with us when we walk the horse, and you can sit on his back," I offered Kathryn. "But you have to help clean him up every day."

The girl's eyes shone with delight. Suddenly, she would have an opportunity to escape her cramped surroundings and her four brothers, and she was also about to make a real friend. Because we lived so close to Wildfire's stable, we often took him home for lunch. We sat outside on our patio furniture as Wildfire looked on, sticking his nose into our dishes from time to time to inspect what "the humans" were eating. When we did so, we often invited Kathryn over. The little girl and Wildfire soon became close friend. He would allow her to scratch him behind the ears as she sat at the table, and he would even put his head into her lap. After three weeks, we had a phone call from her mother.

"Tess, this is Sue. I am Kathryn's mother. I just wanted to thank you for everything you have done for my daughter."

"I haven't done anything," I replied, surprised.

"Yes, you have. Since she knows Wildfire, Kathryn is a changed person. She always had problems adjusting socially. She was shy and withdrawn. Now she has even become more outgoing with the other kids. She has so much more confidence now. And if the kids at school give her a hard time, she tells herself: "only two more hours until I get to see Wildfire." She used to hang around with bad kids, who were into drugs. I was really worried she was going to end up just like them. But now that she spends her afternoons with Wildfire, she has better things to do with her time. She stays away from the bad kids. She tells Wildfire all her problems while she is brushing him. The horse blows into her face, and her world is right again."

Naturally, I was pleased that my horse had been able to make such a positive impact on someone else's life. I told Kathryn she could visit as often as she wanted to.

While Kathryn was still learning about horses, I broke my foot and ended up on crutches. This rendered me unable to take Wildfire for his customary rides and walks.

"You will have to take him for a walk by yourself today," I announced Kathryn the day after I had broken my foot. Usually, I had always come with her, controlling the horse as she either walked beside me or sat on his back. "Do you think you will be able to keep control of him?"

She nodded. "Of course, no problem."

Together, we drove to the stable and I watched as she groomed Wildfire to prepare him for the walk. This done, I handed the young girl the lead-chain and - leaning on my two crutches - hobbled to the car.

"I will drive ahead to the beach and meet you there," I instructed her. "It shouldn't take you more than ten minutes."

Half an hour later, I was still waiting at the beach, and

waiting... When Kathryn and Wildfire did not show up, I went to look for them. To my surprise, I encountered them coming out of the driveway of an elegant, white house.

"What happened to you two?" I asked when I caught up with them.

"Wildfire dragged me right to that guy's front door," Kathryn explained sheepishly. "He must have a fascination with driveways. He just wouldn't budge until we were on the doorstep."

I laughed, not knowing what else to do. It was either laugh or cry, and out of the two, I always prefer to choose the former. The slender girl, 13 years of age, had obviously been taken for the proverbial ride by my horse, who knew full well that he was stronger than her.

"What happened?" I wanted to hear the rest of the story. "When you got to the doorstep, I mean?"

"Well, the owner came out and he asked what the horse wants on his doorstep. 'I don't know. I think he wants a carrot', I told him, not knowing what else to say."

The hapless man had replied: "I don't have any carrots, but I have an apple. Is that okay?" Kathryn nodded, and he had gone inside the house to cut up an apple for Wildfire. When he returned, the horse chewed the apple and then willingly walked out of his driveway and back on the road again to continue his walk.

After this, Wildfire learned that driveways equaled snacks. For the six weeks it took for my foot to heal, Kathryn and Wildfire turned up on many doorsteps of our exclusive neighborhood, shaking the "proper" New England mansion and house owners out of their "properhood." Even our landlords were not immune. They lived in a huge mansion adjoining our property, and were frequently visited by our horse. He clopped down their cobblestone driveway with a happy expression on his long face, typically squashed a few daisies in the yard and curiously looked through their front door window as Kathryn or myself rang the doorbell.

Hope, the landlady, would take one look at the front door and - being confronted with a big, black horse-nose on the other side of the window - would shout upstairs to her husband: "Dick, Wildfire is here." Dick, a retired Admiral and politically well respected member of Newport's elite, would rush downstairs to satisfy our horse's demands. He bought, especially for this occasion, carrots by the sackful and he kept them stored in his fridge. When Wildfire came to call on them, he rushed outside and fed him. After Wildfire had snacked to his heart's content, he often posed for photos with Dick and Hope before we went on our way.

Soon, Wildfire's and Kathryn's driveway antics earned us a reputation as "the horse-beggars." People thought we were using the horse to beg for its food! I decided that we would only call on people we knew, and who appreciated the hungry equine's visits. The impromptu visits of Kathryn and Wildfire to people's driveways at the horse's discretion had to stop. This meant that I could not let them go out alone anymore. Looking for a new solution to put the horse through its exercise program, I trained Wildfire to beside my car as I drove, holding on to the reins. For the remainder of my "crutch period," I exercised him by driving on the road, my right arm on the wheel, left arm hanging out of the window, holding him as he walked orderly by the side of the car. It took some training, however, to teach Wildfire that a car was not a toy and one could not walk in front of it while it was in motion. During our outings, Kathryn followed us either in foot, or she sat in the car with me.

Kathryn's mother called to give increasingly positive reports of her daughter's changes. I was glad to hear that Wildfire had been able to make such a great difference. I always tend to think it is so much nicer when you can share your blessings with those around you. Phil and I were even gladder to hear that Kathryn had become a straight A student and that she had transferred from her public school to a private one, having been awarded a scholarship. The girl had completely changed, and we encouraged her as much as possible. Soon, we invited her to our house to brush Tiny and Mike. When we went to the beautiful Newport beaches, which was always a special treat for the dogs, Kathryn came with us and ran with Mike along the beach while Tiny and myself watched.

After several months, Wildfire moved stables. We were in search of a bigger riding ring and transferred him to the "Swiss village," a lovely arrangement of old stone buildings that had been erected more than a century ago by a wealthy Newporter, who had grown up in Switzerland and missed his homeland's building style. This was another accidental find. When Phil was sailing at the historic Fort Adams State park one day, I had decided to visit him. Driving by the Swiss Village, I could see a horse being ridden in a newly erected sand ring.

Immediately, I turned the car and drove toward the horse to investigate. For all I knew, the "village" was an exclusive drug and alcohol treatment center. Not anymore! I was pleasantly surprised to encounter a very pretty young lady by the name of Jennifer who had just signed a 10-year lease with the owners of the Swiss Village, to convert the facility into an equestrian center. She had just arrived with her horses and had opened the facility to the public only the day before. Willingly, Jen gave me a tour. The stables were carved into elegant stone buildings, much larger than usual. I knew that Wildfire would be very happy there. I knew that I would be, too, especially because there was an outdoor riding arena, which did not exist at the other, private stable.

"Can we move here?" I asked enthusiastically, and was told that there was still one stall available.

At the end of the month, Jen's partner Frank picked up

316

Wildfire from his old home. Now we had lost the opportunity to have our horse conveniently located, only two streets up from where we lived. We could no longer bring him home for breakfast, or take him to the beach for a walk. But we had a wonderful riding ring and we met some amazing people at the Swiss Village. Here was truly an exclusive opportunity for meeting the most fascinating characters from all walks of life.

First, there was Jennifer herself. A tall, blonde beauty with piercing blue eyes, she came from a wealthy North Carolina family. Jennifer's father was one of the top cancer researchers in the country. Her brother held multiple degrees in philosophy from such universities as Cambridge and Berkley. Jennifer herself, who looked more like a model than a horsewoman, had a Masters in fine arts from some prestigious university or other. She let it all go to open a horse-farm. The love of horses had won over her parent's expectation of academia. Slender as she was, Jen worked hard each day to clean the stalls, carried full water buckets one in each hand, and stood in glaring sun or pouring rain to give riding lessons back to back, sometimes up to eight hours at a time.

To her, it was all worth it. She was crazy about her favorite horse, a huge chestnut thoroughbred that she named "Red." The two could frequently been seen goofing around the stable. Happiness shone in Jen's eyes as she received "horse hugs" from her giant equine.

Then there was Frank, Jennifer's partner. Frank was 50 and not supposed to be alive. He had fallen off his horse from a heart attack some three years earlier and had been clinically dead. Revived with CPR, and a triple by-pass operation later, Frank was back in the horse-business. Ignoring his doctor's advice not to work anymore, Frank had set off in his truck around the country to buy horses and open a stable with Jen. He was gruff, but kind beneath his rough exterior. Frank was someone everybody worried about, because nobody knew how long he would be able to hold out with his fragile heart. At the time of writing, Frank is still going strong, ignoring everyone's warnings to slow down.

There was a riding teacher, aged 38, who smoked although he shouldn't have done so. Having been born with a defective heart, he had survived a stroke and had been told not to smoke. He did so anyway. The man appeared at the village, gave a few lessons, patted Wildfire on the nose, and was gone within six weeks of arrival. I don't know what became of him and nobody ever told us.

There was another riding teacher who did not last long. He arrived at the same time as a gay stable lad from Puerto Rico. The two eloped and rode off into the sunset, never to be seen again.

The most colorful character was Kate, a most gifted storyteller. Kate had been married to a very wealthy man. In 1990, they had set out on their 45 foot yacht to sail around the world. Kate told wondrous stories of life in the Caribbean, Portugal, South Africa and even out of the way places she had visited during violent revolutions. I just about killed myself with laughter when she spoke of going hunting for wild chickens in the Marquesas, and even from how she described the time their boat rolled over in a hurricane (fortunately without any damage or injury).

Kate was one of those women who seemed to have it all. She had an amazing life, a great affinity with animals, and she was a top pilot and a really nice girl. It was not unusual to see Kate riding one of Jen's horses with nothing but a halter and a lead rope, calming the jittery equine by her voice alone. After her divorce, Kate was now engaged to a lovely man by the name of David, a former Air Force pilot and now a successful engineer. David owned his own plane, and Kate and David took Phil flying with them. As for me, I like to have both feet firmly planted in the ground. Tiny, Mike and I watched from the tower as the three of them took to the skies. When they came down again, Tiny was allowed to sit in the cockpit. Like a child, the little Pekingese obviously got a kick out of being "at the controls" and proudly grinned into the camera as Phil photographed "the pilot" after his daring flight.

A heartwarming story was that of Karen. Karen, with a mane of beautiful blond curls, was a gorgeous University student studying for a Masters degree in psychology. She lived in a mansion with her parents. Karen was the most amazing horse rider in the Swiss village. Beautiful, kind, and wealthy, Karen's life seemed like a fairy-tale, but it was far from it. Talking to her mother, who always came to watch her daughter ride, I learned that a few years ago, Karen had been on the junior jumping team and had been destined to go to the Olympics. Then she was in a devastating car accident: Karen had wrapped her car around a tree and almost died. She spent months in hospital, somewhere between life and death as her desperate mother sat by her side, holding her hand. When Karen finally woke up, it was not clear if she would ever be able to walk again. She had iron plates in her arms and legs. Naturally, the horses had to be sold and her dreams of going to the Olympics went up in smoke.

The once happy girl became withdrawn and depressed. She refused to go outside. She slept all day and saw no more future for herself. Physical rehabilitation was slow, but finally she was able to walk again. One day, her parents happened to find out about the horse farm. They knew Frank and brought a reluctant Karen to the stable. Slowly, she came out of her shell, and eventually started riding again. As she rode, she gained back her desire to live. Her mother remarked how Karen was rehabilitating herself even as we watched her ride, pointing out to me what was invisible to the eyes: how difficult and painful it was for Karen to move her arms and shoulders, effortless as it may have looked.

As we watched, Karen jumped around the hurdles, executing each jump perfectly. After a few weeks of being around the horses, she had begun to smile once more. Finally, she even took part in a competition. It was touching to see her elegant mother walking through the horse manure, helping her daughter groom the horse, assisting in any way she could. After the competition, which she won in several divisions, Karen was a changed girl. Riding, she had gained back her former self. She prepared to finish her Masters degree, made plans to learn Spanish, bought the horse she had been riding from Frank and moved to Paris to study at the prestigious Sorbonne University. The last I heard, Karen had even been parachuting...

There was also Annabel, a stunning twenty-year old. Annabel not only looked like a model, she was a model. Half British and half American, her beautiful face graced the title pages of various local glossy magazines. It was not unusual to go to a local supermarket and see Annabel's face smiling from the checkout stand's magazine rack. Like many professional models, Annabel always looked elegant, no matter what she did. When she cleaned stalls at the horse-barn, her silky, blond hair fell beautifully over her evenly tanned shoulders. When she rode a horse, her jodhpurs clad tightly to exquisitely shaped legs and a sexy Barbie-doll waist. Nobody would have guessed that here was another beautiful face that hid a tragic story: Annabel was a diplomat's child. Her father, an American embassy attaché, had been blown-up by terrorists while he was stationed in Greece. When it happened, Annabel had just entered her teens. She was old enough to grasp the full extent of the horror of what had happened. For the rest of her life, this stunning beauty, who had grown up all over the world and had finally been educated in Britain, would have to live with the memory of her father's violent death. This she tried to forget while riding Frank's horses...

There was, last but not least, Frank's daughter: 16, blonde and determined, the girl had overcome the trauma of her parent's divorce by becoming a financial whiz kid. At 16, she had $200,000 in the bank, all of which was her own money.

"How did you do that?" I wanted to know.

"Well, my grandmother died," she began, "and she left me some money. Then my aunt died and left me some. Then my other aunt died and also left me money. So I had $20,000."

"And?"

"So I called one bank and said: listen, this other bank is paying me so and so much interest. How much will you give me if I come to you? They offered me more, and I changed. A few months later, I called the first bank and asked: how much will you give me to come back? It's easy, you just have to change banks from time to time. Then I asked my mom to buy some stocks for me, and I sold them just before the crash."

She aimed to become a millionaire before she was 25, the ambitious young woman told me. "So I can support my boyfriend, because he doesn't have a cent. And I want to go to vet school, that will be expensive, too."

Lucky boyfriend...

These were not the only ones of Wildfire's friends, just some of these I knew about. It turned out that my horse actually had friends wherever we went. After he had been at the stable for two weeks, I would frequently find total strangers walking up to me and have some woman or man greet me like they knew me: "Oh, so you are the owner of Wildfire. Hi Wildfire, how are you?" With amazement, I would watch as my horse nuzzled the person affectionately for a carrot. "So, you know my horse, too," would soon become my standard introduction. Wildfire was a horse with a captivating personality and a mischievous streak. He made use of his charms to the fullest to entice people to come by his stable and spoil him. A little girl, I learned, who lived in a mansion, came by once a day to feed Wildfire with baby gourmet organic carrots. I rest my case...

My biggest surprise came one day as I was brushing

Wildfire in the stable and a group of kindergarten children arrived with their teacher. "Oh, there is Black Beauty," the little girls exclaimed and made straight for my horse. Wildfire graciously lowered his head to allow the little girls to pat him. As I watched in amazement, dozens of tiny hands held out carrots to my horse, who hardly had time to chew one treat before the next one was being offered to him.

"I hope you don't mind" the kindergarten teacher addressed me. "The children are all in love with your horse. We come here once a day to give him treats."

Of course, I did not mind in the least. On one of our outings, Wildfire and I even stopped at the Kindergarten to allow the little girls to take photos with the horse. Little arms went around his neck as wildfire stood patiently for his photo to be taken. I am told that the photos of "Black Beauty" with his lady friends are now on proud display at the wall of the kindergarten...

Soon, we discovered that the buildings on the back of the stable, still on the same estate, housed the Shake-A-Leg foundation: a housing and living development for people with paraplegia. Actor Christopher Reeve, paralyzed after a horse-riding accident, was due to visit soon. He was involved with the Shake-A-Leg's horse therapy program and would be in Newport for three days. Reeve indeed arrived, sailed on an old America's Cup yacht and afterwards visited Shake-A-Leg. Wildfire, I was told, missed out on meeting him because Reeve's tight schedule did not allow, as he had planned, a visit to the horse-stable before he was off with his lovely wife Dana to one of the many functions which had been planned for him.

Having missed Reeve and the chance to find out about the horse therapy program, Wildfire and I decided to do our own "hippotherapy." After Reeve had been and gone, we made it a point to go riding through the grounds of Shake-A-Leg, happily waving to the astonished counselors who saw us as they got out of their cars to go to work. We hoped that one day we would happen to come across some of the facility's residents, and be able to make their day.

And one day it finally happened. Wildfire and myself were walking casually around Shake-A-Leg's grounds, with me leading him on a long rope to allow him to eat the grass on the side of the road. It was a lovely summer's day, with birds singing in the trees as the sun warmed our backs. Such pleasant a day had not gone unnoticed by the residents of Shake-A-Leg, and we came across a young man and a young woman in their wheelchairs as they were going for a walk/drive with their counselor. Longingly, they looked at the horse and stopped their automatic wheelchairs to admire him.

"Would you like to pat the horse?" I asked. The girl nodded eagerly, trying to lean forward in her chair.

"I don't know if that's such a good idea," the counselor replied. "The horse might kick or bite, and then what? They can't move out of the way."

"Not Wildfire," I assured her. "He would never do that. Wildfire loves people. He will be very careful, I promise."

The counselor agreed reluctantly and watched with a worried face as I led Wildfire closer to the two wheelchairs. Gingerly, the horse bent down his head in put in the lap of the girl, so she could stroke his white blaze. It was as if he knew that there was something wrong with the two people who were sitting before him, that they could not move like his other friends to get out of his way, and that therefore he had to be careful with his usually rapid movements.

The disabled girl's eyes shone with joy as she patted the horse, and soon her companion wanted to join in. Carefully, I led Wildfire to the other wheelchair. It took so little to make these two, who had such a hard lot in life, happy for a moment in time. I could have sworn I saw a smile on the face of my horse when we walked away. They must have told their friends, for I could afterward often see wheelchairs come to the stable

323

just around sunset, driving around the beautiful grounds of the equestrian center. Maybe they were looking for Wildfire, the friendly horse with the big heart...

As much as he enjoyed helping out the less fortunate, Wildfire had a definite taste for things rich and stylish. We found this out when I took him on his first tour around the lavish Newport mansions. The riding stable was set in the midst of a very expensive area of Newport, which was characterized by quiet residential streets with huge estates. Wildfire stopped at every driveway we passed, making a point to look at the houses with great astonishment, as if to ask, "Wow, do people really live here?"

He had an enormous fascination with one house in particular, a lavish twelve-bedroom mansion that stood on six acres of ground and overlooked the ocean. The house was for sale for the bargain price of three million dollars and Wildfire - clearly - had already worked out that we were going to move in. Whenever we passed the house, he stopped and gazed longingly at the house, as if to make out where his stable would be and where he was going to graze...

"If I had a few million to spare, I certainly would buy this house for our horse," I told him as I dragged him on and added "But I don't, so sorry." Wildfire is actually sulking to this day because we did not buy him the house and will still stop each time and try to enter the house through its long, winding driveway.

Wildfire's fascination with driveways extended far beyond this one house, into all of the living grounds of the super-rich. Most of these houses, we learned, were in fact vacation homes for rock-stars, sport-stars and other famous people who came all the way from New York. Riding out, for instance, we met a famous baseball star, several football stars and basketball greats... all of them jogging in the beautiful Newport summer's evening. There was not one driveway that Wildfire did not wish to enter.

One evening, we did him the favor. Kathryn and I were walking Wildfire on a lovely summer's evening when we heard music coming from one of the mansions. Wildfire stopped to look. The driveway wound for a long time before it could be seen from the house. We decided to let the horse catch a brief look. "If we do not walk within view of the house, they won't even know we are there." Warning Wildfire to be discreet about our invasion of whoever this was's privacy, we advanced carefully along the driveway. Wildfire walked proudly, with his ears pricked forward, prancing toward the house. To my utter horror, he stopped just before we came into view of the party guests, lifted his tail and with the most exquisite expression on his face left a huge, brown calling card - plunk - in the middle of the elegant driveway. So much for being discreet! We turned Wildfire around as soon as he was done and got the hell out of there. We could only imagine the "joy" on the guest's faces when they prepared to leave and found the gift that our horse had left for them...

"It wasn't us," I told Kathryn and the horse as we jogged away. "They only have circumstantial evidence. They did not catch us in the act. If anyone asks, we've never been near the place. We never saw that house. The ground rule is: deny, deny, deny. All right guys?" The horse and the little girl agreed and we got away as fast as we could. The following morning I walked past the same house to see that the manure had been neatly cleared away, the driveway pedantically scrubbed clean. Luckily, they never caught the offending party...

Chapter 28

A Tear And A Smile
Or: Mike, Wildfire And The Extreme Games

Sometimes, the sun shines as the sky caves in. Sometimes joy and pain ride on the same train. Sometimes tragedy and happiness live under the same roof. Sometimes a smile and a tear form a rainbow. As the dogs of a journalist, these things happen to Tiny and Mike just like they do to everyone else. Because of my line of work, sometimes they happen in a dramatic way. Or in an extreme one...

In the middle of 1996, the Extreme Games came to Newport, and with them the world's most daring athletes. There are twenty-three events in nine categories, with strange names such as: sky surfing, in-line skating, street luge, bicycle stunt, sport climbing, bungee jumping, skateboarding, wakeboarding or barefoot jumping. I was there to interview some participants of the sky-surfing competition. Because their competition took place at the beach, or rather, above it, I decided to take Mike along. Because of the heat and Tiny's susceptibility to it, we left him behind with the cat.

Three days into the games, the first jumps of the sky-surfing competition started. When getting my accreditation, I was told that I did not need an extra pass for Mike. "I think canine journalists can come in with their owners, though we never had a case like this before," the man at the Press Office said.

Newly accredited, Mike and me drove to Newport's beautiful Second Beach. What a great environment this was to be working in. The water was warm and inviting and relaxed journalists in shorts and hats shared their sunscreen lotions with each other and looked out to sea as we waited for the action to begin.

I knew nothing about sky surfing, and was informed by

327

a colleague that it is the most fascinating, but also the most dangerous sport of the Extreme Games.

"I hope they are paid well, then," I replied.

"It's not that kind of sport," he explained. "Nobody here is paid large sums of money. People who sky-surf jump for the sheer love of their sport. You will see their eyes shine with joy when they come in to land after a jump."

I opened my media guide and learned that the roots of sky surfing stem from skydiving. Skydivers first began experimenting with boards in 1980. The initial manoeuvre of lying down in flight was replaced after seven years with standing up on the board. Today, sky-surfers jump in professional competition teams of two. These consist of a camera flyer and a surfer. They are judged according to the camera work as well as the acrobatics with the surfboard. Incredibly, all of this happens while they fall at an average speed of 150 miles per hour.

The defending world champion, I read, was a young man by the name of Joe Jennings. He had lost his partner, Rob Harris, a few months earlier in a skydiving accident while they had been filming a television commercial in Canada for Mountain Dew. Rob's parachute had failed to open. Joe was jumping and videotaping his friend at the time of the accident, having to watch helplessly as Rob plummeted toward the ground. Their friendship and Rob's loss, I learned, was the X Games biggest story this year. I also learned that Sky-surfing is the most fascinating sport of the games, because it is so unusual, and that most of the spectators suffered his loss alongside Joe Jennings.

Because the sky-surfers' maneuvers happen high in the air, the videos of their jumps are transmitted to the public via large screens. The fans follow their heroes on these screens, until they are low enough to open their canopies. Then, they watch them "live" as they glide into the landing zone.

A media tent had been installed on the beach, opposite

the big screen. I came to sit next to a charming, older gentleman who introduced himself to me as: "I am Joe Jennings's dad."

"You must be very proud of him," I commented.

"Yes," the man replied. "I sure am. It hasn't been easy for him to come here. After Rob's death, he decided to retire from competition. But he is doing one more season, because they had planned to defend their title this year. It had been their dream to come here together. Joe is doing this for Rob."

I watched Joe and his new partner Patrick de Gayardon (a French Count who became a sky-diver and sky surfer of legendary reputation and who also invented the bird suit that allowed longer freefalls than previously possible) perform their sky-ballet on the big screen. It was a performance of astonishing elegance and beauty. When Joe came in to land, his father got up, walked to the dividing fence and gave his son a long hug.

"I am proud of you, son," he told him.

Next, I watched Joe hug and kiss his wife. I watched him hug and kiss his friends. It was evident that he was going through a very rough time. He seemed to be held together only by the support of his family and friends, and barely at that. Inside of him, everything hurt but on the outside, he smiled and he jumped, as a tribute to his dead friend...

Never having met Rob, I was still able to imagine his love for the sky. It hung in the air and it shone through the teary eyes of his friend Joe. It was even evident in the pain of his other sky-surfing friends. They all had him in their hearts and they were jumping with him.

Later that afternoon Mike and me went to the drop zone. As we watched the competitors re-pack their parachutes, I interviewed Vivian Weygrath, an attractive world champion sky-surfer from Switzerland.

When I asked her about Rob, she replied: "It was a big blow to all of us. At first, they only told us that he had been killed, but not how. It was most important to me to know why

329

he died, what exactly had happened. Once I knew, it was easier to deal with. Initially, it was difficult to go back to jumping, because there is someone missing now. Sky-surfers are a close knit group. We all travel together. We love each other like family. When someone dies, it is like losing a family member. Rob was always so happy, full of smiles. I know he'd have rather gone like this than any other way."

Talking about her friend Rob, a lump formed in the young sky-surfer's throat. Mike, sensing that something was wrong, walked up to her and sat in her lap. As is his custom when he wants attention, he worked on the girl's arm with his paw, demanding to be petted.

"That's quite some dog you have there," Vivian remarked, smiling again. It was difficult to imagine that the sad girl who sat with me on the field, playing with Mike, was a world champion sky-surfer and that she jumped out of a plane in flight with a surfboard strapped to her feet...

In the evening, Mike and myself went to dinner with the sky-surfers. A table had been set up with soft drinks, and people formed lines to get a plate of chili, tamales and hamburgers.

"For top class athletes, they don't feed them very well," I remarked to Phil. We decided to pass on the food, being used to more healthy fare. Instead, we watched the others eat, Mike making friends here and there as people hurried by to get to their tables. After dinner, most of the sky-surfers got together with their camera flyers to watch and analyze their afternoon's videos. Others sat on the floor in a big tent, which was marked "athletes only" and packed their parachutes for the next day's competition.

Journalists were not permitted in the tent, but this was no problem for Mike. A quick dance for the doorman, a delighted exclamation of "My, isn't he cute" and we went in as the delighted doorman, besotted by Mike, said, "Go on in, you're free to pass."

We spent the evening with Amy Bailey-Haas, whom I interviewed for a profile. Amy was interviewed for part of a series entitled: "Ordinary pilots, extraordinary lives," because her life is extraordinary indeed. During the week, she flies a plane for UPS. On weekends, Amy sheds her pilot's uniform and turns into one of the world's most daring athletes. Add to this her infectious smile, her pretty face and a sweet personality, and you know why Amy charms everyone she meets. Including Mike!

Mike was smitten with Amy. While we were talking, he jumped up on her lap. I had to interrupt the tape several times, to give Amy a chance to play with him and share the last of her dinner with him. He had already guilted her into giving him her every second bite. Other competitors came up to see what we were doing and thought Amy had gone nuts, sharing her food with the little dog.

Macho guys and Shihtzus? Forget it. We became a standing joke among the competitors: "See, there is a difference between men and women after all. No matter how hard they fight for equality in the sky, they still remain sissies. One only has to look at that damn dog to see the proof. As if two guys would ever be caught dead doing an interview with a dog in their midst!"

Oh well! You win some, you lose some...

Amy and me grinned happily at the guys, ignored their whispered remarks about Mike, and kept talking and feeding Mike. When Amy and me had finished the interview we made tentative plans to travel to Latin America the following year - accompanied, of course, by Mike.

The next day Mike marched from athlete to athlete, "inspecting" their parachutes.

"My dog wants to have a look at your parachute," I explained to one astonished macho-competitor, as Mike pranced across the canvas floor towards him. Despite himself, he took time out from packing to pat Mike.

"We are writing a book about him," I explained. "That's why I take him on all my assignments. I hope you don't mind. We are going to write a chapter: Mike at the Extreme Games, you know."

"What a splendid idea," the man replied. He confided that he was a dog-lover himself, having owned a spaniel until recently. "But then I started competing seriously, and so I am never home. I decided to give the dog to my mother for now."

"Why don't you just take him with you?" I suggested.

"Perhaps I ought to consider it," he reflected. "I must say, the thought of taking a dog on the road has never occurred to me. Mike is the first dog we ever had at the Extreme Games..."

Mike danced around the parachute, scored a biscuit from the man's pocket, and then we had to be on our way. I thought I heard the men around us mutter something like "Women!" and saw them shake their heads as we walked out the door...

The following day was the day of the sky-surfing finals. Once again, I watched Joe on the big monitor. He and his partner executed their spectacular sky-board routine. Together with the other journalists, I walked over to his family when he came in to land. There were tears in his eyes. We stood by as he gave first his wife and then his mother a long hug. They all cried. We could not help being touched by these people, and most of us journalists cried, too. We could not even explain why. I got a better idea why we were all so moved when I met Harris's girlfriend Chrissy. She wore a locket around her neck, which she opened for me. On the left side was a photo.

"That's Rob," she explained. Then, indicating the right side of the locket she said "and these are his ashes." Despite the warm sun, the words of Rob's beautiful girlfriend and the contents of her locket chilled me to the bone.

Soon after, I met Joe's mother in law, Lynn. We started

talking, as she confided: "The last jump was especially difficult for Joe. We haven't made it public yet, but he jumped with Roy's ashes on his wrist. He released them in the air during the jump. He's done that at drop-off zones all over the world, releasing some of his ashes over each drop-zone they had once jumped together."

Now I understood why everyone had cried. The idea of a man releasing the ashes of his dead sky surfing partner during his final jump of a world-class competition, in free-fall, was very moving. We both cried again.

"I think it is great he is doing that for Rob," I told her, sniffling and fumbling for a tissue.

She sniffled back: "Yes, isn't it? He is jumping this final round of competition, before he retires. He is jumping not only for Rob, he is jumping it with Rob. It will be the very last time the two of them jump together. After that, Rob will become part of the air. Now, because Joe has his ashes still with him, they still exit the plane together..."

There we stood, a couple of tearful ladies, in the sun outside the drop zone. We watched as the competitors went for the victory celebration. Joe's father and wife never left his side. Joe stepped on the podium and accepted the Bronze Medal, together with his new partner. Many of the other competitors let their tears flow freely, as did most of the journalists. It was a sad moment, and yet a happy one, because Joe had come to fulfill the dream of his friend.

He and Patrick, his new partner, had not been able to retain the title, but a third place in the world championship was not bad either.

During the medal ceremony, Sissy's mother and me cried through another couple of tissues. "This is so sad," I sniffled. "Would you like to go and visit my horse? He'll cheer us up again. My horse is very funny. He is stabled just round the corner from here."

Lynn said that she would love to. We asked the others if

they wanted to come along, but they preferred to go straight back to their motel. Joe's group was, rather surprisingly, staying at Newport's Motel 6.

"This is where Joe and Rob had been staying last year, so we wanted to reconstruct the trip as closely as possible to how it had been for the two of them," Lynn explained.

On the way to the horse, we drove by an old cemetery in downtown Newport. "Have you ever seen the movie 'The Fugitive Kind' with Marlon Brando?" I asked her.

"No, why?"

"Because it makes the most beautiful statement about graveyards and living," I told her. "At the start of the movie, Brando's girlfriend takes him to a graveyard. She asks: 'Can you hear the dead people talking?' 'Dead people don't talk', he replies. 'Oh yes, they do', she says. 'If you only know how to listen to them. They say: Live, live. It's the only advice they can still give.'

It's so true, isn't it? Ever since seeing that movie, I think of this when I drive by a graveyard and I tell them in my mind: Yes, guys, I'm living. I'm at it..."

"That's really nice," Lynn replied. "I'll do that from now on. Rob would probably tell us this, if he could still talk."

"Tell me about Rob," I encouraged her, sensing that she needed to talk.

"He was very kind and outgoing. He always had a smile for everyone who crossed his path. Not many people knew that he was brilliant in most of what he did. He would shoot to the top in whatever he tried his hands at. In addition to being a world champion sky surfer, he was also the first person to solve the rubic cube. He was invited to become an Olympic breakdancer, but he turned it down. He was the foremost DJ in California. And he was very modest about it. He never talked of his accomplishments. He came to sky-surf and that was it. People didn't even find out about all the other fields he had excelled in until they began to research his life after he was

334

dead."

"Wow," I replied, trying to construct a mental picture of the person she described to me. When I tried, what came to mind was the image of a brilliant man who loved life, and who had skydived to find absolute freedom. Rob, young as he was, had left behind a life well lived.

Wildfire, my horse, sensed that the woman I brought with me was sad about something. He raised his mouth to her cheek and blew her a soft kiss. Lynn was instantly enchanted. She spent a long time patting wildfire and the ponies he shared his paddock with.

"Thanks for letting me come here with you," Lynn addressed me as Wildfire searched her pockets for a carrot. "This means a lot to me. I was having such a difficult time at the games, it's doing me good to get away. Sometimes, when your soul is broken and needs mending, an animal can be the one to do it best."

I nodded. "Somehow, they always seem to understand when something is wrong, don't they? They don't fumble for the right words to say. They are not embarrassed by your grief. They just come up to you and tell you in their very own, special way that you are loved."

Wildfire rested his head on Lynn's shoulder as she stroked his beautiful white blaze. The horse twisted his forehead into the right angle, to guide Lynn's hand just behind his ears. "He wants you to scratch him there now," I explained. "It's his favorite spot."

Lynn started scratching as instructed. Wildfire put on a wide horse grin and took his head off her shoulder, letting it drop lower and lower until it almost came to rest on her feet. Eyes half closed in blissful enjoyment, Wildfire leaned Lynn's shin as she scratched him.

"Your horse is quite something," she remarked. "He's really more like an overgrown Labrador than a horse, isn't he?

I've never met a horse quite like him. He is so affectionate."

We stayed in the paddock with Wildfire for over an hour. Far from the beach and the sad memories of Rob, Lynn found her smile again.

"I wish I could stay here forever," she sighed. "What a wonderful place!" With great difficulty, she finally tore herself away. "I suppose we better get back to the others," she said. "But you must promise to send me a photo of Wildfire and his Pony-friend. They are such dear animals. Actually, they are really just furry people. I am so glad I met them. I feel so much better now."

Chapter 29

Summer in Narragansett - TWA 800 hits close to home

July and August are the biggest tourist months in Newport. The town gets so congested that traffic jams block the beautiful cobble stone streets, restaurants and even grocery stores are overcrowded and - to top it off - Newport turns from a friendly little town into a nasty place. Greed becomes its motto as the town charges highly for use of the beaches, where it suddenly disallows dogs until 6pm and bans horses completely,

There are also high charges for parking almost anywhere, including the parking lots of grocery stores. These kick you off their car parks as soon as you are through shopping, courtesy of a guard. You are not even given one minute more, to perhaps shop at a neighboring store as well. Newport in summer is not a very friendly place to be. We decided to get out of our house for July and August and go somewhere else for the summer, hoping to turn these two months into a working vacation.

The nicest vacation spot for the summer, we learned after asking the locals, was the area of Scarborough/Narragansett. Situated on beautiful beaches, the picturesque location was topped only by one other spot: Harbor Island, an exclusive community within five miles of Narragansett. One nice afternoon in June, Phil, the dogs and I set out across Newport Bridge and into Narragansett, in search of a summer cottage. We went to Harbor Island first, on the off chance that there would be a place for rent. As always, fate smiled on us. As we drove onto the exclusive community, we happened upon a waterfront road. Following it all the way to the end, we came to a private beach club. Seagulls soared in the wind, above a row of carefully maintained jetties on which impeccable yachts were anchored. A couple of tables and a barbecue pit mixed with my imagination as I saw Phil, the dogs and myself sitting there for our evening meals...

"Wouldn't it be great to live here?" I asked. Phil watched the dogs run happily along the length of the beach and agreed. "We could have a wonderful time here. But what are the chances of a house being for rent in this district? Especially if it's only for two months, and then on the waterfront? "

As he spoke, a young woman walked up to us.

"May I help you?" she addressed us. "This is a private beach club."

"Yes, we know. We were looking for a place to rent for the summer. That's why we came here."

"In that case, I might be able to help you."

"Really?" Phil and me could not believe our luck. "How come?"

"See that house on the waterfront there? In the back is a duplex bungalow. I am renting the upper half. I know that my landlady is looking to rent out the lower half for July and August. So far, she has not put the ad in the paper."

Three weeks later, we took possession of our summer home. The drive from Newport was stunning: across two bridges, above the open sea, with sailboats peacefully floating by, then through lush foliage, along the beach, across open fields and finally onto "our" community of Harbor Island.

What followed were blissfully lazy weeks, during which I only worked half-day. The rest of the time the dogs and I spent exploring Harbor Island, making new friends, taking the cat for a walk on its pink leash. On weekends, Phil's banker friend Win drove up from Boston to fit his 6 foot 2 frame on our futon-bed/couch for two nights, so the men could go sailing together every Saturday and Sunday. As I had envisioned, the three of us sat on the beach during warm summer's nights, eating fresh squid curries as the dogs looked on...

Lisa, the young woman who lived above us, was only 26, but she had her hands full, with life and responsibilities! One day, my car had broken down and Lisa took me and the little dogs (who always insist on coming) to the grocery store. The young mother was at the end of her tether when she found out that her tax returns - to be picked up at her PO box on the way from the store - had not arrived as scheduled.

"You're under a lot of stress, aren't you?" I asked.

"Wouldn't you be, with two little boys and an unemployed husband?" she asked me. "You can't imagine how difficult it has been for me."

Lisa, it turned out, had started young: pregnant at 16 with her first child, she had married the child's father straight out of high school.

"But he became a drinker, so I left him. At 20, I was an unmarried mother with no job."

"What did you do?"

"I trained as a nurse's aide, finally as a nurse. Today, I run my own nursing home service. Right now, I look after a woman who once was very wealthy. She was paralyzed in a car accident and her husband left her. She kept their house, but had to convert all of her liquid assets to hire private nurses. She cannot move very well, but I think her biggest problem is loneliness. She gets panic attacks from being alone all the time. So either I or one of my employees go over to sit with her. But she can't afford to hire us around the clock. There is not enough money. So we provide companionship, and basic functions such a cooking, for eight hours of the day. The rest of the time she is alone."

"Screaming?"

"Perhaps," Lisa replied. "There is nothing I can do about it. You may not be used to it, being from abroad, but here in the States, there are a lot of lonely people. We all die from it, sooner or later."

"How do you mean?"

"We get cancer from worry, we suffer from panic attacks, or we commit suicide. Sometimes we just die inside from lack

339

of kindness. That's enough."

"That's terrible"

"That's life," Lisa shrugged. "Even I ... I have a husband, but I am still alone in all essence. All the responsibility is on me. I have nobody to talk to about my own problems. If I don't make ends meet, the kids don't eat."

The husband, I learned, was her other high-school sweetheart. After having left the first one, she married him and had a second child with him. "He is not the father of my first boy, but he adopted him. Still, it's not easy. We argue a lot, because there is never any money."

"Why doesn't he work?"

"He is a car mechanic, but he is not licensed for the state of Rhode Island. He would have to go back to school. But I can't let him do that for now. I need him to baby-sit. I work two jobs, and we need every cent. After all the expenses, there is no money for a baby-sitter. Still, it is tough on everyone, most of all for Carl, my oldest. I simply don't have enough time for him, since I work weekends as well."

"He is a smart kid," I complimented the young mother.

"Yes, he is. He gets straight A's in school. He wants to be a doctor to help poor people. That's wonderful. I am proud of him. He is also very kind. I have done my best to instill values in him: to be kind to people and animals, that we are all worth the same, rich or poor, black or white. The other day, I saw Carl stop to rescue a beetle in the middle of the road so that it wouldn't get run over. But he needs more attention. He is hyperactive because nobody looks after him."

"Well, Lisa, I suppose the dogs and I..."

"Would you? Would you let him come and play with your dogs? Oh, that would be wonderful. I know it would make such a difference to him."

"Of course. The little dogs and I make it our duty to help out wherever we can. Just send him down in the morning, and I'll take him on walks with us."

340

The stressed young mother smiled at me with gratitude. "You don't know how much that means to me."

"Anytime we can help out, just ask. I suppose we could come with you to cheer up the paralyzed woman if you think it could do any good..."

The dogs and I had just gotten our first "assignment" while on vacation. We never made it to the paralyzed lady's house, but Carl came by every morning to accompany the little dogs and their cat to the beach and on their daily walks...

When we had the time, Phil and me took all three of our little animals to the big beach of Point Judith. This was a prime tourist spot, attracting not only the tourists from Rhode Island and Massachusetts, but also anyone who went to Block Island, since the ferries left from there. The cat walked on the leash and the little dogs went off on their own along the white sands of Point Judith, their shapes beautifully contrasting against the setting sun. It was an image of such peace and beauty that once again we thought ourselves lucky to have such a varied life of travels. We were glad also to be able to allow our little animals so much of the world, enabling them to visit so many beautiful places in their short little lives. As we had expected, the three of them attracted attention as people flocked around them in big crowds, charmed not only by the two cute little dogs but also by "the furry thing, what is it?" which they later identified as a cat.

Mike, true to his nature, often scored with groups of tourists who were having barbecue on the beach, more than once by jumping on their tables as they were eating. Luckily, everyone was in a summer kind of mood and instead if scolding him, there were reactions of "what a cute little dog," and morsels of grilled meat for the bold Shihtzu.

Our best friends a couple from Boston, whose vacation home was only a few houses up from ours. Cindy was the charge nurse of the Intensive Care Unit of a big Boston hospital. We often met on the beach: her two big dogs, Mike, Tiny and our cat. Stanislaw, one of her dogs, was instantly intrigued with the cat. He came up to sniff it but Mike - as disdainful as he treats the cat in our home - was immediately there to protect it. Only after Stanislaw had proved his honorable intentions by wagging his tail and giving a friendly grin did he gain permission from the "body guard" to come closer and sniff the cat. Before the summer was over, the cat fit in perfectly with the dogs and came to consider himself one of them, leash, walks and all...

"We are writing a book about the dogs," I announced proudly to Cindy. "They had so many adventures that it would be a shame not to. I don't think there are many dogs who have been to as many places as we have been together."

"Oh yes?" Cindy asked curiously. I shared with her some of the little rascals' escapades. As we sat together at the picnic tables, watching a seagull soar from one end of the beach to the other and back again, I told her about Ian Stephens.

"That is such a nice idea," Cindy remarked. Her open, compassionate face betrayed a deep sense of caring for the less fortunate. I was not mistaken. "You know, at the hospital where I work, so many of my patients are very lonely. Most of them do not have a chance of survival. They spend their last weeks and months all alone, in such a cold institution. Many of them do not even have visitors. I know that a pet can make a big difference to them, the same as yours have done with that poor man dying of Aids. Our hospital does not allow dogs, but I sometimes bring them photos of Stanislaw, or even of this beach here. It cheers them up so much. Animals are so important."

"The hospital in Montreal did not allow animals either," I confided.

"What did you do?"

I told her. "This may be a crazy idea," Cindy began. "I don't mean to impose on you, but do you think you could

342

possibly... with Tiny and Mike ... nah, forget it, I probably shouldn't ask."

"What?"

"Do you think you could put Tiny in a bag and visit some of my patients one day? I am always on my own at night, so if we timed your visit for 11pm or later, you would only have to get him past security at the gate. Once you are up in the unit, you could let him out and we could go into the patients' rooms together. I know that just the sight of the little dog walking in would make a huge difference to some of them. It would really make them smile, and most of them do not have much to smile about anymore..."

And so the little dogs and me got our next "assignment," even as we were on vacation!

Our tranquil time was shattered with the crash of TWA flight 800, when it dropped out of the sky shortly after take-off from New York's JFK airport. The jumbo, which was bound for Paris, had exploded in mid-air for unknown reasons, killing everyone on board.

We had watched reports of plane crashes before, but never had one hit as close to home. A journalist friend of mine at NBC had lost a close friend and colleague, who had been a producer at ABC and had been on board with his entire family. Further, we were shocked to find out through Time magazine that Pamela Lychner had been on board of the plane. Although we had been on opposite ends of the political spectrum during our stay in Houston, this did not change the fact that I had always admired her resourcefulness and strong spirit. I felt terrible for the beautiful young mother and her two little daughters, who had been on the flight with her.

"This can't be," I said to Phil. "I never know anyone in plane crashes. Pamela could not have possibly been on board that plane."

How I wished I could bring her back. How I wished

343

we could argue once more about the capital murder appeals process in Texas, or about the "bleeding heart liberals" who were "soft on crime." How any political adversity faded in the face of her death. How I wished to have taken more time to understand her. How all life suddenly became nothing in the face of death, how all importance of who was right or wrong faded and disappeared...

Three days after the crash, Phil and I sat with our friends at a beautiful restaurant with an outdoor patio overlooking the ocean. We watched the waves crash to shore below us as we cracked fresh Maine lobster and watched the sun set. Nobody spoke much, the TWA crash still being on all of our minds. Somehow, we got talking with a young couple who sat next door to us. They, too, lived on Harbor Island. I don't know who mentioned the plane crash first, but I came to mention that never before had a plane crash hit so close to home.

"For us neither," the woman replied. "You know that air hostess from Harbor Island who was on the flight?"

"Yes, I remember reading about her."

"She was our neighbor. She and her husband lived in Connecticut, but they used to come out here every weekend. They were such a lovely couple. Been married for a long time, too."

"Is her husband still in Connecticut?"

"No, he came here as soon as it happened. We haven't seen him since he arrived. He has locked himself inside the house, won't come out. He is not talking to anybody."

"That's terrible. I guess he must have had a big shock. You don't expect your wife to crash with a plane, especially when she is an airhostess and has flown so many times before. Is there nothing anyone can do for him?"

"I don't think so. We try what we can, but I think it is going to take a while until he recovers from his loss. They were not a young couple. She was in her sixties, and they had been married for a long time. They have been looking forward to retirement together."

"Listen, I have two charming little dogs. They can cheer up anyone. Do you suppose that we should go and ring his doorbell?"

She listened with interest as I told her about the dogs and some of the "cheer-up" work we had been doing. We talked about it, and finally decided that knocking on his door might be too much of an invasion of the brand-new widower's privacy.

"But why don't I give you the address and you take the dogs for a walk, right outside his house? All he does is sit and stare out of the window all day. If you walk by his house, he is bound to see you. If you do this, he won't have to engage in any kind of interaction with you, but he will still see the dogs and maybe this will cheer him up a little. At least if they are as cute as you say they are."

"Oh yes, they are, take my word for it."

Said, done. She gave me the address of the airhostess' house. The next morning, the sun smiled down on Harbor Island as the little dogs and I set out for our walk. It was not a pleasant experience. Every shrub we passed on the way to the dead airhostess's house reminded me "this is what she saw on her final day. This is where she drove past as she left Harbor Island to catch her flight. This street she looked at hundreds of times when she came to visit here..." It was eerie to re-live the dead woman's final journey away from her beloved summer vacation spot, eerie also because I realized full well that what had happened to her could happen to anyone, even to me and the little dogs. God knows we were flying around the world enough...

I realized how fragile life was. You never know when you will see something for the last time. You never know which day will be your last. I looked at the little dogs with even greater appreciation, understanding that as secure as we felt that there would be a tomorrow, we did not know how much time we had left. We did not know it anymore than this woman had known. It bothered me that she had come from precisely the same place that we had chosen for our vacation. It bothered me that he death had invaded our carefree summer and driven home thoughts of our own mortality. It bothered me because she had reminded the three of us of facts we would rather ignore. At least her death had reminded me ... as for the little dogs: I don't think they knew or cared one way or the other. How blissful it would be sometimes to just be a little dog, I mused. To live each day with the full expectation that new one would arrive, to live unaware of your own mortality.

We arrived at the airhostess' house to see the American flag outside her house blowing gently in the wind, at half-mast. All her neighbor's flags were at half-mast, too. It was a sad sight in such beautiful a location. It seemed absurd that tragedy could invade a spot as peaceful as this.

"I don't think there is much we can do here, guys," I told the little dogs. "But we can try at least."

We walked up to the man's house, and made a point of passing right in front of it. Though the large windows, I could see him sitting at his living room table, staring out over the ocean. He did not see us. We walked back. Up and down. Up and down. Finally, he noticed. He lifted his head and looked at us a long time, with the faintest hint of a smile. When we left, his eyes followed us until we were gone. Did it help him to see these cute bundles so full of joy, bouncing around outside his house? I have no idea, but if even one ray of sunshine got through the black shroud of that poor man's grief, it was all worthwhile...

Chapter 30

Mike The Air-Show Groupie
Or: How Mike Charmed The World's Best Pilots And
Became An Internet Star

These things are always somebody else's fault. The cat and the horse were Tiny and Mike's fault. The airshow pilots - well, they were Wildfire's fault, in a manner of speaking. If Wildfire had not made friends with Kathryn, this chapter would never have been written.

It started when Kathryn and me had spent a nice summer's day with Wildfire at his new stable. Driving back, into the setting sun, we breezed down Ocean drive, passing cliff-walk. Over Newport's first beach, we suddenly spotted three small airplanes. They were flying the most amazing stunts in formation, loops, then straight up again only to plummet down again at breathtaking speed.

"Wow, this is so beautiful. Let's pull over and watch," I exclaimed, stunned by the aerobatics.

I had never seen aerobatic flying before and I was instantly fascinated by the aesthetics of it all. Traffic on Ocean Drive came to a standstill as drivers of dozens of other cars fell under the same spell. Soon, almost a hundred impromptu spectators lined up on the wall that bordered ocean drive, completely taken in by the amazing pilots and their sleek, silver planes. They flew before the panorama of the setting sun, dancing in passionate embrace with each other, making magic in the sky.

"I bet there is not a single woman in these planes," I remarked to Kathryn and to a woman who stood next to us holding her small baby. "It's a pity these things are always men's sports, isn't it? I wonder where these people are from."

"I think I know," Kathryn volunteered. "There is an

airshow at Quonset every year, and it's on again this weekend, starting tomorrow. "

I knew nothing about airshows. I had always thought they were noisy, military kind of things, and I hate noise. But if airshows were like this ...

"Is Quonset far from here?" I asked.

"About twenty minutes by car."

"Great, let's go there tomorrow."

The following morning, Kathryn, Phil and me set out for our first ever airshow. Thousands of people had turned out at the Quonset military base on that fine summer's day, to watch the best aerobatics pilots in the world as they put their planes through their paces. As I had anticipated, I hated the noisy military planes, with their strange shapes and grey exteriors. The civilian airshow planes, however, were a different matter...

Spellbound, the three of us watched as the same air ballet formation that Kathryn and me had seen the previous night performed again at the show. This time, there was a forth plane flying with them. I learned that they were the Northern Lights, a new sensation on the airshow circuit. A Canadian team, they flew beautiful formations to the music of Canadian ballad-singer Susan Aglukark.

When they had completed their performance, I was so thrilled that I wanted to watched them taxi to their hanger. We walked across the entire airshow display to get to the hangers where the planes would come to a halt. The cockpit of the first plane opened. A handsome man stepped out. The cockpit of the second plane opened, and out came a less handsome but very athletic man. The third cockpit revealed a handsome one again, this time with big muscles. The forth plane's cockpit opened, and out stepped a slender figure, the flight suit tightly clinging to its waist. The helmet came off to reveal a mass of stunning red hair.

"It's a girl," I exclaimed, hardly able to believe my eyes. "There was a girl flying with them. It really is a girl!" The girl turned around to reveal her pretty, even-featured face. "And an attractive one as well," I gasped. "I would have never thought ... there's a story in that, for sure."

I waited until she had finished signing autographs. Naturally, the male fans were crazy for her. Stepping closer, I noticed that she spoke English with a French accent. An attractive French girl who flies aerobatics as skillfully as any man - no wonder the guys all went nuts over her!

Later, I was to learn that her name was Michelle. She was Swiss, not French. As other planes taxied by on their way to take-off, Michelle and me sat on the grass outside the hanger and she told me her life story. It was simple, really, the story of a dream that wouldn't die. People in Switzerland, I learned, do not grow up to become airshow pilots. She wanted to become one, and she did. She bugged her parents so long until they gave in and sent her to flight school in the United States.

Soon, Michelle flew better than anyone else, and she clawed her way to the top of one of the most competitive industries in the world. She became the only woman to fly in Canada's top-notch aerobatics display team.

"Today, I live a life of total freedom. I am happier than I could have ever been in Switzerland, boxed into a nine to five life. I am 27, and I have reached my dream," Michelle told me proudly.

Michelle and I finished our chat just in time for me to see a black Biplane dancing in the sky. Whoever was in there was not merely flying, but making love to the sky. I had never seen a plane handled with such skill. Thousands of people held their breath as the little plane did what Biplanes simply cannot do. Ever. Under any circumstances. It hovered, like a helicopter, on the spot, almost at a complete standstill. "That is impossible," I exclaimed. Mesmerized, my eyes followed the little Biplane's every move until it came down to land again.

Whoever had flown this show had been born with the sky in their soul, there was not a doubt about it.

"Who on earth was that?" I asked the man standing to my right. He was obviously an airshow enthusiast, as I could see that his program contained the autographs of many pilots. "Only the best aerobatics pilot in the world," he replied. "He is quite something, isn't he? "

"You bet."

"Many pilots have tried to imitate that maneuver," my new friend explained, referring to the make-a-biplane-stand-in-the-air-like-a-helicopter episode "They can't. Nobody can figure out how he does it."

"Guys, I think we may have another story here," I said to Kathryn and Phil. "Let's go find the man."

Locating the pilot was not a problem. After his flight performance, he was signing autographs. Hundreds of fans lined up to meet him. I stood by and watched. It took him almost one hour to sign everyone's requests. When he was through, I introduced myself and we retired into someone's private office for an interview. The pilot's name was Sean Tucker, aviator extraordinaire, with film star looks and a charming personality, the combination of which captivated his fans as much as his flying did. He also turned out to be a flight instructor to various film stars such as Tom Cruise, and an avid follower of sky-guru Richard Bach's philosophy, with one of his own to match. The interview grew long and increasingly interesting. The highly intelligent pilot provided a wealth of information, not only about flight, but about life in general.

"Aerobatics is dangerous," he stated. "Each day could be my last. I live more honest that way. There is no time for masks or lies. If you knew that tomorrow you could die, what would you do different today? Whom would you tell that you love them? Why haven't you done it? What would you decide was not worth worrying about? What would you still want to do? What wouldn't you do?"

I left the interview with Sean, and arrived at the airfield in time to see someone climb around a plane while it was in full flight. As I watched, the plane made a loop. The person stood on top of it, upside down, and waved his hands.

"Is this guy crazy or what?" I asked Phil, just as I joined him and Kathryn again.

"It's a girl. They just announced that it's a girl. Her name is Teresa something-or-other."

"A girl?"

Phil nodded. I had never realized just how far equality of women could go. In the sky, there were different rules. Here on earth, at least in my line of work, women had to fight twice as hard to be accepted. We couldn't write literary fiction as well as men could, they said. T.E. Lawrence, better known as Lawrence of Arabia, had once stated that if all women writers had been strangled at birth, the world of literature would be no worse off ... In journalism, we weren't as good as investigative journalists, we were useless as combat journalists because we cracked under pressure ... and so the prejudices went. But in the sky, there seemed to be an entirely different set of rules. If this crazy person up there was indeed a girl, then there was true equality of sexes amongst airshow pilots.

"There is another story in this," I remarked for the third time that day.

I watched, together with Phil and Kathryn, as the plane landed and the girl took off her helmet to reveal a mane of long, blonde hair. Her golden curls contrasted seductively with her black flight-suit. She stood on top of the plane as it taxied past the crowds, smiling and waving to the cheering fans. Close-up, she looked like any other young woman, in reality, she was anything but.

As she tidied up her plane a little later, I caught up with her and we arranged for a phone interview later the following week. I learned that she was an aviation artist from Texas, who had one day .".decided that wingwalking seemed like good fun and wanted to try it." Today, she is one of only a handful of top women wing walkers in the world.

In the evening, I edited my interviews and wrote them up. They were great material. From the initial one-woman interview, it was rapidly growing into a series: women with wings, the heirs of Amelia Earhart. "Actually, that would be a nice book title," I mused as I sat up until the wee hours of morning, finishing the stories.

"What do you think?," I asked Tiny who, as usual, sat up with me. Mike and Phil were fast asleep. Wollen wir ein Buechlein schreibeln? I asked Tiny in German baby language, "Shall we write a book?" Tiny wagged his tail. As always, he was game. He carefully balanced from his chair over to mine and playfully bit me in the nose.

Having gained the Pekingese's approval, I drafted a fax to the director of the literary agency in Germany. He called me back the following morning.

"Yes, go for it. It sounds like a wonderful book."

We also discussed the possibility of a book on the life of Sean Tucker, with Richard Bach's son Jonathan as the author.

I returned to the airshow at once and sought out Sean Tucker.

"I know you admire Richard Bach. Would you consider writing a book together with his son?," I asked him.

Sean agreed. He also agreed to help me with access to the other women pilots.

"How many more are there?," I asked. "I mean, the really top women flyers?"

"At least another ten of them," Sean informed me and promised to put me in touch with them.

We exchanged phone numbers, and arranged to meet up one week later at an airshow in Boston. Meanwhile, I called Jonathan Bach. He had just written an interesting and touching book about his relationship with his father, the author of "Jonathan Livingston Seagull." I had been impressed by his style that, because of his training as a professional journalist, surpassed that of his father. In his book, Jon came across as a humble, kind young man. I rightly concluded that he would probably be like that in person as well.

"Hi Jonathan," I said when he picked up the phone. "This may be a bit out of the blue, but would you like to do a book with Sean Tucker?"

Jonathan agreed. Sean Tucker agreed. The women agreed. Head first, I had jumped into the fascinating world of airshows. Take it for granted that I asked my two little dogs to help me get the job done....

Several months later, I had conducted a great number of interviews by phone. To finalize the American leg of the series, I set out with Mike and a photographer for an airshow in Smyrna, Tennessee. Here, we were to meet up with Sean Tucker and the female aerobatics champion, Patty Wagstaff. Since TWA 800, I had become weary of flying. So we decided to undertake the twenty hour drive to Smyrna in Brian the photographer's car.

"I can't believe the dog is coming with us," Brian remarked when we picked him up at his home and left our car there to change over to his. Brian was a very proper young man and did not suffer little dogs gladly.

"Of course he has to come," I replied. "He is a journalist. Let's get on the road." It was good luck for Brian that I had decided to leave Tiny at home, because the drive would have been too much for the little Pekingese.

Mike's first notable encounter came at a rest stop just past New York City. We had pulled over to use the facilities and to take Mike for a walk in the lovely woods that adjoined the rest area. When we had been walking along the trails for several minutes, a minute creature jumped out of the woods to our left and blocked the path before us.

"What is this?" Brian exclaimed. "A rat?"

I shrugged. "No idea."

The "rat" turned out to be a dog, a Chihuahua, who made for Mike at lightening speed. He was an energetic little thing, jumped over Mike's back and bit him in the tail.

"He's just a pup, you must forgive him," a muscle-packed man who emerged from the path below us said with a laugh. "Shall I call him off?"

"That's okay. It'll do Mike good to get a little exercise," I replied. The man walked up to join us and then the three of us stood and watched the dogs running around. The little one was like a rambunctious child, driving Mike almost insane with his antics. When Mike had enough, he growled. The little thing backed off, ran away, only to "attack" again at lightening speed.

We all laughed as we finally introduced ourselves. "That's Brian, my photographer. I am Tess, and this is Mike, our dog."

"Photographer? Are you a model?" the man asked.

"No. We are journalists, on our way to an airshow in Smyrna."

"An airshow? That's great. I love planes. I used to be a fighter pilot," our new friend, John, informed us.

"What do you do now?" I asked him.

"I drive a truck. That's why we stopped here. I am on my way to Florida. I love the freedom I get in this line of work, and the fact that I can take my dog on the road with me."

I wondered by what strange twist of fate a macho-guy like John had ended up with a dog like this. People like John I usually associated with Rottweilers, or other "man-type" dogs. German Shepherds, Pitbulls ... anything that's large and intimidating. But a little weasel like that...?

As we watched our dogs romp around the woods, the three of us sat down to chat. "Tell me about army life," I urged him. "Is it as tough as people say, the ground training, I mean?"

"The psychological aspect of it is toughest," John admitted. "They tear you down before building you up again. They scream at you almost all the time. If you make a mistake, they treat you worse than a worm. They teach you total obedience. You are not allowed to question authority. In effect, they turn you into a human machine, trained to blindly obey commands without reasoning for yourself. But that is good."

"How can that be good?," I wanted to know.

"If you are in a situation of war, let's say you have to raid a village or something ... can you imagine what would happen if you had soldiers second-guessing their commander-in-chief? We would lose the war in no time, and many lives with it. If you want to defend your country, you have to learn to obey and let someone else do the thinking for you. You just don't question your commanding officer."

"That's a tough life, though, isn't it?"

He nodded. "It can be."

"What made you decide to enter the army?"

"I wanted to see the world. I am 37 years old now, and I have been around the world twice. I have seen foreign lands and learned about new cultures. I come from a small town in Pennsylvania. In my hometown, it's as if life has been at a standstill. I sometimes return to visit, and meet up with my old high-school mates. They are in the same place they were when I left. They have become plumbers, or they work in restaurants and pizza-parlors. I have nothing in common with them anymore. I have seen the world, and they have only read about it. I am glad the army has given me the chance to have a real life, when theirs has passed them by."

"Do you have any regrets?"

"The post-traumatic stress is hard to deal with," John

confided. "When you have been in combat like myself, you take the memories home with you. To this day, I jump and hide when I hear a loud bang. It is an automatic reaction and there is nothing I can do about it. Just the other day, some truckie's tire blew and I jumped under my own truck to hide. The others laughed at me, but once I explained, they understood. I am damaged, but it is a price I gladly pay for all the good experiences I have had. I have Pee-wee to help me through this. He is my best friend."

Figures. The tiny canine carrying the tough guy on his twig-like shoulders. Dogs are amazing creatures...

Having spoken, Mr. Macho got up and gathered his minute friend into his muscular arms. "It was great talking to you, but we'll have to get going or we'll never get to Florida on time."

We watched the two of them get into his heavy truck and disappear, leaving us to eat their dust...

Just outside Memphis, I had a sudden craving for Japanese food. Being used to traditional Asian cuisine, my stomach rebelled against the "Western" fare I had been eating for the past day and a half.

"We need to find a Japanese restaurant," I said to Brian. "It is urgent."

"Now?"

I nodded.

"I wouldn't know where to go," Brian replied. "We are in the sticks somewhere. Can you wait until we get to Memphis?"

Memphis was more than an hour's drive away. "I don't think so."

We pulled into a McDonald's by the roadside and searched the yellow pages for the nearest, half-way decent sized city. There was one, and it even listed one Japanese restaurant. Happily, we obtained directions from McDonald's and got on our way.

When we got to the restaurant, it was closed. We had just driven 30 minutes out of our way, and we were not about to drive back without getting our food. It was 4 p.m. The restaurant, we learned from a sign on the door, was going to re-open at 7 p.m. I peered through the window and saw some people inside. A group of Japanese were sitting around a table, eating. Rightly, I assumed that they were part of the management.

I knocked on the glass door. "Can you please come here for a minute?" I screamed through the glass with urgency.

A man got up and came to the door. "What do you want?"

"A seaweed salad?," I asked meekly.

"Come back at 7."

"Please, we have just driven all the way from Rhode Island. I am really hungry."

"Try McDonald's."

"I don't eat McDonald's, I am used to Japanese food," I told him.

The Japanese man couldn't care less. He was about to walk away when he became aware, who had come to join me.

"That's a very nice dog you have there," he remarked, suddenly much friendlier. "It's a Shihtzu, isn't it?"

I nodded.

"Do you suppose that I could pat him? " the man asked. "I love Shihtzus, we had them in my family when I was growing up."

The door opened, out came the restaurant owner. Trust Mike to take care of the rest! Fifteen minutes later, Mike, Brian and myself sat outside the restaurant in the grass, watching the traffic pass as I dug into my seaweed salad...

We arrived in Nashville in the wee hours of morning. Not knowing where to go and tired enough for our eyes to fall shut by themselves, we pulled into the first motel exit we could find. We ended up at a Howard Johnson's motel, which was run by an Indian family. Naturally, the motel had a no-dog policy.

"This is not a dog," I explained, indicating Mike. "This is a journalist with fur. He is writing a book about his life and we are here for him to interview some airshow pilots. Are you sure you can't make an exception? Mike is not like other dogs, he is very responsible."

Out came Mike from the car. At 2 a.m., he performed his motel check-in dance routine to perfection. It worked. The Indians were charmed, and we stayed.

The next morning, we drove to nearby Smyrna airport, which was the location for the weekend's airshow. It was fascinating to be there three days before it started, together with all the performers. It gave me time to observe them in their hangars, during practice flights, and as they maintained their planes.

When we arrived, Sean Tucker was the first to greet us. As usual, he was surrounded by a small crowd.

"Hi Tess, Hi Brian," he shouted over the heads of his fans. Sean knew Brian from the Cleveland airshow, where Brian had gone on his own to take some spectacular aerial photography. Mike was still a stranger to the famous pilot, but I needn't have worried. Sean and Mike hit it off on the spot. They both had a lot in common: they were charming, great entertainers who knew with perfection how to work a crowd.

"Come and meet Duncan," Sean said and took the three of us along with him. "He is with a famous Country and Western Band, Sawyer Brown. Do you know them?"

To my disgrace, I didn't. In my private life, I listen exclusively to classical music.

Duncan was a nice man who was not just a singer, but also an accomplished pilot. I learned that he flew himself to

358

most of his concerts, in his own airplane. Because he was a country singer, he was based in Nashville, the Mecca of country music. Sean and he had the same sponsor, and arrangements had been made for them to go flying together. As the cameras and Mike and myself watched, Duncan climbed into the plane behind Sean and the two men took to the skies. A CBS crew recorded their every move on film.

While the two men flew, the CBS producer and myself began to talk. He told me that he was from Australia.

"Hey, I used to live there," I told him. "I studied journalism there. I was working in Australia before I came here."

The world of journalism is small, and we soon found out that we knew a lot of people in common. We also had something else in common, a background of current affairs journalism that had left us burnt-out and cynical.

"It's much better to report on these guys, whose world consists of loops and wings, isn't it?" I asked. "Less heartbreak, cleaner lifestyle."

As we watched Sean and Duncan fly, we commented how absurd their "proper" world seemed to us, after where we had been. "Man, a few years ago, we saw people die in wars. Today, we report about airshow pilots. It's a strange world, isn't it?" Wayne asked me.

"You said it, mate," I replied. "It sure is."

Wayne, the cynical former combat journalist, squatted down to play with Mike. "That's a pretty crazy idea, writing a book about canine journalists, you know," he remarked.

"I agree," I replied, happily enough. "But you know what? I don't give a damn. As far as I am concerned, when I gave up full-time journalism, that was like dying. This is my second lease on life now, and I do whatever I damn well please. I don't care about the ifs and buts anymore. I have stopped taking myself so seriously. Perhaps the rest of the world is as burnt out with hearing about tragedies as we are with reporting them. What is wrong with two little dogs traveling the world and writing about it? At least it will give people something to smile about."

Wayne picked up Mike and cradled him in his arms. "You know what, mate?" he concluded. "You are right. Why not have a bit of fun, we can't change anything out there anyway."

Imagine my surprise at what happened when Sean and Duncan had touched down again. Wayne and his crew rushed over to interview them.

"Duncan, could you please put the dog on your lap in the cockpit?" Wayne asked the celebrated country star. "I want to get a few shots in with Sean, you and Mike. I've decided to put the three of you on the evening news tonight."

Following Mike's television session with Duncan, Mike came to consider himself a true star. Wherever we went, a crowd followed us. Mike became "the" air-show dog. Because he hung out with all the airshow stars, the fans soon figured that to get close to their heroes, they had to make friends with Mike. Mike met hundreds of people, bouncing from one fan to the next as they offered him treats and attempted to involve me in conversation about Mike and his famous pilot friends. Mike danced. Mike ran back and forth. Mike wagged his tail. On our first evening at the airshow, Mike collapsed into bed, completely exhausted like a real star...

The next day, Sean and me took time off from the busy life at the hangar to pick up some lunch at the local supermarket. Mike came with us as we got into Sean's rental car and set off. We left the car in the parking lot, with Mike inside. Mike jumped up to the windows and looked after us with a pleading expression in his eyes. "All right, all right," Sean smirked. "I get the message. It looked like I'll have to feed the dog, too."

As we selected fruit from the supermarket shelves - like Sean, I had learned to eat healthy - we discussed Jon Bach and Sean's book project. "I am going to meet Jonathan after I am finished here," I informed Sean. "Then we can finalize the deal."

"Are you going to take Mike?"

"Of course, I take Mike to all my meetings," I grinned. "That dog is a whiz-kid in business like you wouldn't believe."

"I'll take your word for it," Sean said with a half-serious expression on his face. "Come on, let's get the whiz-kid something to eat."

We loaded our cart with dog biscuits, canned dog food and assorted canine snacks, and then we made our way to the checkout. As we waited to pay, I was once again reminded why Sean Tucker had such enormous crowd appeal. As often, the checkout girls were somewhat frustrated, tired and underpaid. Before the young girl had finished ringing up our groceries, Sean had everyone in the supermarket smiling. The young girl felt attractive out of the sudden, coyly brushing a lock of mousy hair from her face. The boy who packed our groceries blossomed before our very eyes as Sean treated him like an interesting person, with enormous respect and joked with him as one would with a best friend. Within seconds, everyone was in a good mood, their dreary day shattered by a ray of sunshine named Sean Tucker.

"I don't know how you do it, but you sure do it," I remarked to Tucker on the way back to the car. Sean turned out to be almost as good as Mike, when it came to crowd-pleasing. I wondered what the two of them could do in combination. I was soon to find out...

First, there were more photo sessions to come. Sean and I gulped down a hasty lunch, and then he was off to meet with more sponsors. As for the "airshow star" and me: we went in search of two-legged airshows stars to photograph.

On the way to the hangar, we met Suzanne Oliver, America's best female skywriter. The attractive, kind Blonde had granted me an extensive interview at a previous airshow. I liked Suzanne, who had worked her way up to the top with enormous determination. She had come a long way, from being the youngest person ever to obtain a commercial pilot's license to becoming the first female skywriter with the commercial Pepsi Team. Her infectious ambition and total freedom continue to be an inspiration to anyone who is lucky enough to meet her.

Suzanne flies in a team with her husband Steve, who walked alongside her as we met them at Smyrna. Steve, who is known as Skydancer, took one look at Mike and went completely gaga over him.

"Oh, this dog is so cute. I am so glad that we have another little airshow dog. You know, Suzanne and I used to have a little dog. For fourteen years, she accompanied us, from airshow to airshow. When she died, it was like a death in the family. It was as if our child had died. We were devastated."

Like Phil and I, Suzanne and Steven are childless. When you lead a life that puts you constantly on the road, it is almost impossible to raise a family. Our dogs become our children, and we go gooey over them.

"Steve, I know exactly what you mean," I replied. "I don't know what I would do if anything happened to these two. When you are on the road all the time, they become the only permanent fixture on your life, don't they?"

Like a movie star, Mike posed for the camera with Steven and Suzanne, in front of their airplanes. The look on Mike's face clearly indicated that he considered himself to be the true celebrity of the photo shoot, with Suzanne and Steve mere extras....

The chance meeting between Steven and Mike turned into an instant male bonding event. From then on, Steven was the First to greet us in the morning when we arrived. Usually, he had a dog biscuit or two in his pocket for Mike. If it hadn't been for me being there, I am sure that Mike would have gladly gone home with the Olivers, even though "home" in their case meant an RV that they drive from one airshow to the next during the season. Mike wouldn't have minded one bit. He was as charmed with the aviator couple as they were with him. Had they lived in the same town as ourselves, I have no doubts that Suzanne and Steven would have taken over from Debbie as the "good aunt and uncle" of Tiny and Mike.

But a famous dog's got to do what a famous dog's got to do. Mike bid his good-byes to Steven and Suzanne because it was time for us to make our rounds with Wayne, the CBS journalist. He had asked me to help him with producing a special on Patty Wagstaff, the world's foremost female aerobatics pilot. Patty is widely considered to be our modern day's Amelia Earhart. Her good looks, courage and high intelligence are only being surpassed by her flying skills. In fact, Patty's plane is on display alongside Earhart's at the Smithsonian, and the stunning aviatrix is everyone's darling. Crowds formed instantly as we prepared to interview Patty. Mike looked on, basking in the limelight and the attention that Patty's fans showered on him. After the interview, Mike and Patty posed for photos together in front of her airplane.

After we were through, Patty excused herself and retired for the day. Not so Mike. As soon as Patty had left, we were mobbed by her fans. "Is this Patty's dog?" they wanted to know.

Over and over again, I had to explain the story of Mike, the canine journalist. Over and over, we agreed to requests for photographs.

When we were finally done for the day, Mike and I went to Nashville with our photographer. After we ran into his limo driver, we set up an impromptu interview with a singer by the name of Colin Raye, who was getting some music award that evening. Record company executives and a selection of "Who is Who" of Nashville society darted in and out of the exclusive restaurant where the function took place. Mike, the limo driver, Brian, Raye's fans and I waited outside. The ceremony dragged on and on. Finally, tired and overworked, we gave up waiting.

"Can we have a photo of you and Mike instead?" I asked the limo driver. "Limo drivers to the stars are the next best thing to a photo shoot with the star, or not?"

The limo driver cradled Mike in his arms as we took photographs. Watching was a group of wannabe country singers, and Colin Raye fans. When they heard that Mike had met and befriended Duncan of Sawyer Brown, everyone wanted to pat Mike. Apparently, Duncan's group was quite well known, and Duncan was some sort of semi-God to his fans. It seemed that touching the dog that had been in Duncan's arms only a few hours ago was the next best thing to touching Duncan himself. I must admit, I will never understand the celebrity hype. Mike, however, loved it. It left me wondering whether I ought to send him on tour with Duncan and his band...

The following morning, the actual airshow started. The quiet hangar was transformed into a circus. There were people everywhere, and plenty of noise from the planes as they warmed up their engines for their performances. It was too much noise for Mike, but what could we do? We looked around for solutions, and were lucky to meet Mr. Howell who ran a business out of Smyrna airport. He became our airshow angel when he offered Mike a refuge in his offices, and an array of goodies to munch on.

"There's coffee, tea, donuts, bread, milk, yogurt, anything you want. Feel free to come in here anytime and help yourself. As for Mike, he can stay in my office for as long as he wants. Nobody ever comes in here, and it is well away from the noise outside."

We gladly accepted his offer of kindness. While Howell and Mike became the best of friends, Brian followed me to the hangars and we set up interviews and photo-sessions with the pilots in between their performances.

When the show was over for the day, I took Mike along to interview its director, a charming older gentleman.

"What makes you decide whether to book a certain act?" I asked him.

"Flight skills, definitely, but also good showmanship. If a pilot is a great flyer and also knows to charm the crowds, then he is going to be one of the top acts in the industry. That is why Sean Tucker gets so many bookings. He flies a spectacular show, and the crowds love his personality."

The old man spoke with Mike on his lap, occasionally being interrupted by the Shihtzu's attempts to kiss him on the chin. Finally, he gave in and allowed Mike to plant a wet kiss on his lower lip. Then he continued as if nothing had happened...

" For instance, I have seen Mike here work the crowds. He is a great showman. All he needs is an airplane and a few aerobatics lessons, and I'll book him anytime. If Mike could fly, he would be our top act..."

That evening, Mike decided to team up with Sean for a fan session. What a success they were: children came from everywhere to have their photograph taken with Sean and the new, charming little airshow mascot. We have photos of Sean, Mike and blonde children; Sean, Mike and brown-haired children; Sean, Mike and assorted tough guy pilots with their children... As a team, Mike and Sean were unbeatable. I found myself wondering whether we should turn them into a permanent act...

Sunday was the final day of the weekend's airshow.

365

Thanks to Sean, who had arranged for an all-access pass for us, we were able to get to all the performers without problem. None of them could refuse the charming little dog's request for a photograph when I was through interviewing them.

Mike had indeed developed some true star-qualities by now. When it came to having his photo taken, he posed so professionally that he could have passed as a canine model. We met with two beautiful women from the Golden Knights parachute team, Mitchi and Helen. After the interview, Mike and Mitchi posed for a photo. Helen, the pilot for the Golden Knights, posed together with a friend and Mike.

After the two girls, we went to meet Leo Loudenslager, multiple aerobatics world champion and another great star of the airshow sky. Leo was a fascinating, handsome man, with somewhat of a shy, introspective personality. I am not sure what went through his mind when I handed him Mike to pose in front of his famous, custom-built airplane. Being a very straight-laced man, he probably considered us to be completely nuts.

I would not even like to speculate what the thoughts of this reserved sky-hero must have been when Wayne came over with his camera crew just seconds later, asking for the same thing, and adding: "I would like you and Mike on the evening news." It must have been something like "Oh dear, not another one. Have all the journalists gone insane? It must be the sun..." By all reports, Wayne had been a perfectly normal journalist before he met Mike ... As for poor Leo, who lived in Tennessee, he probably had some explaining to do to his friends who had watched him on the evening news cradling a somewhat idiotically grinning Shihtzu!

For Christmas that year, we sent cards to Sean Tucker, Leo Loudenslager and Patty Wagstaff, enclosing a photograph of Mike and them. We signed the cards from both us, with a paw-print from Mike.

Patty Wagstaff was so impressed with her photo that she posted it on the internet, on her personal performer's page. Considering that over three million people turned up at the world's biggest fly-in airshow at Oshkosh; that Patty is the most famous female pilot in the world; and that fans from all nations hit her webpage to access her schedule, I would say that Mike's photo is being seen by millions of people around the globe - millions, who are perhaps asking themselves: "Who is that charming little dog in the photo with Patty"?

Well everyone, here is your answer: He is Mike, one half of the world's best canine journalist team...

FINAL WORDS:

As we prepare to leave the Unites States for Europe, only a few things remain to be said. On the way home from the airshow, we met Jonathan Bach, spent a few days at the University of North Carolina at Chapel Hill and even took Mike to visit snobby Princeton for an interview. When we returned to Rhode Island, Tiny and Mike met and charmed a Holocaust survivor/international book author because we had set out to buy some fresh farm eggs. I swear, these things just happen to us...

We sat in her living room as she told us of her experiences in the death camp of Auschwitz, pulling back her sleeve to reveal her concentration camp number. She was stuck in time, I realized, even forty years later, still crying as she re-lived her experiences when she told us about them. Steven Spielberg was about to interview her ... were we to stay in Rhode Island, the next chapter would probably have the title "Steven Spielberg, Tiny, Mike and the Holocaust survivor."

The Auschwitz survivor, Judith, was charmed by Tiny and Mike. She gave us three crates of eggs: "You don't have to pay for them, not with such charming little dogs. They just lighted up my life," she told me as she thrust the eggs into my arms. Then she reminded me: "You must overcome whatever life throws at you. Look at the sun, the trees, the stars. Enjoy the sheer fact that you are alive. Look at me, it hasn't been easy, but I have overcome what happened to me. In life, you have to leave bad memories and experiences behind, go forward into the sunshine. And look at you, you have nothing ever to be unhappy about, you have two very charming kids...," with this, she indicated Tiny and Mike. Tiny had just given me a lick on the nose. "There's a lot of love there," Judith said as she saw us to our car. "Just remember that."

She was very right. Our family might be small, and mostly made up on non-humans, but there is certainly a lot of love, for each other and for those we meet as we travel the world. There are always plenty of them. Recently, we have entertained two major publishers from New York, who came to stay with us and were utterly smitten with our "zoo."

We have all grown a little older now. I have a few lines on my face that were not there before. Phil has grey temples, Tiny's muzzle has turned white and Mike does not run in circles as much as she used to. Wildfire and the cat, the latest additions to our family and the youngest, still show no signs of time. They remind the rest of us to keep going. Far from slowing down, we keep our spirits as young as ever and are always in search of new adventures.

At this time, Tiny and Mike are planning a second book. It is going to be called "The further adventures of Tiny and Mike - two canine journalists in Europe." In Europe, they once again expect to meet the famous and the infamous, and also to discover historic Europe through their unique, canine eyes. I am currently working on a book about Anthony Burgess, and we look forward to meeting his widow in Monte Carlo. Readers of Burgess will know Liana from the dedications of his books. Already, she is in possession of a photograph of Tiny and Mike, and she recently told me that she cannot wait to meet them.

We plan to visit Jon and Helen Peters, of course, and some refugee camps, prisons, hospitals and who knows what and who else. Wildfire, having been bitten by the writing and the pet therapy bug as well, plans to come along. We will buy a horse trailer in Europe and visit traumatized children everywhere, just to see if a certain black equine can put some sparkle back into their lives...

While they are on the road with "their" cat and "their" horse, Tiny and Mike plan to edit a book titled "Favorite Animal Stories from around the World." Already, they have been able to obtain charming contributions from my colleagues and some of their own human friends. Perhaps I can help them out with a few contacts. Recently, I met with one of New York's top literary agents, a German gentleman by the name of Bobby Lantz. He is one of the top power-players in the industry, with clients like Elisabeth Taylor. Despite of this, Bobby clearly knows what is truly important in life - recently, he sent me a photograph of his prize-winning dogs, and I sent him one of Tiny and Mike...

Tiny and Mike hope that you will join them again for their next book. They will be out there in Europe, comforting those who need it and charming everyone they meet. But their exciting lives would mean nothing to them without a "family" of readers to tell about them. They tell me that they cannot wait to meet everyone again in the next book.

For now, it is time to say good-bye. The little dogs are busy, planning their move across the Atlantic. Tiny, taking his job as world-leader very seriously, still spends his nights sitting up with me by the computer so he can "edit" my work and make sure I do the job right. In these final weeks before our move, he is a very busy Pekingese indeed.

In two weeks, Wildfire will go to New York for his pre-flight quarantine. After that, he will catch a flight from New York to London. The little dogs and the cat get to fly in the cabin with us, a few weeks later. We will probably live in Germany first, then France, then Monte Carlo and perhaps Italy. Whatever happens, it will be an adventure. We hope to see everyone again for the first chapter of their new book: "Tiny and Mike fly to Europe" - my guess is that there will be plenty of adventures to tell from the airport. For now, the canine reporters sign off, eager to pack more adventures into the years to come. They will be back soon with stories of assorted canine, feline, equine and human friends...

THE END

POSTSCRIPT:

LEO LOUDENSLAGER DIED ON JULY 28th, 1997 AS THE RESULT OF A MOTORCYCLE CRASH.

FRENCH ARISTROCRAT COUNT PATRICK DE GAYARDON, JOE JENNINGS' SKY SURFING PARTNER AT THE EXTREME GAMES, DIED ON APRIL 13th, 1998 AS THE RESULT OF A PARACHUTING ACCIDENT.

TINY DIED IN ENGLAND ON JANUARY 13th, 2001 AS THE RESULT OF VETERINARY NEGLIGENCE. HE WAS 13 YEARS OLD. HIS LAST ACTION WAS TO GROWL AT THE VET.

Epilogue:

Wallace Sife, Ph.D.

"But I don't want to go among mad people," Alice remarked.

"Oh, you can't help that," said the cat. "We are all mad here. I'm mad. You're mad."

"How do you know I'm mad?" said Alice.

"You must be," said the cat, "or you wouldn't have come here."

But we have come here, and must now admit that all pet lovers are probably a little mad. And that is wonderful! As we have seen in the adventures of Tiny and Mike, even those who don't own dogs were vulnerable to their charms. All of us are freshened by our companion animals' perspectives on things. It must be marvellous to be able to realise this and sing it out into the world. And that is just what Tess has done. In addition to being a very interesting narrative, this book is also the story about the unusual lives of her two celebrated dogs, and the joy they brought to so many, who even briefly touched their lives.

At first, writing about Tiny and Mike as canine journalists can be seen as a pretty crazy idea. Yet it doesn't take the reader long to appreciate why some credit must go to them, too. They are certainly an important part of this journalist's team. When on the road all the time, they became the only permanent fixture in her life. Even when temporarily separated from them, she felt their presence and influence. All pet lovers can understand that. The unique bonds we have with them can be nurturing and supportive, as well as spiritually rewarding. In many ways these relationships are stronger, purer and far more intimate than with others of our own species. We feel loved and secure in sharing our secret souls with them. How often can this safely be done, even with another person who is very close?

Yet there are many who can never accept this, and would even try to belittle it. That is their loss.

There are some people out there, always looking for some peg to hang their anger on. I am reminded of one of Abe Lincoln's favorite expressions, "There are always going to be some fleas a dog can't reach." Unfortunately, these self-appointed critics and judges can make life uncomfortable for us, at times. But with the explosive growth of the media, the world is fast becoming much more appreciative of the great intrinsic value of pets. Everywhere around us we can see appealing examples of this. One can't even watch an hour of television without seeing at least one adorable pet on the screen - whether in ads or in the programs themselves. We are becoming a modern civilisation of pet lovers and are ever improved by the perspectives and love these special companions can add to our existence. The unusual lives Tiny and Mike led with Tess brought smiles to everyone who met them. By writing this book, she has made it possible for these fine dogs to reach into our lives, as well. What a wonderful tribute that is.

Ultimately, all life is change and growth. Otherwise, it wouldn't be worth living. This can be a very hard lesson to learn, but a necessary one. Perhaps it is not surprising to realise that our pets have turned out to be the best guides we could have through our tough and lonely times. If only we could discover ways to better see the trees, despite the forests! I have learned from my many years of pet loss counselling that we must learn to cherish our every day. That is one of the wonderful things our animal friends can teach us about life, even after they leave us. As Tess declares, earlier in the book, "You have to leave bad memories and experiences behind, go forward into the sunshine."

Our beloved animal companions have an innate wisdom that is natural to all living things. In our all-too-busy and preoccupied civilisation we humans tend to lose contact with much of this. But thank goodness for such friends! They can always teach us good things about ourselves, and enrich our journeys - if we are open to what they have to offer us. Life can be seen as a metaphor of a merry-go-round on which we ride with our companion animals. The rest of the world keeps swinging around, encountering us in singular ways, because of their presence. As we come across new people and experiences we are often reminded how fortunate we are because of these special partners. They keep our spirits young and joyous, sharing our life's experiences and adventures.

Some special animals seem to have an innate sense of empathy, and always know when something is upsetting or delighting us. Each, in its own unique way, expresses how loved and appreciated we are, regardless of how good or bad our lives may seem to us, at the time. I am sure that some readers must have been surprised as well as delighted to see how Wildfire was so empathetic and caring. Most people have not given much thought to the real nature of our everyday companion animals so it must be surprising for them to see how sensitive and therapeutic a friendly horse can be. A remarkable new field of pet therapy has only recently begun to emerge, capitalising on this newly discovered, but ageless phenomenon. Tess had to sneak her dog into hospital, to give him the opportunity to heal with a smile and a wagging of his tail. But today, more and more hospitals, nursing homes and special care facilities welcome trained companion animals to visit and warm the hearts of those who are confined there.

We are all in this world for a brief span, and our dear companion animals offer us an unique kind of love to accompany us on our journey through life. But even after the beloved Tinys and Mikes in our lives have passed on, their effects on us remain. What we have become and will still achieve is a loving memorial to them, and we are all better people because of them. They will live on inside of us.

As with all good books, reading these delightful pages

can broaden our comprehension of the world around us, as well as within us. The adventures of Tess and her special pals have given us all some smiles, as well as new perceptions on life. And that is good.

Life is a ceaseless process of discovery and growth, and if we are lucky we come to realise that each of us is capable of wonders. When reaching deep down, into our very being, we can come up with some truly amazing things. And our beloved pets with their ever-understanding, ever-accepting love, help us achieve this.

Wallace Sife, Ph.D., is a noted expert on pets and their influence on our lives. When his beloved dog, Edelmeister, died unexpectedly, he was suddenly forced to evaluate his own life from a new perspective. As a result of this personal trauma he wrote his award-winning book "The Loss of a Pet," which has been acclaimed as the seminal work on this subject. Dr. Sife is semi-retired, but still in private practice as a psychologist in Brooklyn, New York where he is currently working exclusively in this specialty. He is considered to be the leading authority on pet loss and bereavement, and co-founded the Association for Pet Loss and Bereavement. The APLB has become the recognized international authority for disseminating help and information in this field. Dr. Sife has also written several columns and major magazine articles on pet loss. He has also written five other books, on different subjects, and was nominated for the Pulitzer Prize in poetry for "Modern Rubaiyat."